The LATINO CENTURY

How America's Largest Minority Is Transforming Democracy

MIKE MADRID

WITH MARCOS BRETÓN

SIMON & SCHUSTER

New York   London   Toronto   Sydney   New Delhi

This book is dedicated to my mother, Rosalina Arguelles Madrid, whose most impactful gift to me as a teenager was a blue paperback Roget's Thesaurus inscribed simply, "Write beautiful things."

Contents

Prologue: *It's Not All Black and White*   1

1 The Latinization of America   15
2 Lessons from My Nana   25
3 Becoming a Republican   39
4 Political Director of the California Republican Party   47
5 *Un Nuevo Día*   67
6 First He Came for the Mexicans   79
7 Political Odd Couple   89
8 The Lincoln Project   103
9 The Bannon Line and the New Southern Strategy   113
10 The Latino Voter   133
11 Beyond the Politics of Immigration   147
12 The Flip Side of Machismo   159
13 Nevada: Labor and Working-Class Latinos   165
14 Florida: The Cuban Exception   173
15 North Carolina: What Opportunity Looks Like   185
16 Texas and the Rio Grande Valley   195
17 Arizona's Valley of the Sun   203
18 The Challenge for Republicans   211
19 The Challenge for Democrats   217

Epilogue: *A Case for Optimism: Pluralism over Tribalism*   225
Acknowledgments   237
Notes   241
Index   249

PROLOGUE

It's Not All Black and White

As a political data guy I often see the world in the black and white of data points, but there are other ways of seeing. Politics is a careful balance between science and art; you have to understand both to be successful. As hard as I've worked to gain a mastery of the data and science behind electoral patterns, I truly also believe that politics, since it's all about understanding people, will always be more of an art form. I'm also a painter, and as a painter I pay close attention to story and character—to what I see in a face—and also to the power of color in all its distinctive shading and tone. In any one painting, I can use dozens of different shades of blue or green or red and each tells a story. I can also use dozens of shades of brown, each with its own identity. Because brown is made with so many other different colors it becomes the glue that holds a painting together. It flows seamlessly throughout every other color without the eye even noticing it. That is how I think of my fellow Mexican Americans, and of Latinos in general, dozens of shades of brown, dozens of different groupings and subgroupings. As essayist Richard Rodriguez once put it, "The essential beauty and mystery of the color brown is that it is a mixture of colors." Brown is functional. Brown is beautiful.

My story as a third-generation American is not remarkable, but my experience as a Latino political consultant is. I am one of the few political consultants who has worked at the highest levels of campaigns on both sides of the aisle and I have seen firsthand how both parties work. As a Latino growing up in Southern California, I witnessed the changing demography of the Golden State and, from an early age, began to ask what that meant for the future of our country and the electorate as a whole. As a product of the public school system, I was one of the many Brown kids it failed, but also redeemed. After attending Moorpark College, I applied and was accepted into the School of Foreign Service at Georgetown University, the catalyst to a thirty-year career as a political consultant focused on data points and closely following Latino voting trends.

Upon graduation, I could have stayed in D.C. and gone to work on the Hill. However, I chose to return home to California, a state I love, and launch my political consulting career. California plays a special role as the largest state in the Union. It has become a microcosm of the country and a blueprint for the electorate and its mood. And living and working in the Golden State, I have had a front-row seat to the changing demographics and emergence of what is becoming the Latino Century.

For more than twenty-five years working as a top-level Republican operative, and ultimately a cofounder of the anti-Trump Lincoln Project, my strength is identifying electoral patterns. I know what it takes to move the needle in an election. Politics is about understanding people and what makes them vote. This book is not about predicting the outcome of a specific election. It's certainly not tied to the 2024 presidential contest where Joe Biden could easily bring Latinos back into the traditional range for Democrats after a decade-long slide. Conversely, we could also see Trump break out into record territory for a Republican, surpassing George W. Bush's numbers when he cracked 40 percent. This is a recounting of a unique demographic transition that is taking place over generations and is literally changing our democracy through cultural and political attributes that will define this century.

Here's the blunt reality: we as a country are in a demographic foot-
race between an emerging generation—younger, browner, poorer, but
more optimistic about the promise of America, despite having few reasons to believe in it—and an older generation, the wealthiest, most
privileged generation of Americans who has ever lived, whose lives
have been shaped by an era of relative peace and U.S. global hegemony,
yet they still have the most negative view of this country and America's
future than any generation in modern polling history. Here is the math
that is probably going to be our saving grace. Every day, 10,000 Americans turn eighteen, and every day, 7,500 people die in this country. Our
spirit is slowly being replenished by the young. Our national sense of
optimism—and ultimately our commitment to pluralism—are being
rejuvenated by a younger generation and its increasingly Latino demographic makeup, and this regeneration from within is what's going to
save this country, if only we can last that long. Can the new breed of
opportunistic right-wing extremists unleashed in the United States,
typified by Steve Bannon and his Leninist, tear-it-all-down ideology,
inflict so much lasting harm and pollute the political environment so
much in the next twenty years that this country is beyond redemption
after that? That's the foot race. Here's the bad news: It's going to be
close. Like photo-finish close.

We have to quit imagining we're somehow going to convince bomb
throwers not to throw bombs. We're not going to fix anyone and—
poof!—turn them back into Reagan- or Bush-style Republicans. This
is a party we've watched double down—and triple down—on the
crazy right. No politician is going to ride up on a white horse and save
us—not even on a brown horse. Not happening. Meaningful change
takes time, and only through the slow drip, drip, drip progress of demographic change will the culture change, and our politics change, and
everything about us change. That's the lever to watch exert itself, rather
than sitting around and waiting for a lot of Republicans to evolve and
see the light.

Latinos will be the key driver of this demographic transformation. Latinos will reinvigorate the American experiment with our uniquely blended cultural attributes; our inspiring confidence in democratic institutions, despite them sometimes being used against us; our unrelenting optimism about America that has always defined this country's allure; and our comfort with pluralism as a people defined by our blended European and Indigenous DNA. Latinos have much more faith in our institutions, much more faith in police, academia, media, government, the military, voting. We have a far more optimistic view than any other group in America and we're the fastest-growing. For most of what ails the American body politic: Latinos are the solution. We will put a face on a time of change and growing optimism I call the Latino Century.

Recent elections have shown what I have been saying for decades as a political consultant, researcher, writer, and activist working to focus the country on the largest ethnic demographic change occurring in our history: Latinos aren't understood by either party, but the one that is able to define itself as the party of an aspirational multiethnic working-class party will dominate American politics for a generation. For the moment, Democrats are struggling to keep their working-class roots and Republicans are resistant to the multiethnic future that is America's destiny. Both are struggling to be aspirational. The inscription at the base of the Statue of Liberty famously depicts Lady Liberty as "the Mother of Exiles" and adds, "From her beacon-hand glows worldwide welcome." And what about this? " 'Keep, ancient lands, your storied pomp!' cries she with silent lips." A timely reminder. Only then: "Give me your tired, your poor / Your huddled masses yearning to breathe free / The wretched refuse of your teeming shore."

I grew up with the Statue of Liberty as a sacred national symbol, and not only because my grandparents were part of the huddled masses yearning to breathe free who came to this country to pursue a better life for themselves and their children. For me, the Statue of

Liberty is so personally important a reference point that when I did a series of paintings combining iconic imagery of American culture with iconic images of Mexican culture, I depicted the Statue of Liberty in a style that also evoked the Virgen de Guadalupe. Recent years have seen those values trashed and tarnished by a generation of Americans who have stood on the shoulders of the blood, sweat, and tears of the generations that came before.

Sometimes we need a little help from the rest of the world to remind us why our ideals still matter in a world too often grown cynical and calculating—a world in which we have come to expect those ideals to exist without any struggle. Vladimir Putin's obscene power grab in sending troops into Ukraine, and embarking on a scorched-earth strategy of trying to kill as many Ukrainian civilians as possible, galvanized the West behind the Ukrainian cause. I saw for myself, firsthand, just how important Ukrainian resistance was for the world; as President Volodymyr Zelensky put it in a December 2022 speech to a joint session of the U.S. Congress, "This will be the basis to protect democracy in Europe and the world over."

I was in Ukraine in May 2022 at the Ukrainians' request to offer advice on political communications strategy. Just weeks after Russia's incursion into the Donbas region, I felt compelled to head into the conflict to experience what it felt like to be among people truly fighting for freedom and basic rights and against tyranny. In America these words had become hollow and overused to describe the refusal to wear a mask during a pandemic or in organizing a trucker's convoy to protest oppression. Another Lincoln Project cofounder and I met with Rustem Umerov, at the time Zelensky's choice as chief Ukrainian negotiator with the Russians. The mere fact of Zelensky, a popularly elected Jewish leader of Ukraine, selecting as lead negotiator a man born in the Soviet Union to a Crimean Tatar Muslim family amounted to extending a middle finger to Putin, a move I liked a lot. Umerov also struck me as down-to-earth, passionate, and visionary.

"This is about seeing if a pluralistic democracy can work," Umerov told me late one night in Ukraine, deep into a marathon conversation at the absurdly lavish dacha of some deposed oligarch.

Umerov's words should not have been so striking to me, but they were. He was articulating a vision of this conflict as more than just a centuries-long battle between Slavic people and more than a struggle about East versus West or democracy versus authoritarianism. Umerov and his Ukrainian countrymen viewed this as a battle to prove that pluralism could work. They were fighting to prove that a multiethnic democracy could work. This was not a battle *against* something. It was a battle *for* something.

"That blows my mind," I told Umerov. "That's *our* mythology. That's the American mythology. That's what I'm fighting for, too."

"How's that working out for you?" Umerov asked sarcastically, smiling wryly as he leaned back in his chair.

It's easy to let noble words shrivel and die on the vine. Words like "pluralism," which to me evokes a political philosophy that emphasizes the value of diversity and difference fruitfully thriving side by side in a democratic society and blending together to make that society stronger and more able to adapt and regenerate itself. The blunt truth is that even in its finest moments, the United States has shown only a partial commitment to pluralism. That unfulfilled potential excites me, even as it inspires in me a deep feeling of dread. What if we as a still relatively young country can truly come into our own and bring a vibrant and sturdy pluralism front and center? What if we really made pluralism work? And thrive? What if we could move beyond endless iterations of the same old fights and blame games, one side using historical oppression and injustice as a weapon to club opponents, another embracing reactionary racism? What if race and cultural difference could be viewed merely as components of that which makes us who we are, along with questions like basic decency and character, commitment to treating other people with respect and openness, generosity and kindness, both personally and in the larger sense of how we see society? What if we could finally get past the academic and theoretical questions of what the Founders wrote compared to how they lived and find out if a multiracial society could become a nation based on ideals and values?

Democracy worldwide is under threat. American-style democracy faces its own specific set of challenges. The list is long and daunting: rising authoritarian tendencies, the destruction of social norms in public life, a growing toxic tribalism whose adherents espouse a pernicious religious populist nationalism, eroding confidence in social institutions that are simultaneously being viewed as partisan weapons, the atomization of information that has allowed social media to divide us algorithmically, the interference of foreign actors into our public square, and an electoral college system that gives advantage to the fastest-shrinking demographic in the country. But for all the gloom and doom that coagulates our social media and news feeds predicting the demise of democracy, there is a rapidly emerging portion of our population that, through its cultural characteristics, blended race, ethnic heritage, and recent migratory experience, is better prepared to see the world differently—and more optimistically.

Let's move beyond black and white. Let's talk more about brown in all its shades. America's whole racial discourse over 250 years of history, its whole national story, has to date literally been defined by black and white. Whiteness in America was created in contrast to the Indigenous, the slave, and the Mexican on this continent. We can move beyond the argument that if you're not white, then you're some shade of oppressed. And we can move beyond the equally ridiculous attempt on the right to argue that race doesn't matter, which really means: the more white you behave, the more we'll accept you.

This is not an argument to forget our history of injustice and oppression—quite the opposite. It's an attempt to more clearly define and understand it, while also moving forward out of the trap we've been stuck in for two and a half centuries. It's also a declaration that working-class "people of color" are increasingly viewing their lives through the prism of economic class, and not race, and are voting that way.

I hate it when I hear people say Latinos are "apathetic." My decades of experience working with Latino voters have taught me that as a group we are keenly aware of historical injustices, but often tune out day-to-day politics because so many of us don't have the economic luxury of engaging in civic life. It's difficult to focus on past oppression when you have mouths to feed tonight and rent to pay on Friday. Too often we chide those who don't vote as "apathetic," when the stark reality is the poor and working poor rarely see any change in their lives based on who is in control in Washington. Poor people don't vote in large numbers and that's the same whether you're Black in the Deep South, white in Appalachia, or Latino in East Los Angeles.

I came of age as a conservative at a time when "family values" were often cited as an important touchstone, but if you're looking for real family values, look to Latinos. We're passionate about our families and also our friends, who we treat like family. My fellow Mexican Americans might be the ultimate exemplars of the adage that true wealth comes from a richness of connection to your family and your circle of friends, and that matters—for the moment anyway—way more than material possessions or bulging bank balances or the insatiable consumerism that has come to define modern American culture.

As more intermarriage between different ethnic groups helps power a trend toward greater racial blending, especially on the part of Latinos and Asian Americans, social science research indicates this demographic shift could actually ease tensions rather than the converse. As Richard Alba, Morris Levy, and Dowell Myers reported in a June 2021 *Atlantic* article,

> Notably, the narrative of racial blending was especially reassuring to white Republicans, who felt most threatened by the conventional

majority-minority account. In our most recent study, 67 percent of white Republican participants expressed anxiety or anger after reading a news story modeled on the majority-minority narrative, compared with 29 percent of white Democratic participants. Among those who instead read a story of rising multiracialism and blending, anxiety and anger were much lower, reported by 26 percent of white Republicans and 13 percent of white Democrats. Moreover, Latino, Black, and Asian participants in these studies expressed overwhelmingly positive reactions to the story of racial blending. . . . Eighty-five percent of Black, Asian, and Latino respondents expressed hopefulness or enthusiasm after reading this account—more than the approximately two-thirds of minority respondents who expressed these positive emotions in response to the majority-minority story. For all the talk about racial polarization in America, the broad consensus is that an expanding and more diverse mainstream portends a better future.

That's good news. And it's one of the main messages I want to underscore in the pages of this book: demographic trends are pointing us in a better direction. We're entering a far more complex time in which we must learn to acknowledge the experience of different groups and subgroups and the individuals within them. The ebb and flow of racial groups in America's future won't be considered in the bilateral framework of Black and white we've historically used to discuss race, but going forward it will increasingly be both. Most Americans surveyed feel optimistic about the emerging multiracial world because there is a growing realization that race is becoming less static and more dynamic. Within that complexity are the seeds of a future where race is no longer a zero-sum consideration.

Latinos as a group embody a true, honest, family values–oriented conservatism, call it classic conservatism, for which I've worked for years. This is different from the "social conservative" narrative so easily drawn by the media and pundits. There is a blue-collar culture in

America today and there always has been. It is a culture worlds apart from that of the college-educated, high-income earners in emerging industries. Latinos are the segment of the blue-collar workforce that is most rapidly expanding and those values are renewing America's mythology and changing our politics.

The battle for the future of our country will hinge on the extent to which visionary leaders in the Democratic Party and Republican Party can overcome myriad past mistakes to do better at speaking to—and especially listening to—my people. Latinos are emerging to say: Wait a second. Yes, there are racial problems. There are problems of being alienated. But we don't have a legacy of slavery or even the need for government assistance to break through the current system. Despite the history of very real oppression that continues in many nefarious, if often more subtle ways, we have not endured the pernicious legacy of slavery, nor much of the systemic suffering that falls harder on Black Americans and endures to this day. We are, by most measures, achieving middle-class status generationally like so many groups before us. We are increasingly college-educated, and increasingly homeowners. Interracial marriage rates are more than 50 percent, meaning it's more likely you'll marry a non-Latino than a Latino. These are all indicators of what we used to call assimilation, but that term no longer applies. The size and scope of the shift are so massive that it's fair to project, as I do, that non-Latino Americans will be becoming as much or more like Latinos than Latinos are becoming like Americans. That makes it hard to sort out what's happening using a racial vocabulary we've been relying on for 250 years. In one sense, Latinos are like other groups, many ethnic Catholics, whose assimilation shaped the development of the United States at the turn of the last century. However, the size and scope of the change represented by growing Latino numbers that began at the turn of this century is unprecedented—and it's impossible to believe that we can be anything other than forever altered by becoming a non-white-majority nation. In this way, to compare the

Latino experience with that of ethnic and racial groups of the past does not appreciate or respect the experiences that occurred at the turn of the last century and what is happening now.

Our racial imbalance was set from the day we enslaved people and forcibly brought them over to this country. It continued as we massacred our way through Indigenous populations and took lands from Mexicans as the spoils of war. Our racial narrative was further complicated by the Civil War, segregation, and Jim Crow. This historical infamy is cast as the entire narrative of how we talk about diversity or policing or systemic racism. When the country was founded, roughly 20 percent of our population was Black and enslaved. Fears of whites being "outnumbered" were more justified, especially in the Deep South, but more recently Blacks have constituted just 12 to 15 percent of the U.S. population, which has held steady since the end of the Civil War. That does not add up to any kind of "great replacement." There has been no actual numeric threat. There has been no basis for the fear of Black Americans—let's get real here—driving the Great Replacement Theory. The fear of being "replaced" by non-white people is driven by the explosive growth of Latinos during this century. The fear of "replacement" is driven by the acknowledgment of America's original sin of slavery and its systemic treatment of most non-white people, specifically Blacks. Politically there is a lot undermining the powerful motivator of the Great Replacement Theory as a fear tactic, but most of it boils down to: *Are they going to treat us like we treated them? Are they, with growing power, going to be as brutal, discriminatory, and even barbaric as we were?* In short, white people are understandably taking on many of the characteristics of a minority group as they become one.

The term "melting pot" as a central idea of U.S. assimilation and culture was not always part of our national heritage, not by a long shot. Well over a century went by with a much different standard, that of diversity and pluralism. The "melting pot" gained currency in the Progressive Era at the start of the twentieth century during the presidency of Republican Theodore Roosevelt. In 1908, a stage play premiered in Washington, D.C., with Roosevelt in attendance, titled *The Melting Pot*, helping to promote the concept. The play earned rave reviews, which, whatever its artistic merits, tells you something about the mood of the times. The *New York Times* gushed that "'The Melting Pot' symbolizes America as a crucible wherein all nationalities are fused into an American type, a being with the dominant characteristics of all that is best the world over." The Washington *Evening Star* reviewer called it a "remarkable play," in which "the expression of intense feeling . . . has the shock and appeal of a human cry" in evoking its vision of a melting pot "in which racial hatreds must be fused and transformed." The *Evening Star* added this description of the play's central concept: "'The Melting Pot' is a term symbolical of America itself; the crucible in which the various nations of the earth are melted and fused together, to the end that the typical American results." For the first time, America was "nation building" here at home. President Roosevelt gave a widely cited anti-hyphenated-American speech at Carnegie Hall in 1915, telling the gathered Knights of Columbus, "There is no room in this country for hyphenated Americanism. . . . [A] hyphenated American is not an American at all."

What is "typical American" supposed to mean? It's a question we have wrestled with since our founding and we stand on the precipice of great change in coming to a renewed understanding of it. Maybe it's time to move beyond the patently absurd idea that any such thing exists. We are, all of us, typical Americans, all in our own way. Our distinctness is as important as our sameness. Generation by generation, we see more intermarriage and more breaking of old racial barriers and divisions. We see a growing generational comfort with natural diversity and pluralism; it's changing the culture. It's overwhelming the melting pot. We've moved beyond the old model of all blending into a bland nothingness where culture is left at the doorstep, as well as language, religion, and identity; just wrap yourself in the American flag, screaming eagles, and the Fourth of July, hot dogs as the national food, and consumerism as the national religion. The rise of Latinos—what I call the Latinization of America—offers another way.

As serious as I see the threats facing this country, and the spread of the cancer of populism, the truth is that I'm actually very optimistic about where we find ourselves as a country. People cite Thomas Jefferson's quote about "[t]he tree of liberty must be refreshed from time to time, with the blood of patriots and tyrants" and use it to mean whatever they want it to mean, but the fundamental idea is renewal and fresh growth. Character is forged through conflict. We'd like to believe that as a country we have achieved enough progress that everything will be automatically okay all on its own, but that will never be true. There will always be threats to our way of life. In the same way that an individual's character is defined by the adversity through which you have to struggle, how you wage that fight and who you become in the cauldron of conflict, we as a country are dealing with our most protracted and challenging existential fight since the Civil War.

Together we are forging a new American character. In a controversial if memorable phrase, Art Torres, the chairman of the Democratic Party in California during the 1990s, described a racially charged political campaign about undocumented immigrants as "[t]he last gasp of white America." In retrospect it's much more likely we were witnessing an old way of thinking about race than we were watching the demographic end of white people in the state.

As much as it feels, correctly, as if a part of America is dying, we should not look at these as pangs of death, but pangs of birth. Something new and promising is being born. Maybe that's the Mexican in me talking. Going back to our Mayan ancestors, there was always the belief that if the world ended in an apocalypse it would usher in a new life cycle. What we in the United States are going through now is difficult and for many it's scary, but we're giving birth to a potentially truer reflection of what the Founding Fathers envisioned. Look, they knew they were not being true to the high-minded ideals they were writing down on parchment. They were slave owners! They knew! But they were setting down an aspirational framework. The struggle of the American experiment is to continually push to get there, where they wanted us to get.

As a younger man, I bought into the bullshit that American ideals meant we as a people were fundamentally above nationalism and jingoism and narrow self-interest. I really believed it. Recent years have taught me how wrong I was about that. My Republican convictions have taken a deep hit. But I still believe in our founding documents, words penned by flawed human beings whose vision of what we could become was still empowering and ennobling. The American idea is not restricted to blood and soil, and geography. As a country of many colors, a country going back to its origins as a laboratory of the power of people with profound differences living side by side, working together toward some larger end, we have the potential to show that these are universal ideas available to all, a truly global transnational idea. Now, more than any other generation of Americans, we have the potential to live up to that challenge, a country of many shades of brown, a country that at long last is moving beyond black and white.

The continuation of the American experiment will not be a function of government reforms or updating processes. It isn't about how we regulate social media platforms or place more or fewer guardrails on free speech in the internet age. (It's not about regulating "dark money" or creating third parties.) It isn't even about our military might and international influence as the world again stands on the precipice of another global war. No, the future of American democracy literally resides within us. Every day that we awake and find the country still here, functioning and operating, is a demographic step closer to an America truer to the professed mission statement outlined in our founding documents.

- 1 -

The Latinization of America

Since the 1980s Latino voters have been telling pollsters who they are. And who they are contradicts the conventional wisdom that Latino voters are, as it is usually put, "not monolithic." The truth is, we are and we aren't. Latino voters are younger, poorer, less college-educated, and more optimistic than voters in non-Hispanic white communities. All four of those are important, especially, I would emphasize, optimism. All four characteristics show up broadly in voting trends, polling, and exit polling whether your family background is Cuban, Puerto Rican, Venezuelan, Mexican, or any other of the many distinct nationalities that make up "Latinos."

"Latino" describes an ethnicity, which means it has a distinct culture. That culture is fluid and changing—sometimes blending, sometimes maintaining its distinct identity. Politically this presents an extraordinary challenge. Perhaps more than any voter group I have ever worked with, Latinos are both the hardest and easiest voters to define. The struggle to identify group versus individual identity is unique in our political system. Some have described it by saying that while there may not be a Latino vote, there are Latino voters. The most consistent steadfast rule is that there are exceptions.

The Latino voter is an economic populist who supports blue-collar industries, except when the environment is threatened. They are a culturally conservative voter who regularly polls to the right of many

Americans on many social issues in the abstract, such as abortion or marriage equality, but tends to be more moderate on these issues as they move from the abstract to the real. They are a voting group that identifies far more with being "a typical American" than an aggrieved racial group, but that is also more politically responsive than non-Hispanics to attacks on immigrants and other people of color. The Latinization of America will also lead to a "feminization of America," not in the sense of effeminate characteristics, but rather in Latino culture not being afraid of having strong women lead our communities on issues of culture, race, and politics.

The Latino is a swing voter, a base voter, and a voter showing natural assimilative tendencies. While most Latinos are Democrats, it is inaccurate to say that most Latinos feel at home in the Democratic Party. While there is a rightward shift toward Republicans, it is inaccurate to say most Latinos feel at home in the Grand Old Party. In fact, Hispanics have among the weakest partisan ties of any ethnic group in America.

For over thirty years, nearly every quality survey of Latino voters has identified jobs and the economy as the top issue on their minds. Over those same thirty years, almost no political campaign from either party has developed an economic working-class agenda for Latinos as its primary message. That is how strong the desire is to characterize Latinos as a niche-aggrieved racial minority motivated by immigration, farmworker, and border issues. This remains one of the most striking and obvious blind spots in American politics: the most rapidly emerging voter group in the country is quantifiably telling the political parties what it needs to hear and both parties summarily dismiss those concerns because they believe they understand these voters better than those voters understand themselves.

For more than a decade, the data has told us that Latinos differ in how they identify as Americans based on how far removed they are from the immigrant experience. Back in 2012, according to the

Pew Research Center, Latinos were divided almost evenly over how much of a common identity they share with other Americans. Nearly half (47 percent) said they considered themselves to be very different from the typical American. And just one in five (21 percent) said they used the term "American" most often to describe their identity. But on these two measures, U.S.-born Latinos expressed a stronger sense of affinity with other Americans and America than do immigrant Latinos. It is the U.S.-born, non-immigrant Latino share of the population that is the fastest growing in the country. By 2021, according to Pew Research, Latino babies born in the United States had driven more growth in the overall Latino population than newly arrived immigrants. Pew found that the share of U.S. Latinos born in another country peaked in 2000 at 40 percent and has declined since then. Meanwhile, the share of U.S.-born Latinos has risen from 59.9 percent in 2000 to 67.3 percent in 2019. Among adults, the share of U.S.-born Latinos has increased from 45 percent in 2007 to 55.2 percent in 2019.

With the exceptions of Cubans and Venezuelans, all Latino immigrant groups who have migrated to this country for economic concerns have overwhelmingly voted for Democratic candidates. Cubans and Venezuelans, who are fundamentally political emigrees fleeing communist or dictatorial regimes, voted with Republicans. Mexicans, the largest bulk of Latino immigrants, are no exception, and the voting patterns of naturalized Mexican immigrants is routinely over 70 percent for Democrats.

The Latino population is assimilating, and today the dominant segments of the Latino vote are second- and third-generation voters. This is changing the country's politics, and political professionals are wholly unprepared for what is coming. By 2019, English-language proficiency among Latinos had risen to an all-time high: 72 percent of all Latinos aged five and older indicated they spoke English proficiently, up from 59 percent in 1980, according to the U.S. Census Bureau. In perhaps the greatest indicator of pluralism and social blending, interracial marriage rates among Latinos, for example, are among the highest of any racial or ethnic group. Higher-education attendance and graduation rates are improving dramatically. According to the Census Bureau, the number of Hispanic people ages eighteen to twenty-four enrolled in college doubled in just fifteen years, increasing to 2.4 million in 2021, up from 1.2 million in 2005. The share of all college students ages eighteen to twenty-four who were Hispanic grew, too. The lowest share during the period (11.4 percent) was in 2006; by 2021 it had swelled to nearly 20 percent.

These young, overwhelmingly U.S.-born Latinos are a politically different generation than any previous Latino cohort in history. For many Hispanic people in the United States, educational milestones are recent events. In 2021, the majority of Hispanic adults were between ages twenty-five and thirty-four. This young segment of the Hispanic population had the highest rate of college completion (bachelor's degree or higher) as well as the highest rate of high school completion. Contrast that to a generation earlier, when in 1996, 58.2 percent of the Hispanic population ages twenty-five to twenty-nine graduated from high school; by 2021, the share increased to 88.5 percent. The power of the changing Latino electorate is most pronounced in one data point: 22 percent of Latinos will be voting in their first presidential election in 2024, with a surprising 38 percent of the entire Latino electorate—nearly four in ten voters—being new since 2016.

By 2040, 70 percent of new homeowners will be Latino. There is a direct correlation between homeownership and voting. There is also a tendency to become more economically conservative on issues like taxation as well as support for law enforcement. Latinos are transforming the complexion of the working class, donning the hard hats, work gloves, and blue collars while increasing workforce participation rates.

In 1980, when I was nine years old, there were 14.8 million Latinos in the United States, just 7 percent of the total population; by 2021, according to Pew Research, that number had grown to 62.5 million and 19 percent. Lost in most national discussions of Latinos, which carries a strong flavor of East Coast provincialism, is the fact that Mexican Americans overwhelmingly shape the overall identity of Latinos in the United States with more than 60 percent of the total. More than 37.2 million Americans, mostly in the West, have family ties to Mexico, compared to 5.8 million from Puerto Rico, 2.5 million from the tiny Central American country of El Salvador, 2.4 million from the Dominican Republic, 2.4 million from Cuba, and 1.8 million from Guatemala. Mexican Americans as a group will continue to grow in size and impact not because of immigration from Mexico—which has been flat for years now—but because of population growth. Unlike other immigrants and even other Latinos, our country of origin, Mexico, isn't an ocean or even an island away. For many of us it's a day's drive. Even without that proximity, the names of our states, cities, and towns reflect the Spanish names of our people who lived here long before the United States was a country.

The growing class divide in this country is increasingly evolving into a racial/ethnic divide and America's inability to have a nuanced discussion on either topic has added to the alienation of this critical voter group. The failure of both parties to develop an aspirational working-class agenda is manifesting in lower voter turnout. When both parties focus primarily on stereotypical issues of immigration when Latino voters are saying clearly they are interested in economic concerns, it should come as no surprise that there's no inspiration to show up and vote.

Most Latinos do lean toward Democrats, but as I have argued for decades, there is every reason to believe that as Latinos age, get college degrees, become homeowners, interracially marry, and work increasingly in high-tech, white-collar, college-educated jobs, they will become more Republican. Three of the last four national general elections have demonstrated that. In effect, as Latinos assimilate into all facets of American life and reflect the tapestry of this country, their politics are beginning to reflect that diversity as well.

As fewer and fewer Latino voters are immigrating and naturalizing, we can expect the fastest growth in the Latino electorate to be of second- and third-generation voters. This will have a considerable impact on key issues from immigration to abortion and will also change the research methodologies and manners in which we communicate with Latino voters. It will also present challenges to how both parties have historically approached them. Far less Spanish will be required and a growing emphasis will be on bicultural and bilingual messaging. Bicultural messaging can range from using dark-haired and brown-skinned people in your campaign ads to including regional accents to incorporating cultural imagery that is commonplace in Latino households. Many political campaigns have begun to incorporate these themes to great success; a cultural nod to the Latino voter by showing children playing loteria, a common Mexican game similar to bingo, the use of Spanglish terms in campaign scripts, or a picture of the Virgen de Guadalupe hanging on the wall, for example.

Bicultural messaging requires extreme nuance, and when this is lacking it can easily cross over into what I refer to as "sombrero politics," which incorporates crass stereotypes like the ubiquitous use of mariachi bands, *folklórico* dancing, and eating tamales in everyday settings. There is a very fine line between skilled use of cultural messaging and going over the deep end into playing sombrero politics. Quantifying the difference is almost impossible to do, but it's like former Supreme Court Justice Potter Stewart's statement on pornography—it's difficult to describe, but you know it when you see it. This delicate balance requires a keen understanding of Latino culture and explains why both parties struggle with messaging to Latino voters. This includes cultural aspects within the Latino community; Cuban and South American cultures are very distinct from Mexican and Central American culture, and vice versa. There are very few Latinos in decision-making capacities on either side of the aisle, even though Latinos are voting in record numbers. Chuck Rocha, a prominent Democratic Latino political consultant, estimates from his own firm's research that just eight companies controlled the messaging and strategy for over 90 percent of the top fifty congressional races for Democrats heading into the 2022 midterms. All were majority-owned by white women/men. My experience in Republican politics would suggest it's the same or worse on that side of the aisle.

Because our overall numbers are growing, Latinos will set turnout records in every election for the rest of our lives, even though Latinos have the lowest turnout rates of any of the four major ethnic and racial groups: whites, Blacks, Asian/Pacific Islanders, and Latinos. So Latinos have the least reflection of our population by voter turnout. In fact, most spikes in voter turnout have come because of perceived attacks on our community. The post–Proposition 187 years in California in 1996 and 1998, the racist actions of former Maricopa County sheriff Joe Arpaio in Arizona in 2018, and of course the arrival of Donald Trump as a presidential candidate—all led to significant spikes in Latino voter turnout.

Demographers and political data experts like me focus on numbers and facts that feel important. My mother's influence trained me to see the same story through a different prism: that of family, and community, and communities that feel like family, and of a broader shift away from American myths of rugged individualism and the white man's lonely struggle to prevail and dominate. All that Max Weber stuff; you know, the "Protestant work ethic" and making a religion of hard work and self-sacrifice to the point that your value *is* your work. The Protestant notion of individualism through both salvation and economic success is about to run into a new cultural reality. The Latino work ethic has matched or eclipsed that of white Protestants in today's economy, but it's certainly not driven by the same notion of individualism.

Those notions may have served a purpose in helping build a young country in a previous era, and I would suggest a necessary cultural characteristic of creating the great gift of America. This country is in many ways the apex of Western Protestant thought, but to put it bluntly, for many other cultures in the world it is no way to live. We as Americans in the twenty-first century must do better and be better, for ourselves and each other, and my Latino friends and I are here to help. We are here to help America achieve the dream of a society truly committed to making pluralism work, to be inclusive and respectful, and get past the age-old musical chairs game of newer immigrant groups to the United States struggling for the power of established groups and everyone stepping on everyone's toes.

For me it all goes back to the words of my mother about always showing one another respect, about respecting our various cultural traditions as an important part of life without ever having to get in the way of seeing ourselves as united in being part of the larger fabric of U.S. life. "I would like to see the Latino influence as being accepted for what we are: intelligent people, hardworking people, respectful people, not only respectful of our own families, our own parents, our own culture, but of others, too," she once said. "I was raised in a very poor neighborhood, but I was raised to respect everybody, every religion, every ethnicity, every handicapped person, every economic aspect of our world."

Mom's words remind me of conversations I had as a young man with older people who had grown up during the Great Depression and never saw themselves as poor, or different, because in those years everyone was struggling. Maybe it's childhood innocence. Or maybe affluence does compound human difference. I don't know, but I tend to believe that a shared struggle creates a uniting bond that makes us see more of what we have in common than what divides us. Even in today's polarized political climate. In fact, the blue-collar working-class perspective is one of the strongest unifying characteristics among Latino voters.

When I imagine this country moving forward, I see a world in which the role of Latino women—of Latinas—has been especially important in turning away from tribalism and factionalism with more of a focus on improving lives around us one by one by one by one. America will be a much more female-oriented culture—that is, a worldview shaped through the eyes of much more women in power. If you look at the college-education gap between men and women among Latinos, it's big and growing bigger. Only 26 percent of Hispanic men have an associate's degree or higher compared to 33 percent of Hispanic females.

This "diploma divide" is bigger than for any other racial or ethnic group, so over time Latinas are going to be in higher levels of private enterprise and corporate power structures. They're going to be much more college-educated and much higher income earners. They're going to be in more positions of political power and authority. We don't talk about it nearly enough, but the Latinization of America will also lead to truly a feminization of America. Not just politically where we are electing a lot more women, but also the social perspective of women in leadership on the social safety net, economic concerns, and the use of both hard and soft power in foreign affairs.

– 2 –

Lessons from My Nana

The modern American story is one of different groups living side by side, each new wave of immigrants starting out humble and poor, packed into loud, crowded, urban neighborhoods. Then, with time, over generations, the children of these families move away to bigger houses with bigger lots in quiet neighborhoods. I learned as a boy from my mother and from her mother, my *abuelita*—or nana—as we call our grandmothers, the disrupting effects of that progress on families and the essential need to overcome it wherever and however possible.

Betty Smith grew up poor in Williamsburg, Brooklyn, the daughter of German immigrants, and captured the bustling humanity of that tenement neighborhood in her 1943 novel *A Tree Grows in Brooklyn.* "A person who pulls himself up from a low environment via the bootstrap route has two choices," she writes in the novel. "Having risen above his environment, he can forget it; or, he can rise above it and never forget it and keep compassion and understanding in his heart for those he has left behind him in the cruel upclimb."

This American immigrant story is being retold in countless neighborhoods today. It was the challenge that my parents lived with, having moved away from a bustling, active, low-income Los Angeles neighborhood to buy a home in Ventura County. Both my parents were born in Los Angeles during the 1940s, a distant time and place from L.A. in the Vietnam era. My father's people arrived from the New Mexico

Territory, which means that, combined with my mom's family coming from Sonora and Durango in Mexico, we were desert people on both sides of the family. Both of my grandfathers were mechanics who arrived to work in an industrializing post–World War II Los Angeles. Everyone they knew were hardworking, low-income Catholic families, like so many that came to this country at the turn of the previous century. Our communities in large cities like Los Angeles, where I was born, became enclaves of economically and politically dispossessed people often lacking basic amenities and often beset by violence and crime. The focus was on family and providing for family.

My father, Louis Madrid, was deeply suspicious of the growing "Chicano" movement that defined the 1960s and '70s in Mexican American Los Angeles. Chicano activists defined themselves as culturally distinct from both the Mexican and European ancestry they descended from. Chicanos were often just friends from Latino neighborhoods, but Chicano activists gained notoriety on college campuses in Los Angeles during the Vietnam era. My dad saw them as agitators and elitists posing as revolutionaries. Chicanos were too defiantly opposed to a world he was working hard to attain for his family. He did not protest the Vietnam War; he joined the military before he could be drafted. No one in my family and no one my family knew had graduated from a university when I was a child, so my dad couldn't relate to these so-called Chicanos pontificating from college campuses that were not yet accessible to families like mine. They may as well have been from Mars as far as my parents were concerned.

Dad expressly forbade us from identifying as Chicano ourselves because we were American, and an older generation of Mexican Americans resented the word "Chicano," which served to draw our people as distinct after they had worked so hard to be viewed as the same. "Chicano" loosely refers to Americans of Mexican ancestry, which included me and my dad, but he hated the political overtones associated with the label. He also hated their association with Vietnam-era social excesses such as long hair, drug use, and social unrest. But mostly he resented their defiance of the dominant culture that he was struggling so hard to help his family become a part of. We were American, as American as anybody else, and Chicanos were trying to carve out a separate identity.

As a political professional years later, I would come to understand Mexican Americans who identified as Chicano and those, like my father, that did not. "Chicano" was countercultural and defiant. The negative stereotype my father associated with Chicanos was really a personal—and community—struggle to say, "I'm different." I'm not fully Mexican and I'm not fully American. I'm neither and both at the same time. In many ways, Chicanos were my first introduction to the realities of pluralism and taught me that Latinos weren't just diverse as a people living among others in their neighborhood—they were living with that tension among themselves, able to relate to and understand two distinct worlds, while never being fully accepted in either, and also refusing to make the choice at the same time.

My youth in the 1970s and '80s was a time of few Latino role models, so having your dad frame members of our ethnic group in starkly negative terms completed my picture of alienation. Unlike the white friends of my youth, understanding who we were was always a fraught proposition. This is the way it had always been.

I remember once asking my parents—I might have been in junior high at the time—if they had ever protested the Vietnam War, like so many of their baby boomer generation. My mother rolled her eyes at me.

"Protest?" she asked me with a slight tinge of disgust. "We didn't have the *luxury* of protesting. We had bills to pay."

When Mom was in school, she was warned by her Mexican parents to stay away from "gangs" and "gang members," or risk being dragged into trouble. Mom tried to keep her parents' admonition in mind, but once at school, she found it hard to act on. The people she was supposed to fear would ask her if she thought she was better than them. Of course, she didn't think she was better than anyone. Mom walked a fine line, feeling suspicious and frightened of many Mexican Americans like her, especially when she witnessed a gang fight that she found terrifying, but not wanting to put up walls. Instead, she tried to be friends with everyone.

Mom has light skin, spoke English well, and she loved Dick Tracy, John Wayne, Howdy Doody, and Hopalong Cassidy. She also loved the famous Mexican comedian Cantinflas and the Mexican corridos in Spanish she listened to on the radio. By the age of five, Mom was acting as the English-language translator for her parents. She slipped easily between English and Spanish and loved the Mexican songs her parents would enjoy on Spanish-language radio. She was in both worlds, always, which came with its own set of challenges.

Years later, she would tell me she didn't want to sell out to the Mexican part of her. And she didn't want to surrender to the Anglo part of her. Her recollection of the false choices she had to make in her own community made me love and respect her even more. It would have been easy for her to give in to bitterness or to reject her Mexican culture, but she didn't. She was always optimistic, loving, and strong. She always had hope for herself, her family, and especially her children.

More than anyone in my life, my mom has been my North Star— the bravest and best person I know. She refused to allow us to believe we were victims. She also imbued in me a deep love of country, a patriotism that only Latinos can understand. She reminded us often that we were no less American than anyone else in our hometown— but I always wondered if white moms ever told their kids that. The belief in and love for a country where your experience was never quite having a full seat at the table, but loving your country because of those faults, not despite them. Hope and optimism in America hit differently for non-white Americans. In many ways they are more intense and committed because our country's faults are so apparent. I'm convinced that's why social and political criticism from many non-white people is often misconstrued as anti-American or unpatriotic. Because many white people don't see many of the social challenges obvious to non-whites, legitimate criticism often feels overblown. As the number of whites shrink in the population, they're beginning to see the world through the eyes of a minority and that's uncomfortable, to say the least.

My older sister, Juliet, was born while my dad was away during the Vietnam War, serving on the USS *Gridley*, a guided-missile cruiser. Future presidential candidate John Kerry also served on the *Gridley*, which was not a big ship, so he and my dad talked often during the time they were both on board. My dad loved to tell us stories from his days on that ship, crossing the equator, visiting Hong Kong, patrolling the South China Sea in support of Seventh Fleet aircraft carriers. My father was proud of his service as we were growing up. It somehow legitimized our Americanness. I remember my *abuela* proudly framing the photos of her son and nephews who served in the military on the wall in between the only surviving photo of her father and a painting of the Sacred Heart of Jesus that overlooks so many Mexican homes. It was those memories of proving our Americanness that informed so many of my pioneering efforts to target Latino military vets in future campaigns. One of my father's fondest memories was of going shopping in the Philippines, buying tailored clothes at a great price—and also a tobacco pipe. It's the last thing I have from my dad, that pipe. On Election Night in 2020, when it was time to celebrate beating Donald Trump, I pulled it out and fired it up, thinking of him smoking that same pipe and fighting for our democracy in his own way.

When Dad returned from his service, he got a job at a bank in the San Fernando Valley, and that's when my family really started thinking of leaving Los Angeles. My parents thought it was nonsense for my dad to be driving an hour out to the San Fernando Valley and then having to fight traffic for another hour or more on the way back to our duplex near downtown Los Angeles. They also came to the sad conclusion that it would not be healthy for us to grow up where they had. Mom said they saw the encroachment of drugs into their neighborhood. There was a problem with gangs, and with "white hippies." Homelessness was becoming a factor in their neighborhood as well.

As newlyweds, my parents lived for a time in the apartment complex where my mom had grown up, but now that she was a mother herself, she saw the place differently. Times had changed. When my mom was growing up, even the most hardened neighborhood gang members respected the elders. They were mindful and respectful of children. These were lines that were never crossed. As a young mother in 1970, she was a little shocked to see old restraints fall away. "With the advent of drugs, it all deteriorated," she told me. "They didn't care if it was your grandmother or an older man, they were going to beat you up and take away your money."

I felt bad, hearing what she had lived through. It sounded harsh. It sounded harrowing. But when I asked her if life for her back then was good, she answered quickly that of course it was. "Life was good because I had my family with me," she said. "I had your older sister, Juliet. We had the love of aunts and uncles and cousins. I had the support of my mother and father. My goodness, what else did I want? We had the warmth of family. Everybody knew everybody. My mother took care of the kids as a grandmother."

Nowhere did my mother define happiness as a career, income, owning a home or anything material, although she had all of those things. The entire focus of her happiness was based on having family around her. Her answer tracked precisely with the priorities I have seen in focus groups of Latinos for thirty years, defining what happiness means to them.

The idea of leaving our family behind to move elsewhere came from my dad. He would recount for my mother the beautiful stories he had heard from his bank coworkers about the new homes being built in Ventura County. They assured him he wouldn't believe how nice they were until he took a ride out there to see for himself.

My parents made a pact: my mom would consider Ventura County, but they would keep the idea of weighing a move between themselves. They knew if they told their extended family members too soon, they would face strident opposition. Family members would work hard to get them to change their minds. They would tell them it's too far away and too scary. They would plead: *What are you going to do up there without your family?*

The first time my folks made the fifty-mile drive from downtown Los Angeles to Moorpark, in the fall of 1970, was in their Volkswagen Beetle. They drove due west to the literal end of the road: the 118 freeway, which took them through Granada Hills and Simi Valley, and ended in Moorpark, which was then a small rural unincorporated city named after a variety of apricot. Back then, Moorpark was a train stop smack-dab in the middle of Ventura County, the northernmost county in what is considered Southern California. Its agricultural roots, sweeping farmlands, and location within commuting distance to Los Angeles made it attractive to the growing suburbanites of the booming Southern California economy.

Orchards dominated the area. My mother found the landscape breathtaking to behold. "The most beautiful thing I have ever seen in my life opened up," she says now. "I thought I was in the Valley of the Green Giant. I thought: *My goodness gracious, this is not a city like the one I grew up in.* All I knew until then was the asphalt jungle. Here there were trees and greenery everywhere. We thought, *This has got to be it.*"

My parents decided then and there, but kept their plans secret, even from my mother's mother, until after I was born in 1971. My maternal grandmother, Leonides Ballesteros, spoke only Spanish. She never received a formal education and came to the United States at fifteen. Her ancestors were Yaqui, Indigenous people from communities stretching from northern Mexico to Arizona. She met my grandfather, Jesus

Arguelles, who was in his early thirties and had worked in the United States and then returned to his native country to find a wife. She was a girl of fifteen, illiterate, and coming to the United States with a husband in his thirties that she barely knew.

I came to learn that my grandmother, my nana, experienced great cruelty, and yet she never responded with cruelty. In her L.A. neighborhood, she would make juice bars for kids on the street who were on welfare or whose parents were absent or suffering from addiction to alcohol. My mother would solemnly recount stories of learning to read and remembering that her mother would sit with her and say in accented English, "Sound it out," as a way of urging her to keep pushing her daughter to read. It was years later that my mother realized that her own mother couldn't read the words that she was encouraging her child to read.

I think often about my grandmother and her strength of character. That's especially true in times of difficulty, when I need a reminder that whatever challenges I experienced couldn't compare with what she went through. She left the desert hills of northern Mexico for the industrialized city of Los Angeles. She would be the mother of six children and endure abject poverty, the abuse of an alcoholic husband, and the inability to read or write in a foreign tongue. Her story is the immigrant story that so many Latinos today can relate to. Though most of us are not immigrants ourselves, we know them, were raised by them, loved by them, and protected by them. While I've never had the terrorizing experience of worrying about being deported, I know that the trauma of crossing the border into a new world is among the most life-altering experiences a human being can endure. To get through that ordeal, family bonds are stretched tight.

For my mother's mother, the news of our impending move came as a body blow. Telling her we were going to Moorpark was like telling her we were going to the moon. It felt impossibly far away and remote. She had helped raise my older sister, Juliet, who was about four then.

She had taken care of me as a baby when I was in the cradle. We were, like so many Latinos, a multigenerational family sharing food, child-care, and money.

"When I said we were moving to Moorpark in a month, I was ripping you guys away from her arms," my mom told me. "Not once did she say, 'Don't take my babies away from me.' She just said: 'I'm very happy for you. You have to do what you have to do.' And when I think now, if you took away my kids from me at that age, when they were just tiny? That's a horrible thing. What a horrible thing I did, because her grandchildren were her life. Literally."

Our new three-bedroom, two-bathroom home in Peach Hill, the first new housing tract in Moorpark, purchased for less than $30,000 and financed with a VA loan and 3 percent down, sat in a tranquil setting dotted by orchards, open fields, and endless possibilities. Home-ownership was a destination in and of itself. Neither of my parents had lived in a home their family owned. They had been renters all of their lives. They now had a stake in something, and it would change their perspective and priorities. Among other things, owning a home triples the likelihood that you will be a voter—just for the simple fact that you feel invested in your community. My parents had fulfilled the typical trajectory of immigrant families moving, generation by generation, from their home country to the urban core, and ultimately into the suburbs as homeowners, but the transition to a new life came with many uncomfortable adjustments.

My mother, hardened to the daily life of gangs and street crime in Los Angeles, found herself terrified by the unfamiliar sounds of nights so dark the only light was from the moon. "The coyotes would call out at night and I thought they were babies that were abandoned," she told me. She missed her mother and her family. Who would look after her kids when she was at work? What if something happened and she needed her mom's help? Mom handled it the way she handled everything that frightened her: she dealt with it. She told herself there was no looking back. She told herself—and told us many times—that everything was going to be okay.

Mom felt in her heart that moving to Moorpark was best for my sister Juliet and me, and the year after we moved to Moorpark in 1971, my youngest sister, Gina, was born. Mom wanted a clean environment. She thought Moorpark was going to be like heaven for her children because the local schoolyard actually had grass. Mom was overjoyed that her kids would have trees to play in. We weren't going to grow up on a street adjacent to a freeway off-ramp. We weren't going to see any gang members. Safety, security, upward mobility, and a clean environment were becoming primary considerations for the young family, and in that we were not alone.

When we first got to Moorpark, it was a sleepy Mexican American town of just over three thousand people, built on a plateau. Half the city lived up on a hill of orchards being turned into suburban tract homes—where we lived. The other half was below in downtown, largely a poor community of Mexicans and Mexican Americans, many of whom worked in the agricultural fields I could see from our house, or had working-class jobs in construction or manufacturing or, if they were really lucky, government.

Mom had worked in social services all of her adult life, often serving the most economically disadvantaged people in Los Angeles. She didn't see the point in commuting from Moorpark to Los Angeles, so she moved to our new town without a job and only her sense of faith that she would find one. She did, as a court interpreter. She would travel all around the county, often to rural communities where the Mexican farmworkers needed her to explain their legal situation to them within the county court system.

If my life as the grandson of Mexican immigrants could be summed up in a single image, it would be the view from the front porch of my childhood home in Moorpark in the early 1980s before the inexorable creep of suburban sprawl obscured that view. Looking out, I saw vast apricot orchards, where migrant workers from my ancestral homeland of Mexico toiled for piecemeal wages each year as a largely white community sprung up around them.

The image of the farmworker inspired both immense cultural pride and a nagging fear in me, feelings of compassion for the least among us and a sense of foreboding that my existence would be as limited as theirs. I would spend my youth, my entire life, trying to reconcile the conflicting cultural forces of my suburban upbringing on a hill overlooking an agricultural valley, where people of my ethnic group lived and worked in poverty. I would try to process where I fit in my city, state, and country during a time of transformative change. I would seek answers, and sometimes an escape, from what was right in front of me.

Ventura County, one of the richest agricultural regions in California, was a key battleground in the fight to unionize farmworkers led by Cesar Chavez and the fabled United Farm Workers union. This was a fierce battle in the mid-1970s when I was not much older than six or seven. Given my mother's commitment to justice, and to helping humble people, she recognized the UFW movement as a pivotal moment in the political awakening of Latinos in California.

She insisted that my two sisters and I—all of us just beginning to understand the struggle of holding on to being Mexican American while also surviving in a white world—go with her to the harvest fields in nearby Oxnard and Camarillo so we could see the Latino political awakening for ourselves. It didn't turn out that way. The UFW protests devolved into melees as striking workers fought scabs brought on to take their jobs. Hand tools were used as weapons, and enraged men, their faces and features brimming with hatred, sweat, and blood, broke into fights around our car. My sisters and I, just little kids at the time, were terrified by the experience. In one of my formative lessons in politics I learned that disagreements often turn to violence, especially when livelihoods are threatened.

Like most young people, I was more concerned with making my

way in the neighborhood than taking the time to appreciate the signif-
icance of California history. I wasn't interested in thinking about how
my people were on the wrong side of it for more than a century before
I was born in 1971. I didn't appreciate that my childhood hometown
and state once had been land-owned by wealthy citizens of Spain and
Mexico, until it was all legally stolen by the United States Congress. I
didn't even want to speak Spanish because I didn't want to stand out.

I was, however, keenly aware that my roots ran much deeper in this
place than my white friends. I felt a sense of connection to the land and
its history that felt eternal. Yes, my grandparents migrated to California, but it always felt more like a homecoming than a start in an entirely
new place. My grandfather would migrate to California over half a century after it became the spoils of the American war with Mexico in
1850. At the time, as Cris Perez wrote in a 1982 California State Lands
Commission report on the origins of California, "The mood of the
country was of conquering warriors. Mexico had just been defeated in
a war and the United States was not about to give away land it had just
fought for."

In moving to the suburbs, my parents were, in a sense, staking their
claim, acting on their right not to be dispossessed, as so many Brown
people have been. The pain that move represented for so many in my
family reached deep into family history and into our history as a people. I don't think, until I talked about that period again with my mother
as I worked on this book, that I ever truly grasped just how hard it was
for my parents, and their parents, for our family to be divided when we
made the move to Ventura County. "That was like Columbus leaving
Spain to go to the New World," she says now. "How in the world was
I going to leave and go away from Los Angeles to Ventura County?
Leaving the circle of the family was very, very difficult. I only discov-
ered that when I was out here."

Mom talked to her own mother on the phone often, and for years
urged her to come visit us in Moorpark to see our new home. My

grandmother resisted. She found ways to ignore the offers. She made excuses. Years passed. Mom never stopped asking. "I would love for you to come and stay with us because it's such a beautiful county," she kept telling her mother. "You've got to see it. It'll remind you of Mexico with the beautiful trees and the agriculture."

Finally, my grandmother agreed. She made the trip from Echo Park in the heart of Los Angeles to see us in Moorpark, but the visit did not go well. She was overcome by culture shock. She was badly thrown. She couldn't understand why everything was so quiet, the streets so empty. She didn't say much for a few days, taking it all in, but then the questions came flying out.

"Rosie, where are the old people?" she asked my mom.

"Well," said Mom, "the old people are out in convalescent homes."

"And where are the dogs? There are no dogs here."

"They're in their backyards, Mom."

"But where are the children?"

"Mom, they're in day care."

"Where are the cars?"

"They're all in garages."

"But where are the parents? I see nobody during the day. They go into their homes, but I never see them. I see a garage door go up and then it goes down."

My mother stopped trying to explain. She had no answers, not to the deeper questions her mother was posing. "This is horrible," her mother said. "You don't see anybody. You don't hear the children crying or laughing. You don't see the dogs barking. You don't see the old people walking. You just see people wave at each other and walk on. The houses are all the same. The rooftops are all the same. There's no color here. There's no life."

To her, it was like a ghost town.

Mom had a specific fear of what our new environment would do to my sisters and me. "I was afraid that you would not be compassionate people," she says. "That you would not be street-smart. That you wouldn't know how to protect yourselves or how to maneuver in the world. That you would not be able to welcome people to know what I knew in my school: that everyone is part of humanity. I just saw segregation that scared the daylights out of me."

Mom didn't fear that we were going to be segregated based on our skin color. She feared that her kids would experience a segregation of the mind, where they viewed themselves as different from other people. "I didn't want that," she said. "Because I always treated people as if we were all the same."

- 3 -

Becoming a Republican

In my heart, I became a Republican in 1980 when I was nine years old. That was the year Reagan was elected president, a year that also brought the culmination of the Iran hostage crisis, when families like mine relied on network television to stay informed about world events, even staying up late sometimes to watch a new program on ABC called *Nightline*, hosted by Ted Koppel. Back then, there was no story more consequential than the kidnapping by Iranian revolutionaries of fifty-two American diplomats and American Foreign Service employees from the U.S. embassy in Tehran on November 4, 1979. As their months of forced captivity dragged into 1980, I understood that blindfolded Americans paraded for cameras by jeering Iranians were a sign of utter weakness on the part of my country.

My parents had always said that ours was the strongest country in the world, but suddenly that belief was shaken. Generations of American boys like me had been raised on heroic images of American military might triumphing over all adversaries. I was too young to live through the turmoil of the Vietnam War; I was only a few years out of diapers at the time of the fall of Saigon in 1975. The Iranian crisis hit me hard at a formative age. Having American political futility broadcast onto my family TV screen while I was eating dinner marked me with a feeling that I couldn't shake. President Carter was weak in my eyes. His words were unconvincing and unsatisfying. Under Carter the United States had been brought to its knees by a third-rate power in the Middle East and we continued to show our impotence daily. The American crisis of confidence spoke louder to me than anything our president had to say.

Even as a high school kid I saw President Ronald Reagan as a great historical figure who combined strength of leadership with a sweeping vision of optimism and economic opportunity for all and, ultimately, inclusion. Reagan saw U.S. values as a beacon to the world. I knew from an early age that I wanted to be a Republican, and to work hard and make the most of opportunity and not settle for a life of second-best and surviving on crumbs.

The American political crisis of the Carter years coincided with my first realization of our family economic crisis. My parents grew up in a poor, urban Los Angeles neighborhood because that was, as they saw it, all that was available to them. Even though everyone around my parents was poor as well, families knew each other and looked out for each other. Their community was like a warm blanket that brought comfort and solidarity. When we moved to the suburbs, my family traded urban crime and poverty for a sense of physical safety whose price tag was a lonely sense of cultural alienation. Among our ethnic group in Los Angeles, we were like everyone else. In the Moorpark community of my youth, we were different and poorer. We had fewer material possessions than my classmates. Our food and family interactions were a world apart from my friends. My alienation and my family's economic anxiety created the desire in me to embrace the world my parents exposed me to when they became the first in their families to leave the comforts of living near their extended family. Their progression to the suburbs meant that I would traverse two worlds—an old one and a new one—and I understood at an early age that making it in my new world was my only chance. I equated Republicanism with economic success, and I wanted that, and I wanted that for people like me.

From early youth I donned a coat of emotional armor, and I subsumed my feelings of vulnerability until they were hidden behind a sharp and protective veneer that I have carried with me ever since. Reagan offered an alternative to the weakened state of the American republic. He also became a beacon in my life when I needed one. Though Reagan was thirteen years older than Carter, to me he seemed younger. He seemed the type who could scare the Iranians and restore our national sense of strength.

When Reagan traveled to Berlin in June 1987 and gave a speech in front of the Berlin Wall, I watched the ABC News coverage with my parents that night. As anchor Peter Jennings said of the Berlin Wall, "There is no more potent symbol of division between the Soviet bloc and the Western alliance."

"I think it's an ugly scar," Reagan told the camera. "Mr. Gorbachev, open this gate!" Reagan declared that day. "Mr. Gorbachev, tear down this wall!"

The delivery was pitch-perfect and the message was powerful. As a young man, I loved watching Reagan assert the strength of American values. I loved the confidence he projected. There was a fear of overtly poking the bear in the eye, and risking nuclear war, but to me it didn't feel like Reagan was being reckless. I knew it was a high-stakes game that could end in nuclear annihilation, but to me Reagan hit just the right note in putting our best face forward, that of conviction and resolve and willingness to do what needed to be done in support of our deeper beliefs. Reagan, seeking to muster our collective strength to win a larger ideological and military struggle, projected an inner confidence in American values. He saw the big picture.

In my childhood, more than anything else, economic stability over insecurity became an obsession. I wanted to stand with Reagan and the Republicans, who to me projected strength in the world and an inclusive vision of economic prosperity for all at home. "Mom, Dad, you think you're Democrats," I'd tell my parents, "but you don't know that you're Republicans." There was a growing divide between the way my parents were voting and the values they were teaching me.

Decades later, during the 2000 presidential campaign, I learned that Reagan told the iconic Latino political consultant and my mentor, Lionel Sosa: "Hispanics are Republicans. They just don't know it yet." It was a phrase Reagan would use many times throughout his career.

The Sunday after Reagan's speech, I spread out the *Los Angeles Times*, as I did every weekend, and devoured it. The thing about the Berlin Wall that was so shocking was that it was built to hold people back—to deny them freedom. An article that day noted, "Since the 103-mile-long wall was erected Aug. 13, 1961, more than 4,900 people have escaped despite shoot-to-kill orders issued to East German border guards. There have been more than seventy-five confirmed deaths at the wall. There have been at least twenty unsuccessful escape attempts this year, and eleven incidents of shots fired."

To me, Reagan's speech defined a true vision in a way that no American leader for years to come would be able to match. Even more important was the last address of the Reagan presidency, a valedictory he delivered from the White House on January 11, 1989, nine days before he left office after eight years. It's known as the "City on a Hill" speech, and rightly so, given a memorable passage toward the end, but to me, it's really an immigration speech. It's a speech about the United States being a welcoming beacon to the rest of the world.

"Our spirit is back, but we haven't reinstitutionalized it," Reagan said, late in the speech. "We've got to do a better job of getting across that America is freedom—freedom of speech, freedom of religion, freedom of enterprise. And freedom is special and rare. It's fragile; it needs protection."

Then, in his closing lines, he evoked Pilgrim John Winthrop's famous 1630 sermon imagining the possibilities of the New World and proclaiming, "[W]ee shall be as a citty upon a hill. The eies of all people are upon us." Reagan, picking up the theme more than 350 years later, said: "I've spoken of the shining city all my political life, but I don't know if I ever quite communicated what I saw when I said it. But in my mind, it was a tall proud city built on rocks stronger than oceans, wind-swept, God-blessed, and teeming with people of all kinds living in harmony and peace; a city with free ports that hummed with commerce and creativity. And if there had to be city walls, the walls had doors and the doors were open to anyone with the will and the heart to get here. That's how I saw it, and see it still. And how stands the city on this winter night? . . . [S]he's still a beacon, still a magnet for all who must have freedom, for all the pilgrims from all the lost places who are hurtling through the darkness, toward home."

For Reagan, if we put up walls, they had to have doors. And those doors had to be open to "anyone with the will and the heart to get here." Those were words that made me a Republican, and a passionate Republican at that. I only wish that other Republican leaders after Reagan could rise to the challenge of following through in his tradition, both of moral leadership and fighting for his optimistic, inclusive vision of America and its pluralistic future. More than any other speech Reagan gave, it was the "City on a Hill" speech that evoked the most confidence in America for the simple fact that it is a speech on immigration. Only a confident nation has doors open and is available to anyone with the will and heart to get there. Only a people teeming with an inner sense of abundance can genuinely believe that its system can provide for the entirety of humanity if only everyone saw the world as we do.

Ten months after Reagan left office and went back to his California ranch full-time, the news out of Germany was stunning: on the night of November 9, 1989, the impregnable Berlin Wall suddenly turned porous; people streamed through and pulled out chisels and hammers to chip away and pull it down. The fall of the Berlin Wall was easily the most dramatic single development in those years of change as Poland and Czechoslovakia and other countries under Soviet control suddenly gained their freedom, and ultimately the Soviet Union dissolved itself.

When I heard the news that the Berlin Wall had fallen, I thought back to nights watching the evening news with my parents in our living room at home in Moorpark and talking about Reagan and what his strong vision and leadership could mean for the country. I thought of what we took for granted then, having Reagan at his sharpest and most eloquent, ready to cut to the heart of the matter and offer a convincing vision of an important moment in U.S. history.

When the Berlin Wall came down, first there was cheering and then there were questions: *What in the hell just happened? And why?* America needed answers, the *world* needed answers—and President George H. W. Bush sadly never provided them. He talked of a new world order, but never articulated a convincing vision of that order.

Bush missed an opportunity to inspire the world with a vision of a new American pluralism that succeeded, where in the past our promises and proclamations always seemed to fall short. "Liberty" needed to be more than a slogan, but a green light. The collapse of the Soviet empire from within was, in geopolitical terms, an own goal. It failed because it was an inferior system—economically, morally, and practically. But the victory of the United States in the Cold War led us to believe that our system as it existed was the apex of human experience. The end of history, as Francis Fukuyama put it.

Of course, we know now that the end of the Cold War was a beginning, not an end. America had never lived up to its own ideals, and was always, even in its best moments, a work in progress. The important questions were all about: *What now?* It was time to get to work and see what we could create. What did American ideals really mean?

Democracy had scored a victory over authoritarianism, and that was better than the alternative, but for most Americans, it was no time to gloat and no time to chest-thump. Hard questions and hard work remained if we as a country were going to promote, articulate, and *live* a culturally and ethnically pluralistic vision of how American ideals could work. No one has ever put that forth in a meaningful way, certainly not in American foreign policy on either side of the aisle. I'm still waiting to hear that, and a lot of people are waiting with me. An essential opportunity was lost, a vital moment in world history squandered, and we never get that back.

No president since Reagan rose to that challenge. Bill Clinton, who served for eight critical and pivotal years in the 1990s, chose domestic concerns over any sort of foreign-policy vision. George W. Bush had good intentions and good instincts, but they were superseded by the September 11 attacks and aftermath. Barack Obama's performance on the world stage was erratic and underwhelming. None of these three ever came anywhere near articulating a coherent foreign-policy rationale worthy of the victor in the Cold War, which helped pave the way for the rise of Trump.

Trumpism to me is a strain of political gangrene; it spreads where the body politic has already started to die off. Or, if you will, it's what sets in when there is failure in the functioning of the basic organs necessary for a healthy democracy. Trump for years wrote checks to both Democrats and Republicans. Politics to him is simply transactional. His approach, he said, was "smart." Good for business. He wanted to run for president to build his brand and would have run on the Spartacist ticket if he thought that running as a militant Marxist gave him the best chance to win. Instead, telling associates that he thought Republican voters were the most "gullible" (his word), Trump ran as a Republican, except that he purged the party of all institutional memory, all principle, all continuity with the ideals of Ronald Reagan.

Trumpism emerged with the collapse of Reaganism. It provided fear where Reagan found strength. It provided anger where Reagan showed confidence. It was scarcity where abundance once overflowed. Trump instead offered the religion of grievance and the elevation of his own whims to matters of state. Where Reagan boldly demanded that we tear down the walls of tyranny and oppression, Trump postulated that without walls we would be overrun and replaced. Where Reagan saw walls as needing doors, and national strength built on a commitment to inclusivity, Trump saw walls as a symbol of his pyramid-scheme approach to political power, an offer to buy in and back a winner, keeping out the suckers who weren't quick enough or lucky enough to be on the right side. Like all pyramid schemes, it worked for a while, surprisingly well actually, until it didn't.

- 4 -

Political Director of the California Republican Party

"Let me get this straight," I told the guy in front of me, who needed me more than I needed him: "You want me to save the Republican Party's ass and come up with a fresh new way to appeal to Latinos in California, tapping my experience and expertise and insight, but you don't want to give me the title of political director of the California Republican Party? Instead, you want to hire a 'big name' who will make the money I should be making, but not really do jack shit? Is that pretty much it?"

He stared back at me. We were at a chain restaurant near party headquarters in Glendale, a TGI Fridays or something like that, but I'd completely forgotten my half-eaten plate of food. I'd have walked right out and never looked back, and my friend Rich Lambros, executive director of the California Republican Party at the time, knew it.

"Yeah, that's pretty much it," he admitted.

Welcome, ladies and gentlemen, to Republican Party politics in the 1990s. I learned working with Lambros and the state party at the time how much Republicans need Latinos, and how much opportunity they have with Hispanic voters, if only they make a priority of appealing to them—which at the time, other than my own efforts in California, and the work of a few other people, they were emphatically not doing.

This was in late 1997—after rabidly anti-immigrant Proposition 187, later ruled to be unconstitutional, was passed in 1994, and Republican governor Pete Wilson rallied support that year by running hard on 187 and whipping up anti-immigrant sentiment. The California Republican Party was dominated by figures like Robert "B-1 Bob" Dornan, born in New York to a former Ziegfeld Follies showgirl, a Southern California Republican congressman who never met a defense appropriation he didn't like and who ran a race-baiting campaign in 1996 against Loretta Sanchez—and lost. The state was going through a transition on immigration, and Republicans were on the wrong side of all these political issues. They desperately needed somebody with a last name that was not Jones, Watts, or Schroeder to get out there and front for them, which I'd been doing as "deputy political director" that year.

I was a true believer in a cause that would define me, nourish me, isolate me, enrich me, condemn me, and expose me to a career of chasing a truth I thought I knew until I didn't. I would be blessed and cursed. I would make friends with the enemy of my friends, and I would be enemies with people who shared my life story.

My journey through Republican politics began in 1992 as a volunteer with my first campaign during my sophomore year at Moorpark Community College, when I worked on the reelection campaign of my local congressman, a Republican named Elton Gallegly. In 1982 Gallegly became Simi Valley's first elected mayor. He'd first been elected to the House in 1986, claiming a seat left open by Bobbi Fiedler's Senate run. In 1992, after historic redistricting that made his district much more Latino, Gallegly's Democratic opponent was a Latina named Anita Perez Ferguson, later honored by *Hispanic Business* magazine as one of the "100 Most Influential Hispanics in the United States."

Not knowing a thing about how politics worked, I sent a letter to the campaign office of my local congressman. When I got word that the Gallegly campaign wanted to interview me for a volunteer spot on the campaign that year, I was ecstatic. I got a haircut, put together some respectable clothes, and planned to arrive early for my interview.

My father helped me shine my shoes the night before. As we watched the evening news together with my sisters, I suddenly noticed that my mom was missing. Where had she gone? I found her in her room, leaning over an ironing board. She had perfectly pressed three sharp-edged, heavily starched white shirts for me. I mean they were *perfectly* pressed.

"Mom, what are you doing?" I asked. "We're all in the living room watching TV."

She looked up at me, her eyes heavy with emotion.

"Michael, I know you're going to do great tomorrow," she said. "I'm so proud of you. I'm sorry we don't have the connections to get you to where you want to go in life. All I can give you is what I do best. I can iron really well, and I can give you perfect-looking shirts."

The Gallegly campaign changed everything for me. In truth, I had no idea what I was in for, what I would have to do, and what I would have to ignore to rise in California's GOP ranks. I didn't know that I would witness the future of Republican politics in California—and in America—by volunteering to help a firebrand Republican take on an upstart Latina challenger.

For me it was all about gaining experience, and credibility. Volunteering for that campaign brought me both. But first Kay Duffy, Gallegly's campaign manager, would put me through a test to make sure I wasn't some kind of spy. Yes, campaigns send operatives to competing campaigns to get information, listen in on conversations, and report back on strategy. Kay was friendly and inquisitive about my conservative beliefs. To her apparent surprise, I seemed to answer everything sufficiently, and she asked me to return the following week.

When I returned to the Gallegly office, it was teeming with older ladies dressed in red, white, and blue and adorned with elephant brooches. They were members of the Republican Women's Federated—the volunteer army of Republican campaigns. It was a little awkward because I wasn't just the only man in the room; I was the only Latino and was younger than everyone by about forty years.

Nevertheless, I was excited to get started, so I took a seat beside the ladies and waited for my instructions while sitting on a folding chair stuffing letters for the campaign.

"Mike," Kay said, "we have another project for you next door."

I gathered my things and headed out the door and down the hall to basically a storage closet with a single desk and chair.

"We're going to have you work here," Kay said.

"Okay," I said humbly but willingly, taking a seat at the desk.

"We need you to work on these," she said, setting a large stack of envelopes before me. "These envelopes have been stamped first class by mistake. We need someone to carefully remove all of the stamps so that we can use both the envelopes and the stamps again. That way we can, you know, save the campaign money."

I would be working alone, in a storage closet, monotonously removing stamps from envelopes. This was how my political career began.

"No problem," I said, mustering as much excitement as I could, feeling emboldened that my work peeling stamps was saving the campaign valuable resources and somehow protecting the balance of power in Congress, while also saving the republic.

"Let me know if you need water or anything. I'll come back and check on you in a bit," she said as she left the room. The door closed behind her, and I began my tedious work, delicately peeling off stamps that could be used again for the important purpose of getting the congressman's campaign message out.

Hours passed by the time I completed my task. I rounded up the stamps and the envelopes and took them back into the campaign office. All of the older lady volunteers had left by this time, as had the few paid staff members. The only person that remained was Kay (another lesson I would come to learn about the long hours a campaign manager works).

"Kay," I said meekly, "I'm finished."

She looked up from her computer, surprised to see someone.

"Oh," she said. "You're still here?"

"Yeah, I wanted to make sure I got this done today so you could use them right away," I said.

"Um, okay," she responded, sounding perplexed.

"Let me know how else I can help," I said. "I've got time and am willing to help out."

"Come back tomorrow. Same time," she said.

I returned the next day to ladies milling about the campaign office. And I was again escorted to the storage closet next door and handed another stack of envelopes. After many more hours of this monotonous exercise, I again returned to the campaign office long after everyone but the campaign manager had left. Kay looked up again from the computer screen, surprised again to see me.

"Sit down," she said. I did.

"Who are you?" she asked.

"Mike Madrid," I responded, not sure what she was asking.

"No," she said. "Who *are* you? What are you doing here and what are you looking to get out of this?"

I passed the test. A campaign spy would have left after a few minutes in the isolation closet I endured. I wasn't learning anything useful for any other campaign. It was clear to anyone but a true-believing kid that I wasn't doing anything of consequence. It was my commitment, methodical work on a menial task, and desire to help that opened the door of Republican politics for me. Only a few weeks later, I was offered a job on the campaign organizing precinct walks and prioritizing which voters we needed to reach.

On the Gallegly campaign I also first crossed paths with Arthur Finkelstein, the legendary Republican pollster whose brilliance inspired me to follow in his footsteps into the savage world of electoral politics. "A canny Brooklyn-born brawler who made his political debut on a Greenwich Village soapbox, Mr. Finkelstein was adept at aggressively wooing disaffected Democrats to his Republican clients' camps in statewide campaigns," the *New York Times* wrote in its 2017 obituary. "His strategy was largely to ignore party labels and focus on the basic beliefs that moved these Democrats. . . . Mr. Finkelstein transformed liberal into a dirty word. His conservative political action committee was instrumental in the surprise unseatings of liberal Democratic stalwarts in 1980, including Senators Birch Bayh of Indiana, Frank Church of Idaho and George S. McGovern of South Dakota."

Finkelstein was tough, he was shrewd, he was ahead of his time—and he opened a whole world to me with his mantra of appealing to what he called "rejectionist voting." As the *Times* explained, he "pioneered sophisticated demographic analyses of primary voters and methodical exit polling, and of using a marketing strategy, called microtargeting, to identify specific groups of potential supporters of a candidate regardless of their party affiliation."

I'd never even heard of Arthur before I volunteered on that campaign. I remember being on a call and hearing this voice on the other end, a distinctive, confident, hard-edged New York voice. I didn't know who was talking, but listening to him made me think right away: *This guy is a wizard!* He is on the phone from New York, and he knew more about my home district than I did, and I knew my community really, really well. I asked how many times Finkelstein had been to our district, and the answer was shocking to me: none.

I said to myself: *This is what I want to do.* I wanted to be the guy who would tell people everything they needed to know about a campaign. I wanted to be the guy that everyone listens to—including the congressman running for office. The real power was not with the politician, it was with the guy telling him what to do, what to think, what to wear, and what to say. I wanted to be the guy whose directions set an entire campaign in motion and whose strategies determined where millions of dollars are allocated to help a candidate win. It's not just finding what's in your gut. It's not just math. It's art and science. You have to be really good at both.

I was particularly interested in the differing Latino reactions I was getting to Congressman Gallegly's campaign and to the emerging issue of illegal immigration. It was at the same time extremely emotional and polarizing and nuanced in a way that people understood different policy options intellectually, but could never get past who was saying it. I would find a lot of Latino voters who had naturalized and become citizens who said they were angry at those who came here "illegally," who should wait their turn as they had. Second-generation Latinos like my parents, the sons and daughters of immigrants, were often the most stridently opposed to any perceived attacks on the "community." To them it seemed they had an obligation to defend immigrants—legal or illegal—in much the way they had been a bridge to this new world for their parents, as my mother had as an English interpreter for her parents. By the third generation, the Latinos I talked to mirrored almost precisely their white neighbors expressing concerns about taxpayer funding for services, growing crime, and overcrowded schools, as well as the state not being reimbursed by the federal government for the problem it had created. All of this fascinated me because I could quantify results through data about what my grandmother, mother, and I all felt about an issue that spoke differently to our community than the people I grew up around.

Non-Hispanic whites gave me similar insights. White Democrats specifically had varied views on the illegal immigration issue, with some voters profiled as the most progressive on nearly every issue emotionally pushing back on immigration broadly and illegal immigration specifically. This was not like any other political issue we were dealing with. It was incredibly intense, visceral, and it cut to the core of who people felt they were.

In much the same way, I would years later find Latino and Democratic voters shocked to learn that Barack Obama had been labeled the "Deporter in Chief" for expelling more undocumented residents than all previous presidents combined—"more than 2.5 million people," between 2009 and 2015, as ABC News reported—or that Joe Biden was erecting more miles of wall, continuing with Trump's planned construction despite campaign promises to the contrary. Latino voters were having a difficult time moving past their predetermined views on how politicians from each party were treating their community.

Conversely, I felt disgusted at agreeing with a lot of conservative whites. Even though we agreed on the policy solutions to the problem, it was shockingly clear what was motivating their beliefs—and it was straight racism. While I didn't agree at all with the sentiment behind their beliefs, it was troubling to arrive at the same conclusions. Opposing illegal immigration isn't racist; it is in fact the obligation and responsibility of a sovereign nation to protect and regulate the flow of migration along its borders. But there were far too many conversations I was having that weren't about that or economic concerns—they were about having "those people" in our country. You know, the "drug dealers, rapists, and I guess some are very fine people" sentiment. I was disgusted that I agreed with them because our reasons were so different.

I started obsessing over getting more and more data points to find greater understanding of the motivations behind political decision-making, and after many months knocking on thousands of doors, I found I was really good at predicting people's responses based on all sorts of criteria. Gender, age, race, last name, neighborhood income. A whole new understanding of the world was opening up to me.

I kept moving in that direction by knocking on hundreds of doors for Gallegly. I talked to everybody: cranky old white people who had had enough. There was clearly a lot of nativist sentiment out there. I would talk to people who were clearly comfortable saying the most racist shit I ever heard. But did I also talk to suburban Latinos, college-educated folks? I did. I heard some of them say that they had been in Ventura County for three generations and that they were happy that someone like Elton Gallegly was talking about securing the damn border. These educated, Latino suburbanites were and are a reality that didn't get mentioned much by the parties or the media. But they are out there. Far more than conventional wisdom lets on. Now, when I was walking for Gallegly, did I talk to Spanish speakers who felt under attack by his words? I did. But what gets misrepresented by both parties is that the Latino community is about more than just immigration. Most of the conversations I had with Latinos had nothing to do with immigration, legal or otherwise. The vast majority of Latinos were worried about their jobs, public safety, the quality of their kids' schools, and health care.

It was also on the Gallegly campaign when I first met Glen Becerra, who would become a close friend and a major influence. Glen was from nearby Simi Valley. He was a few years older than me and was a history major at UC Berkeley who had come home during the summer of 1992 to work on the campaign before starting his senior year. Like me, he was raised Catholic, and like me, he had been a lackluster student in high school and found Moorpark Community College as a second chance at getting his life on track. Like me, he saw a connection between the values of his family and what he found in the Republican Party of that era. "Family values are more than words to me," he wrote in a *Los Angeles Times* opinion article that fall. "Families provide the moral guidance and personal integrity our country needs and the government should support. There has never been a time in our country's history when the rejuvenation of strong family values has been needed so much."

Glen was a student leader and had become very involved in Governor Pete Wilson's administration as the rare Berkeley student who would vocally support a Republican. Unlike me, Glen was much better suited to be a politician. Where I was combative and aggressive, he was conciliatory and looked to build consensus. Where I looked at data to understand voters, he took to working the crowds and trusted his intuition. We complemented each other well, and soon became fast friends; he pushed me to be involved at a higher level than just campaigns.

One night Glen offered up an idea.

"Governor Pete Wilson's office is looking for a student appointee to the Board of Governors of the Community College system," he said.

I paid no attention. I had little interest in governing boards or appointments to anything, let alone policymaking. At that point in my life, what did I know?

"I think you'd be perfect," Glen pursued, not leaving it alone. "You'd be a full voting member of the board that oversees the largest system of higher education in the world."

He eventually wore me down and I agreed to his suggestion, not really picking my head up from the precinct sheets I was organizing. Glen got to work making phone calls and soon a packet showed up that he sternly instructed me to fill out and return promptly. I did, and shortly after that I was contacted for an interview with the governor's appointments secretary. Not long after that I received a phone call congratulating me on being appointed to the Board of Governors. It was my first lesson on the power of relationships in politics.

Governor Wilson and his administration handed me an immense opportunity with my November 1992 appointment. (Ironically, a leader who would be remembered most of all for inflaming anti-immigrant, anti-Latino sentiment would help launch the career of this outspoken Latino.) It would be my responsibility to be the voice for students in directing the system that is the best hope for millions of people to get an education.

In those years, the cost of illegal immigration in California became a leading issue in Sacramento. As the budget deficit deepened, the political winds tilted toward prioritizing California taxpayers before those who were here illegally. It was a sound argument and difficult to refute. I also agreed with it. Needless to say, student activists lobbying me did not see it as I did. For the first time, I was confronted by white progressive student activists telling me that I didn't care about the concerns of Latino students. It still boggles my mind to think about, because white progressives haven't changed much in the ensuing years. Here I was, a Latino student doing everything I could to prioritize services for students like me, and I was being told by white progressives that I didn't care about them. It would not be the last time that white progressives would tell me what was best for me and people like me because I could not understand what I needed as well as they did.

From both a policy and a political perspective, it is not racist to prioritize services to the citizens of the state and country where you reside. It's simply not. To argue that we should be paying for government services for the undocumented while also increasing the cost of services to taxpayers is not going to get you very far politically. Tensions in California were on the rise and racial overtones were seeping to the surface. California was seeing more day laborers in front of convenience stores and bodegas, all of them ready to work for American taxpayers, but for piecemeal wages. Suddenly, you began to see businesses with voice messaging that included Spanish language options. Latino kids were outnumbering white kids in classrooms, rattling anxious whites throughout the state.

On my path I was often alone, the one brown face on campaigns and within the California Republican Party structure. But the people who were always with me, without fail, were my sisters and the elders in my family. I remember visiting my nana in the early 1990s, in the days when I was moving rapidly toward my new life. I knocked on the door of the apartment where she had raised her children in Echo Park. I had been in Los Angeles on an official trip for the Board of Governors and I was wearing my first real suit and wanted my grandmother to see me all dressed up. As I walked up the stairs to her apartment, my cousins who lived next door peered at me dismissively. Far from the exciting encounters we always had as children, I felt a palpable tension.

My cousins, the ones I had grown up with, did not look happy to see me and barely acknowledged me.

"What's wrong?" I asked as I walked past them on the porch stoop and into Nana's house.

"Nothing," one of my cousins said with what looked like a sneer and an eye roll.

I walked into my grandmother's small apartment perplexed and immediately recognized the problem. There on the wall before me was my grandmother's cherished photograph of her father, her framed Sacred Heart of Jesus print and accompanying crucifix. Right next to it, carrying equal weight, was the letter she had proudly framed and displayed showing the latest success of her grandson being appointed to an important state board—signed prominently by Governor Pete Wilson. That's how much my grandmother loved me.

~

My cultural identity was the driving force behind my political aspirations and passions. I simply went right, where my contemporaries went left. The hill overlooking my hometown in Moorpark would become the site of the Ronald Reagan Presidential Library and Museum in nearby Simi Valley. As I stood in the audience on November 4, 1991, the day the Reagan library was dedicated, I was a twenty-year-old moving toward a life that could not have been more incongruous for a young man of my ethnic background. Inspired by Reagan's strength and optimism, a philosophy of self-reliance, and the idea that if I believed in it enough and worked hard, I could escape the part of me that hurt and rise as far as my dreams and the promise of America could take me.

My search for my purpose in life took me to Georgetown University, an amazing development for a Mexican American kid with a 2.1 GPA in high school. I graduated from the Edmund A. Walsh School of Foreign Service at Georgetown in 1997 and wrote a senior thesis that launched my career, focusing on Latino voting patterns in the Southwest. My emphasis was on the distinction between voting trends driven by Mexican Americans as an aggrieved racial minority or, as I argued, a more typical case of gradual integration and assimilation into the broader political and social culture of the United States.

In 1996, I took a semester off from Georgetown to work on a California State Assembly race. I'd already run some Assembly races by then and was brought into a Southern California race we as Republicans really should have won. It was identified as the most competitive Assembly race that year. The candidate was John Geranios, a businessman and business professor at Mount Saint Mary's University in Brentwood who had come out of nowhere to win the Republican nomination. The Democrat, Scott Wildman, was a teachers union representative, and Geranios was a good candidate, personable and clearly intelligent, but it was all new to him. If I'd had more of a veteran candidate, ready to grind out more votes with direct canvassing, I know we'd have pulled this one out. As it was, we lost by only 192 votes in the end. It was a lesson for me that sometimes as a campaign manager you're only as good as your candidate.

Working on the Geranios campaign, I noticed another Greek American Republican running in a nearby district and saw immediate political talent and potential. The candidate's name was Richard Lambros, and he easily won the Republican primary in District 56, which includes Long Beach, but then he narrowly lost in the general election—losing, as it happened, to a Latina English professor, Sally Havice.

I reached out to Lambros after Election Night, just to make contact, because I saw him as an up-and-comer who had the potential to win some races. We got to know each other a little at the time, comparing notes on his Assembly race and the one I ran for Geranios. When he was named executive director of the California Republican Party, I reached out to let him know I'd be happy to help on Latino issues.

At the time, "B-1 Bob" was generating terrible headlines for the GOP with his legal challenges trying to overturn his loss to Loretta Sanchez. Here it was, an early instance of a theme that would rear its head throughout my career, a conservative Republican alleging voter fraud by undocumented immigrants with no actual evidence on which to stake those claims.

"Look, I can help you navigate through this," I told Lambros.

"That would be amazing."

The chairman of the party at that time was a guy named Michael Schroeder, who was very good to me. Michael was the first chairman not from the donor class. A wealthy man in his own right, he worked the grassroots to get to where he was. He also had the distinction of being Bob Dornan's lawyer against Loretta Sanchez, which meant he was rightfully taking a ton of flak from people saying: *You're for Latinos, but you're with B-1 Bob against Loretta claiming voter fraud?* I come out of Georgetown, bright-eyed and bushy-tailed, saying I can help.

They really, really, really wanted me to get on board. I was already developing a national reputation for this stuff. I was aware of my own value to them, a Latino who understood these issues, who had credibility with the media, and who understood campaigns. I had everything that they needed in a political director, but they wouldn't give it to me right away, which I think tells you all you need to know about how seriously California Republicans took Latinos. What they wanted was to find someone with the right name to front for them and pretend like there wasn't a problem, which is still, by the way, what Republicans tend to do. They can't help themselves. There are always going to be people willing to play that game and advance themselves within the party by singing a pretty tune about how everything is wonderful, reality be damned, the Tim Scotts and the Nikki Haleys and the Vivek Ramaswamys of the world.

My ask was different. I wasn't going to waste my time going through the motions. I said: *I'll do it, I'll cut this unholy compromise, but you've got to give me the authority to start moving the party in a direction, as tough as that's going to be. I'm going to say stuff that will not be comfortable, and I don't mean whispered asides to insiders in the party in Sacramento, I'm going to use my megaphone to broadcast my message to the entire state, every Republican in the state who reads a newspaper or watches the evening news, and make an urgent case to them that this party has to change.*

My family did not raise me to let anyone disrespect me. I could be calm and accommodating and even flexible, but I was not about to let anyone roll over me. I was an asset California Republicans badly needed on their side, not just because my name was Madrid, not just because of my brown skin and brown family, but because when it came to mixing it up in quotes to reporters, I brought just enough "I don't give a shit!" honesty to make me unpredictable and colorful. Reporters actually liked using my quotes, they didn't just type them into their articles holding their noses.

It was front-page news in the *Ventura County Star* and other papers in early September 1997 that I'd organized a GOP Hispanic Summit in Los Angeles, the first such event California Republicans had held. As Democratic Party consultant Bob Mulholland told the paper, "The total elected Hispanic leadership from the Republican Party in California can fit into a phone booth." This being the last days when phone booths were still a thing.

It was my first public mention as "deputy political director" of the Republican Party, a title I was working on upgrading. "Mike Madrid, deputy political director of the state GOP, is the organizer of the event," the *Star* wrote. "He says that if Republicans direct their message to Latino voters, the rest will come naturally. 'All we need to do is talk about core Republican Party principles and our Republican Hispanic base will come home in 1998,' Madrid said. 'The heart and soul of Latinos is the heart and soul of our party. The polling data on virtually every issue shows that we're right in line.'"

Talking to the *San Francisco Examiner* for an October 19, 1997, article, I was again blunt: "The honest truth is nobody knows what the Hispanic voter is," I said. "The true test is who can win the heart and soul of the Latino middle class, which is exploding," I told the *Los Angeles Times* that December.

So, at that lunch at TGI Fridays with Rich Lambros, I was blunt, telling him: *Look, I'm happy to make a case. I'm a Republican, I believe this. But you've got to also give me the leeway to one, be honest, and two, commit to actually turning the ship around. Not the way you think you can do it, but the way it needs to be done.*

By the following spring, there I was in newspapers all over the country and on cable news, now carrying the added respect of being "political director, California Republican Party." My job description was to start building the statewide political infrastructure for the upcoming gubernatorial race for the 1998 election cycle. State parties are bare-bones operations in non-election years, so anyone on the payroll is expected to help wherever they can. But as I was organizing voter registration drives, training county chairmen, and recruiting candidates to run for office, the communications team was getting inundated with press calls wanting to know about the GOP's post–Proposition 187 "Latino problem." I would gather that, conservatively, over 80 percent of press inquiries were about how much trouble the GOP was in with Latino voters. How bad was Pete Wilson's image for the party? What messages would we use to attract this fast-growing group? Just how much damage had Republicans done to themselves with the anti-immigrant rhetoric?

It didn't take long for the executive director and party chairman to realize I was being vastly underutilized. There was a huge upside to having someone who had answers to all these questions, and, just as important, had a Latino surname, responding to reporters' questions. I fit the bill perfectly and spent most of my day working with the press from then on and was so good at it that I became the official spokesperson for the party. I rapidly became a source for reporters' stories on the national beat and began working with some of the top reporters in the business, explaining the demographics, the party's problems and challenges, how it could solve them, and what the future would be for the country politically in the coming decades.

Soon Bill Schneider from CNN was scheduling interviews at the GOP headquarters. George Skelton, Cathleen Decker, and Mark Barabak from the *Los Angeles Times* wanted to meet for lunch. Adrian Wooldridge from the *Economist* wanted to talk. Reporters from the *New York Times* and *Washington Post* were looking for story ideas. The *New Republic* and *National Review* would call to see if they were getting their upcoming articles right. I had become a regular on television and radio, and journalists came to appreciate the challenges of my role, but also the candor, honesty, and directness with which I answered their questions. As much as a role like this would ordinarily call for a generous amount of spin, I chose a different path. I was frank in my assessment of the problems the party faced. I was honest about how bad it was, and I was critical of the ugly elements within the party that had gotten us to this point.

On March 15, 1998, I was quoted in the *St. Louis Post-Dispatch* saying, "What we have to understand as a party is that what's happening with the Latino community is so profound that there is not one issue that will speak to them." Little did I know that, twenty-five years later, I'd still be giving interviews reminding people that Latinos are part of a diverse community that needs to be understood for the vivid and varied mosaic that it is.

The *San Francisco Examiner* published an article in May 1998 I was happy to see, reporting, "The Latino population is generally younger than the rest of California, but it is getting older, starting families and settling down. . . . The GOP believes at least some part of this population can shift back to the Republican Party. Mike Madrid, political director for the state party, said the GOP will run a large get-out-the-vote campaign on Election Day targeting Latino communities in Los Angeles, Sacramento and the Central Valley."

That was a strange political year in a lot of ways. For one, that was the first year after California instituted a so-called blanket primary, in which typical restrictions on primary voters, like voting only for candidates of their party, were out the window. Voters could cast a vote for whichever candidate they wanted, in whatever party.

The biggest unknown in 1998 was how voters would respond to Bill Clinton's sex scandals, and I played offense. It was good politics on my part: try to make the "greatest sex scandal in American history" stick to Clinton. Except for one problem: Clinton was massively popular. His approval rating at the time was 65 percent. As Pennsylvania's Republican governor, Tom Ridge, said after election results came in, "If you make it a referendum on a president with a 67 percent approval rating, you shouldn't be surprised if the election goes against you." Newt Gingrich had been predicting Republicans would pick up forty seats in the House; instead, Democrats picked up five seats. Give the *San Francisco Examiner* credit for a colorful banner headline: "GOP Takes a Big Pie in the Face: Gingrich's Boast Goes Up in Smoke; Party's Setback Unmatched in Modern Times."

Later that month—in a quote that applies very much to the present day as well—I told the *Kansas City Star*: "The party was hit with a two-by-four. Whether you're a moderate or a conservative, you do not have a prayer if you do not give people a sense that they are welcome in your vision for America."

The bottom collapsed on us that year. It was the worst year for Republicans in modern history. We lost thirteen seats in the California State Assembly besides the five seats we lost in Congress. The Republicans got their asses handed to them, Newt Gingrich's time as Speaker of the House was up, and in California Gray Davis was elected governor, the first Democrat to lead the state in sixteen years. That was in part because of the Latino leviathan, and the growing power of Latino voters. The trajectory was clear for the state: it was blue and getting bluer. The Republican Party had not been knocked out totally, not just yet, but it was given a standing eight count. Someone bring on the smelling salts. The party was in deep trouble if it didn't adjust, and to be very blunt, even twenty-five years later, as of this writing, the California Republican Party has still not made the adjustments.

- 5 -

Un Nuevo Día

One thing you never say in politics when you're helping put together an event is that it was perfect, but this was perfect. It came off just the way my mentor, Lionel Sosa, and I and our whole team had planned it: former Texas governor George W. Bush's arrival in Philadelphia for the 2000 Republican National Convention played out just how we wanted. I don't think there has been a better example in U.S. politics of how to earn the votes of Latinos. The one Republican who understood how to reach the Latino community better than any other was George W. Bush. He knew never to talk down to voters, any voters, never to patronize them, and he could speak about general themes with what came across as sincere, relatable respect for Latinos. He talked directly to the voter almost as a friend.

To set the stage, the Bush team planned to have him stop along the way to Philadelphia on a six-day tour of battleground states. He was in Dayton and Columbus, Ohio. He was in Gettysburg, Pennsylvania, paying homage to Lincoln. These were high-energy stops the candidate enjoyed, and they made for great visuals for TV and the newspapers. We wouldn't have him arrive at First Union Center, the convention hall in Philadelphia, until the final day of the convention, but one day earlier, we'd hold an event at the Philadelphia Museum of Art on the *Rocky* steps made famous in the beloved Sylvester Stallone movie. Only, there was a twist: this was no ordinary political event, this was a fiesta, a fun, joyous, Latino-flavored celebration, the first time ever in U.S. politics that an American political campaign had placed a Latino-themed event as the centerpiece of their candidate's arrival into a convention city. Pretty unbelievable, when you think about it, but true.

At 10:47 a.m. that Wednesday, CNN moved its coverage from the convention hall across town to the *Rocky* steps, and anchor Bill Hemmer explained that candidate Bush was just about to "address a crowd of Latinos who have gathered here." First, yet another George Bush would speak—this good-looking, twenty-four-year-old, half-Mexican, fluently bilingual George P. Bush, whose mother, Columba, was born in Guanajuato.

Young George rose to the occasion. He talked about the day in 1993 when the great labor leader Cesar Chavez died. "My mother came to me and she was crying, in tears," George P. said that morning. Then he broke off into a flurry of Spanish and explained: "In English, that means, you have to find somebody who finds and represents what you believe, who represents our people, who represents our culture. That person is my uncle, and I want to welcome, and I want you guys to put your hands together for, the next president and First Lady of the United States, George W. Bush and Laura Bush!"

This was the moment Lionel and I and the rest of our team brainstormed repeatedly. It had to be perfect. All the dramatic buildup in the world doesn't matter if you don't stick the landing. So rather than have the candidate simply appear from behind the stage, we set it up so he could walk through the crowd—both a great icebreaker with the several hundred Latinos in attendance and a surefire way to get George W. Bush himself fired up, since he's at his best out with the people. You saw that in his years as a Texas Rangers owner when he would sit with the fans in the rows behind home plate and talk to anyone who approached, including, sometimes, cracking jokes with a player, visiting manager, or umpire.

The branding of the Bush 2000 GOP convention in Philadelphia was: *El Sueño Americano*, Spanish for "The American Dream." When Bush arrived in Philadelphia, "*El Sueño Americano*" placards were everywhere. Legends of the Latino community, such as the late Celia Cruz—the Cuban-born Queen of Salsa—were showcased. There were Cuban Americans, Mexican Americans, and Puerto Rican appointees to the campaign.

The key for Latino message guys is you can't just try to connect with Latinos, which is hard and rare enough anyway, but you've got to do more at the same time. Here's where it gets tricky: you also have to make it sellable to the white consultants who must sign off, and to their audiences, because if it's too much, they're going to say, *No, no, no, we can't be that Latino. We can't be that non-white. We don't want to scare people!* We always had to be cognizant of doing outreach, but also getting white, college-educated suburban women to stick with us. That was always the real brass ring. We had to do both.

Almost the first words out of Bush's mouth that morning in Philadelphia were a shout-out to a figure who counted as royalty in the Latino world, Emilio Estefan of Miami Sound Machine fame, husband of Gloria Estefan, who did as much as anyone to give Latin music crossover appeal in the United States in the 1990s. "I want to thank my friend Emilio Estefan," Bush said. "Emilio was telling me behind the stage he had only been nominated for seven Grammys. I think that you can judge the nature of a man by the company that he keeps. I'm keeping really good company with Emilio."

It was bold and a little brassy to have the Republican presidential nominee staking so much on a Latino-themed event the day before his prime-time speech at the convention, but it worked—big time. We could all feel it. And it worked because, with this candidate, it was seamless and genuine. George W. Bush was more comfortable among Latinos than the patrician, leather-soled WASPs of his New England upbringing. There was no way Al Gore could have pulled this off. This was *not* the forced "sombrero politics" I had seen in GOP politics throughout my career. This was something completely different.

The Philadelphia Museum of Art event set a positive tone for what the party and country was becoming—and what it could be. The campaign was confident and welcoming in a way that expressed the best version of the Republican message. This was no act. Bush loved the Texas Latinos who had given him surprising support as governor and I think he also loved that this was an area where he clearly distinguished himself compared to his father, the former president. George W. was a little goofy sometimes, but compared to his opponent, Al Gore, who also spoke some Spanish, he had a way of coming across likable and relatable in his workmanlike Spanish, even with the occasional slipup—some suggested he was relatable precisely *because* of those slipups—whereas Gore always sounded superior and condescending in Spanish. Funny how that works, isn't it?

The reaction was overwhelmingly positive, first within our target audience, the Latino community, but also in the media. Not that we won everyone over—or ever expected we could. "It was like trying to swallow a huge pill," Bergen (New Jersey) *Record* columnist Miguel Perez wrote in August 2000 in a column that was skeptical but full of grudging respect. "I really wanted to swallow the 'compassionate conservatism' act at the Republican National Convention. Really, I did. If for nothing else, maybe it was just for the pleasure of seeing Democrats stop taking the Latino vote for granted. The much-anticipated and promoted GOP outreach to Latinos had me thinking that it was possible, in such a short time, for rehabilitation to work. I wanted to convince myself that the mean-spirited immigrant-bashers of the 1990s would suddenly turn into rehabilitated amigos of the Latino community." Perez came to the harsh conclusion that "it was all an act," but lamented, "Unfortunately, many Latinos are swallowing it—hook, line and sinker—and now it's up to the Democrats, in their upcoming convention, to challenge Republicans on the specifics of their so-called compassion."

We'd succeeded in shifting the ground of U.S. politics—at least for a time. Here's an amazing first the 2000 Bush campaign established in elective politics. There was no separate "Viva Bush" campaign that was segregated from the Bush 2000 campaign. There was no differentiation between our efforts with Latinos and the rest of the campaign. The press corps dubbed it "the seamless campaign," and they were right.

It was all one campaign, and as someone who saw it up close I can report that it was done the right way, no lip service, but real coordination. Bush 2000 seamlessly incorporated Latino professionals from the highest level of the campaign down to the volunteers. Every effort was made to incorporate the voices of Latinos. Even during the Iowa caucuses there were Latino staffers that were buying Spanish radio ads in the remote parts of Iowa, proving the desire of the campaign to find Latino voters wherever they could. This was the first presidential campaign of either party to have operated this way.

Bush 2000 resonated with many Latino voters because it was pitch-perfect in hitting just the right note, aspirational and patriotic and above all inclusive in its messaging to upwardly mobile middle-class Latinos. The campaign didn't shy away from evoking the immigrant experience, but it was only summoned as part of an overall narrative that attempted to speak to various communities within the Latino community. The campaign placed an emphasis on second- and third-generation Latinos and—this was key, and insightful—on English-dominant speakers. News flash: plenty of Latinos, then and now, don't speak a word of Spanish.

Two men above all others deserve credit for the power of that 2000 campaign's Latino outreach; Bush himself, since he was all in, and Hall of Fame ad man Lionel Sosa, just an incredibly talented and visionary figure who it was my great pleasure to get to know that year. I had just left my role as the political director of the California Republican Party and Frank Guerra, a San Antonio political consultant, had reached out. Frank was a political consultant to Republican congressman Henry Bonilla of Brownsville, Texas, who in 2000 was considered an up-and-coming Hispanic Republican, and he and I started working together. That led to the opportunity to team up with Lionel working on Bush 2000 and watch and learn.

Lionel fell in love with the Republican Party young, much the way I did at a different time and place. As *Texas Monthly* relayed the story in July 2000, "Lionel Sosa was a preteen with an independent streak when his father brought home a television set for the family's San Antonio home in 1952. When he turned it on, Republicans were anointing General Dwight D. Eisenhower as their nominee for president. The youngster was mesmerized."

Lionel remembered his parents telling him, "Lionel, you can't be for Ike—he's a Republican. We've always been Democrats. The Republicans are the party of the rich, and we're poor."

Lionel's response: "The Democrats are the party of the poor? Who the hell wants to be poor?"

He turned Republican partly as a way of rebelling, but only partly. "Sosa, who says he is still the only Republican in his family, realizes that he is bucking a deeply imbedded cultural bias when he asks Hispanics to vote Republican," the *Texas Monthly* article continued. "My No. 1 rule is that I don't try to convert them to the Republican Party," he says. "'Vote Republican' is a tougher sell." What's easier, he says, is asking them to vote for a specific candidate by "tying Republican conservative values to conservative Latino values." So, in the Bush television ads, "we talk about what's important to Hispanics: education, family, creating an environment in which you can achieve what you want to achieve because there aren't going to be obstacles in your way."

Lionel had a vision that at its core was always very optimistic. He was not a culture-of-grievance kind of person, not at all, though when he did choose to go negative in an ad, he could kneecap them with the best of them. He first made his name in politics doing ads for John Tower, a U.S. senator from Texas from 1961 to 1985. With Lionel's help, Tower won reelection in 1978 with 37 percent of the Latino vote when no Texas Republican had ever won more than 8 percent. Soon Sosa was getting a major spread in the Marketplace section of the *Wall Street Journal*, and in 1981, he started his own agency, Sosa & Associates, which was on its way to becoming the largest Hispanic advertising agency in the United States with major clients like Bacardi, Dr Pepper, and Coors. Over the next two decades he'd make a mark nationally as one of the most influential Hispanic ad men ever. "I was so proud to be doing all this, and all of my friends, including my mother and father, were saying, 'Are you crazy? Doing stuff for the Republican Party? They're a party of the rich. You should be doing work for the Democrats.' And the Democrats had never even reached out to me." I learned so much from Lionel. When we were in a street fight, he could gut you. His ads in Spanish for John Tower were brutal. But Lionel's default approach was a very deferential, subtle, soft touch and a warm, sweeping vision.

The whole theme of the 2000 Republican National Convention was an aspirational view of what America was becoming because of Latinos—not despite them, *because* of them. The ads Lionel produced that year were the gold standard in political advertising. He was never afraid of simplicity and directness. My favorite, a thirty-second spot, opens with the words *"Es Un Nuevo Día"* on a blue background with a soundtrack of a crowd chanting, "Jorge Bush! Jorge Bush!" and quickly cuts to Bush onstage, speaking in Spanish. Just after Bush says, *"El Sueño Americano es para todos,"* and raises his arms for emphasis, the screen cuts to the Statue of Liberty, then to a shot of Bush kissing a little Latina girl. Lionel mixes in footage of the flag, rippling in the wind, but only very briefly, very tastefully. Bush talks in Spanish of being able to win in November—and no one watching the ad can doubt that.

Lionel freed all of us working with him to look up and not down.

He freed us to work harder to say what we wanted rather than taking an easy way out. He did all that and always in an understated, agreeable way. He chose to navigate through Republican politics with a quiet humbleness rather than brazen fury. I think it's ultimately a choice Latinos have had to make as they climbed the ladder of success in a white world. Do you play the game the "right way" or conclude that there is no "right way" when your talent is never going to be taken seriously?

I remember working very diligently with Lionel and with Frank to capture George Bush's personality, which is very optimistic and sunny. It's difficult, but we helped Lionel do just that. One of the most prominent ads featured in Bush 2000 was a multigenerational piece that depicted a Latino family in Texas as they gathered on the Fourth of July to raise the American flag and celebrate the idea of America. It was the country they loved and it provided the opportunity for their family to realize their dreams. George W.'s optimism, like Reagan's, was a perfect fit for the optimism of Latino voters. The RNC would back up its commitment with a $10 million ad buy, a breathtaking amount for a Hispanic-focused ad in those days.

We developed a moving thirty-second spot that focused on simply presenting Latinos as proud Americans. We tried to convey warmth and community. In a sense, we attempted to portray Latinos the way George W. Bush saw them—the way we wanted America to see them. It took a great team to pull that off. Frank Guerra was brilliant in his ability to capture the blend of American and Latino culture, and he and Lionel fed off each other. Our working group also included Lance Tarrance, one of the most famous GOP pollsters, who believed that the emergence of the Latino electorate was going to presage the next great American political realignment—after the Southern strategy, in which he played a major part—and Leslie Sanchez, who would serve as the Spanish-language spokesperson for the RNC and ultimately become the director of the White House Initiative on Educational Excellence for Hispanics. The Southern strategy signaled an extraordinary realignment of the race and partisan coalitions in the United States during the last century. The profound ramifications of this shift are still very evident in our politics today. It seems a distant memory now, but Black voters from the end of the Civil War until the late 1950s were an overwhelming and reliable constituency for Republicans—the party of Lincoln, the Great Emancipator. Opposition to Jim Crow segregation and the burgeoning civil rights movement deepened the national racial wounds, particularly in the South.

Meanwhile, white Southern voters, who were strongly anti-Republican "Dixiecrats" as part of the legacy of post–Civil War attitudes, responded to Republican racist appeals first by voting incrementally for Republicans and eventually reregistering as Republicans. This ultimately propelled Republicans into majority party status in Congress by 1994, marking one of the most significant political realignments in the country's history, driven largely by changing racial attitudes and the backlash to them.

Emerging realignments are usually presaged by pollsters identifying a gap between the way a voting bloc registers public opinion and the party they ultimately vote for on Election Day. Since Reagan, Republicans had noticed that Hispanics polled much more closely with Republicans on a range of issues, but ultimately voted for Democrats. Lance Tarrance felt he had found the makings of the next major American realignment. Our group of five would work together, separately from the Bush-Cheney campaign, and take on advertising and messaging duties for the RNC and independent efforts for the campaign. We knew that the country was changing and that there was no counterpart to our work on the Democratic side. If George W. Bush won and ushered in a new day (*Un Nuevo Día*) for the Republican Party, we thought our work would be central to explaining a new American story. We decided to form a Latino-owned firm and buckled up for the pending wild ride.

What's amazing about that year was how little others in politics learned from our example. George Bush wasn't successful that year in appealing to Latinos because he used his rudimentary Spanish at campaign stops. He was successful because he understood the Latino community and he tailored his campaign rhetoric not only to attract Latino voters but to explain Latinos to non-Latino voters. When he was first running for the presidency, Bush allies in the Latino community recognized Bush's ability to frame the Latino community in universal themes without pandering to them.

The data demonstrates that Bush was able to express values in a way that not only attracted Latino voters to his candidacy, but demonstrated how Latino voters are different from Black voters. On religion and faith, Bush appealed to voters in a way that eludes Democrats. In the main, Democrats fear talking about faith. Democrats have ceded faith to Republicans, and in their rhetoric, Democrats have a disrespectful predisposition for turning their noses up at religious people and even openly mocking religion. According to the Pew Research Center, the number of Latino evangelicals grew substantially between 2000 and 2004 and a majority of Latino Protestants voted for Bush in 2004. Bush also won the support of a third of Latino Catholics. This stood in stark contrast to Black Protestants and Catholics who overwhelmingly voted for Bush's opponents.

In addition, Bush gained ground in every category defining Latino voters between 2000 and 2004. He was at nearly 50 percent of Latino males, Latinos aged forty and over, Latinos with family incomes of $50,000 and more, and suburban and rural Latinos. His numbers among younger Latinos were also very respectable. In 2004, 34 percent of Latinos between the ages of eighteen and twenty-nine voted for Bush, and 40 percent of Latinos in their thirties voted for Bush. Nearly a third of Latinos living in poverty voted for Bush, as did 30 percent of Latino voters whose family income hovered between $15,000 and $30,000 a year. Latino independents voted for Bush at 42 percent and

39 percent, in 2000 and 2004 respectively. And Bush also attracted a third of Latinos who identified as moderates or lived in cities of fifty thousand residents and larger. Overall, wrote Pew, "Bush had taken 44 percent of the Hispanic vote—a 10 percentage point increase over his share in 2000."

Going back to his days as governor of Texas, Bush showed he was different. One of his first acts in 1995 was to pick up a tradition started by his predecessor, Democrat Ann Richards, to host the governors of Mexican states bordering Texas. "Friends bring out the best in each other," Bush said that January, welcoming the governors. "May our friendship bring much good to both of our countries." Sounds simple, doesn't it? Those sound like words that every president or border governor should emphasize regularly—and yet they don't.

As president in August 2001, speaking to the Hispanic Chamber of Commerce, Bush went further, saying, "Mexico is a friend of America. Mexico is our neighbor. And we want our neighbors to succeed. We want our neighbors to do well. We want our neighbors to be successful. We understand that a poor neighbor is somebody that's going to be harder to deal with than a neighbor that's prospering. And that's why it's so important for us to tear down barriers and walls that might separate Mexico from the United States."

Bush continued, and it's hard to revisit his words now without wincing: "Oh, I know there's some voices who want to wall us off from Mexico. They want to build a wall. I say to them, they want to condemn our neighbors to the south in poverty." Then he added, to a loud round of applause: "I refuse to accept that type of isolationist and protectionist attitude!"

It pains me to recall Bush's pro-Mexico, pro-immigrant, pro–Mexican American, and pro-Latino stance when considering the ethnic divisions exacerbated in recent years by Trump and his acolytes in the current GOP. Meanwhile, the tradition of Mexican governors attending the inauguration of the governor of Texas ended in 2015 with the election of Greg Abbott, who would quickly become an adherent of Trumpism.

Bush won with strong Latino support—both in the nation that is Texas and the nation that is the United States. He was right about Mexico and Mexicans, and right about Mexican Americans and other Latinos: we are part of the American dream, part of the fabric of America, a vital force in helping build a bridge to the future. If others had the courage to show us the respect George W. Bush did, the sky is truly the limit.

When George W. Bush was in the White House, comprehensive immigration reform seemed at hand. Bush wanted tougher border security, but unlike many fellow Republicans, he also wanted to legalize more than 12 million undocumented immigrants. He wanted to hold employers accountable for hiring practices that exacerbated illegal immigration. He wanted a merit-based immigration system, all sensible ideas. It remains an enduring shame that less than eight months after he was sworn into office, 9/11 sidelined what Bush might have done on immigration reform.

The Bush administration would change, the Republican Party would change—and the country would change. Bush's affection for Mexican Americans had offered the possibility of a total reset of how the largest subset of people within the Latino community were perceived in the United States. If Bush had attempted immigration reform early in his first term, the hope of many until 9/11 intervened, he might have used the power of the Oval Office to normalize Latinos and Mexican Americans in our politics. But all that promise and possibility of a new day in the Republican Party came crashing down with the Twin Towers.

First He Came for the Mexicans

I opposed Donald Trump from the moment he came down the escalator at Trump Tower to announce his candidacy for president of the United States. I was against Trump *because* of my conservatism, not in spite of it. I knew he was a threat to everything I believed, and for me this was deeply and profoundly personal. Reagan had closed his presidency with an inspiring speech that signaled to Mexican Americans and other Latinos that the United States was welcoming of immigrants. George W. Bush made it a cornerstone of his 2000 presidential campaign to reach out to Latinos and Mexican Americans. Now Trump was literally starting his quest for the White House by attacking Mexicans.

"When Mexico sends its people, they're not sending the best," Trump said on that fateful day in June 2015. "They're bringing drugs, they're bringing crime. They're rapists and some, I assume, are good people."

Hearing these words, the bile rose in my throat, but he was far from over.

"I would build a Great Wall, and nobody builds walls better than me, believe me, and I'll build them very inexpensively," Trump said. "I will build a great, great wall on our southern border and I will have Mexico pay for that wall, mark my words."

Trump's toxic politics represented a betrayal of all the ideals that had led me to a life and career as a Republican. Seeing the speed with which he tore through the Republican presidential primary field, and the fervor with which Republican voters accepted this self-styled American authoritarian in the mold of a Latin American strongman, that was my breaking point. Everything I had built and worked for in my career was destroyed by the coronation of Trump as the standard-bearer for the Republican Party.

The Beltway pundits and other brilliant people who discounted Trump's rise through the Republican ranks were failing to see what was plainly obvious: the Republican Party had chosen a brand of politics that pitted white voters against dark-skinned ones. The Republicans who opposed this tactic were washed away like tiny coastal homes in a monsoon. Trump's main skill was shamelessness. His incapacity to be empathetic—and willingness to turn people against one another, to this degree, for his own petty reasons—was a trait our country had deftly avoided in a leader throughout our history until now. Trump's recognition of the depths of fear and insecurity many white Americans then felt in a changing country, coupled with shameless exploitation, would take all of the lessons I learned about politicians scapegoating and using racial wedge issues and turbocharge them. Trump innately knew what was driving the average Republican voter and what the Republican Party was really all about and activated it to his advantage. His rise was a symptom of a disease of bigotry, animosity, and a bottomless well of grievance in our politics. I'm a data guy and I've seen all the numbers as they relate to voters who supported Obama and then Trump suggesting race wasn't a motivation for white Trump voters. I've got thirty years of talking to white voters of all political stripes about immigration and I can tell you with every fiber of my being that what motivated white Democrats in California to support Proposition 187 was no different than what motivated white Democrats in Pennsylvania, Wisconsin, and Michigan in 2016—the fear of a changing America. An America that was becoming less white.

I looked at my past and surveyed my future and wondered what was left for me in this career I had chosen. Reagan brought me to the Republican Party and former congressman Jack Kemp kept me there. My ability to connect emotionally, intellectually, and politically with Kemp's principled Republicanism, built around helping the disadvantaged to advance, had made it possible for me to believe that racism in the Republican ranks was isolated among powerless party crazies. I had spent twenty-five years working to build a more welcoming, confident, optimistic, multiethnic Republican Party and had failed spectacularly.

The last flickering embers of the party I knew went out in 2012 when Mitt Romney lost to Barack Obama. Paul Ryan, who would become Speaker of the House, was Romney's running mate and the last disciple of Jack Kemp left on the national stage. Both men were the last of their kind. Republicans of every kind in California have also gone out of style. Their failure to court Latino voters has been a significant reason as to why. Their stubborn refusal to change had cost them dearly and continues to this day. Except for Arnold Schwarzenegger and one other politician who has since left the GOP, no Republican has been elected to statewide office since the early 2000s.

When Trump arrived on the national stage, my old bosses Elton Gallegly and Pete Wilson both endorsed him. Donors, supporters, and activists who talked about the importance of building a broader-based party all jumped on the Trump train. So did so many you'd have never, ever believed would fall in line. Even George P. Bush came out for Trump—George P. of the Bush dynasty, who introduced his uncle before the 2000 Republican National Convention in Philadelphia. After everything Trump had done to humiliate his father, former Florida governor Jeb Bush, George P. still genuflected before Trump and was nevertheless destroyed in the Texas GOP primary for attorney general with 40 percent of Republicans polled saying they would never vote for George P. because he was a Bush.

When I was starting out in Republican politics in the early 1990s, the type of outright racism that I now saw Trump directing at Mexicans was largely relegated to the rantings of low-level bigots on the fringe of the party. Ronald Reagan, George H. W. Bush, and George W. Bush all actively sought to drive these elements from the dark shadows of the GOP. Each spoke of there being no room in the party for those who harbored those sentiments. Those three men, the Republican leaders of my generation, were all pro-immigrant. They were pro-Latino. They were pro-Mexico.

Even though I clearly identified first as an American, I was and remain proud of my heritage. Reagan, Bush I, and Bush II created an emotional lane for me to be a Republican. I was joining a party whose leaders liked people that looked like me and my parents. All three leaders loved the romance of the immigrant story that was also my family's experience. My motivation to be a Republican was wed to the conservative values of my upbringing with the principles of Republicanism that I felt were perfect complements to my family values: God, country, patriotism, and economic opportunity.

But here was Trump labeling Mexicans as "rapists." There he was repeatedly attacking a respected U.S.-born district judge, Gonzalo Curiel, presiding over a case involving the blatantly fraudulent Trump University, saying Curiel "happens to be, we believe, Mexican," a blatantly racist attack—"textbook racism," Republican Speaker Paul Ryan called it. Here Trump was being cozy with neo-Nazis and white supremacists. There he was attacking Republican icons like John McCain. Here he was supporting tariffs, forsaking strategic allies while embracing antidemocratic Russian strongman Vladimir Putin. There he was, disparaging our intelligence community and every level of every institution and every norm that had made American politics a calling to people like me. He was taking everything it had meant to be Republican and flushing it down the toilet—and there were Republicans going right along with Trump as he gained more popularity the shriller and more bigoted he became.

It was the kind of hell you'd read about in novels and history books, but hoped never to live through yourself. Hundreds of friends, candidates, and consultants I knew who for years, often decades, had claimed to be committed to conservatism flipped in nothing flat. Soon enough they came out as Trumpers of one slimy stripe or another. Anyone helping the man, whether actively and directly or passively, through acquiescence and silence, was beyond deserving any benefit of the doubt. Cowards, every last one of them.

The other painful reality that hit me at the time was that, for all his attacks on Mexicans and Mexican Americans, Trump was actually attracting Latino supporters. Of all the Republican candidates that have run for president in the past twenty-five years, why Trump? Why did Latinos shift to the right for Trump of all people and why, eight years later, is so much polling showing Trump doing so well with Latinos against Joe Biden?

Certain undeniable truths played a role in the recent rightward shift to Trump. Yes, there is more energy and outright advocacy occurring in Latino evangelical churches. Yes, the anti-socialism and anti-communism rhetoric did create a multigenerational Republican voting bloc in South Florida among Cubans and Venezuelans. Yes, effective Spanish disinformation campaigns were rampant on WhatsApp from nefarious sources. Cumulatively, these all did play some role, but it's very hard to prove quantifiably that any of these combined accounted for the size of the national shift that has been occurring since Obama's high watermark with Latinos in 2012.

There's a much clearer and straightforward argument that, combined with all of these factors, gives us a road map to understand what is happening. Put simply, Latinos who have been in the U.S. longer are showing very clear assimilative tendencies that are stronger than the racial and ethnic lens that conventional wisdom suggests they should.

In other words, it's not that Trump did so well in 2016 and 2020, it's that demographics suggest he should have done much better. In fact, the Latino performance of other Republicans like Florida governor Ron DeSantis or Texas governor Greg Abbott suggests Republicans can do as well if not better with Latino voters than Trump. Plenty of data exists to suggest this is not a Trump phenomenon—rather, it's a demographic one as second- and third-generation Latinos tend over time to develop more conservative voting patterns.

Donald Trump's poor performances in 2016 and 2018 were likely the last vestiges of the large presence of immigrants from the 1990s' influx on the voter rolls—the number of which have been decreasing ever since. Where 2014 was a record low rate of turnout of Latino voters, 2020 set an all-time record high. The great migratory waves that changed the demography of the Southwest from 1990 to 2007 is now a U.S.-born Latino tidal wave that is just hitting election booths across the country.

Trump would go on to insult and attack people of all colors, religions, and political affiliations, but it should never be forgotten that he attacked Mexicans first. Those attacks were, as we all know now, just the first in a long line of offensive acts. I for one still bristle with anger when I think about Trump's attacks on former Republican presidential nominee John McCain, saying, "He's not a war hero. . . . I like people who weren't captured." I loved McCain and admired everything about his heroism, but shame on the pundits who claimed that attack was *the* moment when in their eyes Trump showed he was unfit for higher office. Excuse me? I've had quite enough of this kind of quiet bigotry. Sorry, women, the moment wasn't when the *Access Hollywood* tapes leaked with Trump saying he would "grab 'em by the pussy!" If any moment after his attack on Mexicans was the disqualifying moment for you, then you are part of the problem. The moment Trump showed he was obviously unfit for the White House was the day he announced his run for president and immediately demonized the Mexican people. Period. End of story. It all went together. It started with Mexicans and moved on to verbal declarations of war on Muslim people, disabled people, gay people, trans people, women, private citizens, war heroes, former Republican nominees for president, and countless others.

In March 2016, I attended the annual Conservative Political Action Conference (CPAC) in the Washington, D.C., area and was blunt in a workshop I gave on how to broaden the party. "Don't talk about building a wall," I told the McClatchy news service. "We are asking to be irrelevant. We made it very easy to beat the heck out of us." I was clearly still roiling in shock and denial at the growing vulgarity bubbling up in the Republican Party. Trump at that point had already won ten primaries and caucuses with that message.

The GOP descent into white nationalism began long before Trump decided he was a Republican, but after the 2016 election white nationalism became a defining feature of Republicanism. I readily concede that not everyone who voted for Donald Trump was an out-and-out racist. Probably true, but what difference does it make? Anyone who voted for Trump had to be comfortable on some level with voting for a dangerous racist hell-bent on whipping up racial hatred and exploiting it for his own personal and political gain.

That meant a lot of the friends, acquaintances, mentors, vendors, and activists I worked with for years were extremely comfortable supporting overt white nationalism, which is the socially acceptable way of saying "racist." When I say "a lot of people in my life," I mean virtually all of them. Yes, there was the occasional political consultant who would tweet his shock at Trump's latest debasement of the Oval Office. But these cowards were more worried about keeping their business contacts in place. They did not want to risk being disinvited from cocktail parties where any outward display of Trumpism would make them pariahs if they dared reveal it in mixed company.

These cowards enraged me even more than the overt racists. These were the enablers, to whom democracy was just a business, for whom all was transactional, absent of any kind of ethical or moral framework. These were the people who consciously knew what they were doing was wrong, and that the Republican Party had become dangerous. These were the ones that criticized me for speaking out about the rot that the whole party structure had become. Sure, they'd tell the press they were anti-Trump, but they would support candidates that were enamored with him, they took money from a party that empowered him, they encouraged their candidates to endorse him.

There were too many Republican Judases to count, but enough to threaten the life of the republic. My Rolodex in California was full of them.

For all the focus on Trump, he was only a symptom of a disease of corruption and bigotry in our politics. The disease lived within the voters Trump activated. He didn't invent racism in politics. His skill was finding the words that unlocked and emboldened people who put white supremacy over the country. The bottom line was that the voters Trump activated were more than willing to stick with the worst president in American history if it meant keeping the Democrats from office.

No one doubted where I stood on Trump. I made damn sure of that. I was an immediate and visceral Trump critic. Given my background as a nationally known expert on Latino voters and engagement, I became a go-to source, ever ready to supply edgy responses to the growing Trump movement. I was growing angrier and angrier by the day. I had spent decades defending the GOP from withering attacks, only to have all my hard work and the assumptions behind it called into question, and now I had to listen to right-wing trolls describing me as having Trump Derangement Syndrome. They wanted to accuse *me* of being possessed by irrational anger, my emotions boiling over because of Trump.

It was true. I sure as hell was. I had a bad case of TDS, probably one of the worst in the country because it was rooted in something deep and profound, as I would come to realize at that CPAC conference: my sharp sense of betrayal. All the leather-soled Brooks Brothers suits who talked about "big tent" politics were falling into line behind the most obvious fraud in American history. I had spent decades defending these cowards against charges of racism. I'd fought for them. Now, I was finding out, if the choice was between losing their big consulting or lobbying contracts or supporting a two-bit carnival barker cum race-baiting dictator, then sure, that one was easy for them, they would goose-step right in line to keep the gravy train rolling.

The vast majority of Republican-establishment types failed the basic test of morality, common decency, and a basic understanding of the idea of America—and the average GOP voter wasn't too far behind them. For me, taking a check from the Republican Party became untenable. Even my work in nonpartisan races at the local level made me feel as if I were supporting a structure that was enabling the worst elements of society. My very vocal criticisms continued almost daily and led Politico to label me "California's most anti-Trump Republican."

The balancing act of living in two worlds that had defined my life had run its course. Donald Trump forced all Americans to make a decision, to take his side or not, and I was no different. It was tribalism of the worst kind, and it was loudly asserting I was not of their tribe.

How else to explain the Confederate flag appearing more in Iowa, Pennsylvania, and New Hampshire than in North Carolina, Georgia, and Alabama during the 2020 presidential campaign? This was more about a white sense of decline in a changing America than it was about the South Rising Again.

I was faced with the prospect of burning down my life's work.

- 7 -

Political Odd Couple

I always had a knack for being a pain in the ass when I wanted to be. (In Spanish we call it being a *cabrón*.) It's a useful skill, especially as a political consultant. I'd put this skill to work back in my days as spokesman for the California Republican Party, going against one of the most recognizable Latino politicians of his generation: Antonio Villaraigosa. Antonio is among the most talented politicians I've ever worked for or against, but in his days in the California State Assembly as Democratic majority leader (1996–1998) and Speaker (1998–2000), he presented weaknesses that I was happy to exploit. For one, his Spanish was iffy, and he knew it. Two, he was easily flustered, or at least he was easily flustered when he was standing on the floor of the Assembly trying to do a TV interview in Spanish, despite not really having a grasp of the language. He was easily flustered when a wild man from the state Republican Party was crowding around, talking in quick bursts of Spanish to the TV crew filming him, making jokes at his expense, needling him in every way possible. That was the start of my relationship with Antonio. To say we hated each other would be an overstatement. We were both passionate about our beliefs. He was doing his job and I was doing mine. But if a tape surfaced of Antonio in this period saying of me, "I hate that fucking guy!" I would not be surprised. And I had some salty things to say about him as well.

Years later, not much more than a few months into Trump's presidency, Antonio and I would work together and our collaboration said everything both about my political journey and the changing face of politics. I came to the painful realization that my previous path had failed, and I knew I had to challenge myself and my assumptions and core beliefs. I did that *not* by joining the other party, but by finding someone in the other party experiencing a parallel dilemma. I would team up with Antonio and do my best to get this Democrat elected governor of California, and the disappointments of that campaign would show me how, in the 2010s and 2020s, white progressives were increasingly pulling the Democratic Party to the left and Black and Brown voters were becoming the party's moderate voices.

It was a big deal in January 1998 when Antonio Villaraigosa, who years later would become mayor of Los Angeles, was elected Speaker of the California Assembly. At the time, the Assembly Republican caucus was mostly old white dudes—just as it is today—but they were in the minority, with thirty-seven Republicans in the Assembly versus forty-three Democrats. Villaraigosa's election heralded a new, progressive era in California politics.

Born in L.A., Antonio studied at East Los Angeles College and then UCLA, where he was a leader of an outspoken Chicano campus organization. He made a mark early on as a skilled union organizer and advocate for United Teachers Los Angeles and served as president of the L.A. chapter of the ACLU. His early career was marked by a passion for traditional liberal causes, but he would find ways to challenge himself and grow—which would lead us to meet somewhere in the middle.

Antonio came of age in California politics as part of a generation of Latino leaders politicized during the Proposition 187 campaign that would go on to achieve remarkable political success—names like future Assembly Speakers Fabian Núñez and John Pérez; president pro tem of the state senate, Kevin de León; and future United States senator from California Alex Padilla. Each would become friends and colleagues over the years, and each would achieve various milestones—good and bad—as their trajectories mirrored the maturing community.

They were all forged in that political moment and, at least throughout the nineties and the early years of the new century, steeped in a particular vision of how Latinos think politically. That's not to say they don't have their own belief systems and political opinions—they certainly do but, in those days, to achieve success as a Latino politician it was enough to be anti-Republican and anti-conservative and race to what was then often the left wing of the Democratic Party. As the Republican Party collapsed during the course of our careers in California, a one-party state sometimes indicated that Latino political successes meant toeing the party line over the needs of the community. Looking back now, it's easy to see that much of what defined a wide swath of emerging Latino politicians was what they were against more than what they stood for.

For all the talk of the importance of diversity and multiculturalism, there was little ideological room among Latino liberals to hear out a Mexican American Republican like me, even when—especially when—I was right. To liberal Latinos in the California of my youth, I was an outcast. I was the enemy. But the truth was, I was just as Latino as they were, and at some level they knew some of my criticism was on target. Many in private told me they were grateful I was levying criticism of Democratic failures in addressing Latino concerns when they themselves couldn't politically. I was one voice that could help them maneuver to the middle as they were being dragged to the left.

Latino activists would call me an "apologist" for racists. Latino reporters would ask how I could live with myself after the cameras were shut off. I remember one particularly brutal haranguing I got from the general manager of the L.A. office of Univision, the Spanish-language media giant. I heard it all: "*vendido*" or "sellout," "Tio Taco," "coconut," you name it. I would be invited to Latino "community" events so that I could be publicly confronted for my beliefs. Bilingual pejoratives would rain down on me, coming from a generation of Mexican American activists who came of age as fierce opponents of Republicanism in California. But I was undeterred. My story was about living in two worlds, and it was remarkable only because it wasn't remarkable. Latino Democrats of consequence knew there were valid issues affecting the community that were too risky for them to confront within their own party. They were just too cowardly to put their community over their party. The education system was failing far too many children, but disproportionately Latino kids. Housing affordability was affecting us more than any other group in the state. Poverty was disproportionately Latino, as was the prison population. But it was always easier to call Republicans racists than acknowledge that Latinos were falling further and further behind as Democrats accrued more and more power. I heard every day how horrible Republicans were, but almost never how great the Democrats were doing for Latinos—because the truth is they weren't. The shrill voices of both the Republican and Democratic parties dominated the political discourse and activists on either side were not going to force me to make a choice between two parties when I considered choosing my Latino community as the better option.

~

I hadn't seen Antonio in years when our paths crossed one night in someone's private box at a Los Angeles Lakers game during the 2002–2003 season. I quickly buried the hatchet with Antonio—and not in his back. He'd run for mayor of Los Angeles in 2001 and lost to a guy named Jim Hahn, the son of the iconic Los Angeles politician County Supervisor Kenneth Hahn, whom Antonio should have beaten. He was the better candidate, but was struggling with an electorate that even in Los Angeles in 2001 wasn't comfortable with electing the first Latino mayor since 1872. I basically had some tough love for him.

"Man, I think you ought to run again," I told him.

He was surprised to hear his biggest antagonist talking that way, but I was serious.

"I think the time is now," I told him. "I think you were a little bit ahead of your skis your first time. Maybe L.A. wasn't ready for a Latino mayor then. But now they are."

I wasn't the only one giving him that advice, but I'm sure it had an impact coming from a Republican who had spent a good part of his career trying to beat him. I know he took my words to heart. He'd tried to downplay his ethnicity his first time running against Hahn, which made sense politically. He was right to worry about scaring off white voters by seeming too Latino. (A familiar theme, as we've seen.) During that first run for mayor, Antonio had to strenuously downplay his Latino identity, notoriously screaming at *Los Angeles Times* editors every time they labeled him "potentially the first Latino mayor in modern times" when describing him. But, as many thousands of minorities have learned while running for office, you can't have it both ways. Ultimately running from who you really are is always dicey politically. For Antonio's rematch with Hahn, he would play it differently in 2005— and win with more than 58 percent of the vote.

Whatever our personal history, it was a proud moment for me— and my whole family—when Antonio was elected mayor. *El Alcalde.* I remember Mom calling me the next day to talk about what a big moment this was for Mexican Americans. "His mother must be very proud," she said. We both wished my nana had lived to see the day.

Antonio served two terms as the mayor of Los Angeles and earned plaudits for his creative leadership and coalition-building. In August 2005, *Time* magazine named him to its list of the "25 Most Influential Hispanics in America."

"Two weeks after Antonio Villaraigosa was elected mayor of Los Angeles in May, he traveled to Washington, where people lined up to acclaim him as the new standard bearer of Latino political power in the Democratic Party," *Time* wrote. "Expectations were high that as L.A.'s first Latino mayor in more than 130 years, he would usher in a new era for Latinos, who historically have been underrepresented in politics. But Villaraigosa was quick to show that his agenda extends beyond the interests of a single ethnic group." The article quoted Antonio, speaking at a lunch for Latino leaders, saying, "'It's not about Latino power. It's about building a coalition.'" Later that day, Antonio spoke at a convention of Democratic Party activists and told the group, as *Time* reported, "that when he looked around the room, there were too many whites and if they wanted to take back America, they would have to be more ethnically inclusive. Coming from one of the nation's most ethnically diverse cities, Villaraigosa, fifty-two, stands for a bridge-building, post-ethnic style of politics." Antonio would go on to serve as a national cochair for Hillary Clinton's 2008 presidential campaign and chair of the 2012 Democratic National Convention.

I see Antonio's political journey and my own as almost mirror opposites. I guess in a way we've met in the middle. Antonio went from being a very, very progressive guy to understanding his own Latino identity within his political party and at the same time moderating—or better yet, challenging—his party's commitment to his community, which is what I love about his story. His is a unique trajectory where he matured as a politician and became much more centrist as he got older. Most important to me, he came to understand that ideology was hurting our community. Over a bottle of wine, just Antonio and me talking, he later credited me with making some good points when I was in my twenties arguing against many of the policies he supported and a lot of what he proposed. As we got older in the business, and so much happened to make me see the Republican Party through a different lens, I saw I had underestimated the power of race messages and the damage they were doing not only to the social fabric but to the community and to its perceptions of Republicans. Antonio had under-acknowledged how much the orthodoxy of his party was hurting the Latino community. In our own ways and on our same paths we had fallen into the same trap. Our community had never wavered in telling us what it needed from the political system—we both believed too much in our own party's commitment to respond to them.

~

Years after I'd run into Antonio at that Lakers game, he called me out of the blue. A lot had happened since we'd last spoken, including Donald Trump's election in 2016. While my relationship with the Republican Party was becoming more contentious and acrimonious, it was also coming into clearer focus. I remained committed to the purpose that brought me into politics in the first place—to help elevate my community. My concerns about the policies that I saw as growing poverty, limiting opportunities, hindering educational attainment and success had not changed. If anything, I had grown more passionate and committed to them. As the Republican Party was growing white-hot (literally) with the burning resentment of the politics of white grievance, more and more of the data I was tracking on Latino metrics of social and economic success were coming in every day at work and things were not looking good. In fact, they were looking downright awful. Latinos were disproportionately poor in California. Our schools were disproportionately underperforming. Our young men were too often on a pathway to prison. Housing for Latinos was becoming harder to afford than any other group in the state. Middle-class opportunities were shrinking for the first time since the Great Depression. California was a storybook place to live if you were white, college-educated, and a homeowner. The ability for young non-college-educated families to drive out to the suburbs to escape poverty and crime like my parents did a generation before was becoming a disappearing memory. California was becoming what I had warned my parents about twenty-five years ago and it was happening just as Latinos were emerging as the state's largest ethnic group. At a time when we had never had more political power in terms of representation, so much socially and economically was heading in the wrong direction.

As I was becoming more and more vocal about the damage the Republican Party was doing to our social fabric, I figured someone had to have the courage to stand up to the policies inside the Democratic Party and say, "This isn't working for Latinos." I had found that courage was virtually nonexistent in the Republican Party as so few stood up against what was so obviously wrong. Taking a stand against your political party in this country is a surefire career ender. It means the end of your titles and access. The end of your contracts and business. It means the end of "friendships," or at least relationships that political people term friendships.

It may sound naive and foolish after decades in politics, but I truly never comprehended just how much this industry—and it is an industry—is motivated by fear. I did understand that the arguments I had made and fought for as a conservative on behalf of my community were unconventional. I understood that they were unpopular in a wide segment of the Latino population and especially in the political class. I understood that many of the economic arguments and solutions for poverty, housing, and education were not stereotypical views of Latinos in politics, but that's precisely why I chose this pursuit in life. Things were evidently not working for Latinos and I didn't care for convention. I cared about making a difference and improving lives.

I knew I now had to make a life-altering decision. I could not work for a party that so openly embraced the racism, isolationism, and protectionism that were anathema to everything I believed. But could I work for someone on the other side of the aisle who was demonstrating that same commitment to saying, "This isn't helping my Latino community"? Could I support someone who also had the courage to choose to improve the lives of the least among us, the poor, the unrepresented, and the voiceless in a party where the evidence was showing things were getting far worse for Latinos than they were getting better?

So when Antonio called me, his timing could not have been better.

"Hey, Madrid," he said.

"Hey, Mr. Mayor," I said. "How are you?"

"Good," he said, getting right down to business. "Listen, I've got a favor to ask."

"Yeah?" I said.

This was going to be interesting. Antonio Villaraigosa asking *me*, Mike Madrid, his one-time number one headache, for a favor?

"I'm thinking about running," he said.

I hadn't hung up or started laughing, so he took that as assent and kept talking.

"I need you to run some numbers, do some of your work, and talk this through with me," he continued. "We can't do this over the phone. I need you to fly down and walk me through the path and show me if I've got a path to win this thing."

I'd known he was considering a run for California governor against fellow Democrat Gavin Newsom. That was no secret.

"Why are you calling *me*?" I asked bluntly.

It was a fair question, and he answered honestly.

"You're the only guy I can trust because you're not a Democrat," he said. "You're not in my party. There are a lot of people in my party that don't like me. You're really good at what you do, and I know where your heart's at. As much as you've been a pain in my ass, I've never doubted your commitment to our community and you've never doubted mine. I know that you'll be committed to helping me out regardless of what happens."

"That's actually the right answer," I said, laughing. "Okay, I'll do it."

I ran some numbers and went and spent a good long day with him. I was pretty blunt. "Look," I said, "I don't think there's a good chance here, but there is a chance. If you're going to do it, this is the way that I would do the race."

I went through my analysis and he agreed with everything I said.

"Do you want to do this race?" he asked me.

I think I snorted.

"Antonio, you can't hire me. I'm a Republican," I said.

"I can do whatever I want to do," he said.

"Antonio," I said, "you're in a party that doesn't even want to be on the same block as Republicans, and I'm in a party that doesn't want to be on the same block as Democrats."

"Well, isn't that the problem?" he said.

He was right. I decided I'd go for it. I would try my hardest to get Antonio elected governor of California.

I think Antonio and I both enjoyed the novelty of the two of us teaming up, a kind of political odd couple—you could almost hear the famous opening music to one of my favorite old TV shows, *The Odd Couple*, with Jack Klugman and Tony Randall playing Oscar and Felix. That, in fact, was the headline the *Orange County Register* used for a November 2017 article on Antonio and me as a "Political Odd Couple." It wasn't quite—narrator's deep voice reading—"on November 13, Felix Unger was asked to remove himself from his place of residence. That request came from his wife." But it was compelling: "One wants to end the death penalty. The other thinks capital punishment is just," the *Register* wrote. "One campaigned for tax increases that the other opposed. One tried to put Hillary Clinton in the White House. The other helped elect President George W. Bush. What both men believe, however, is that Latinos—California's largest ethnic group—suffer disproportionate levels of poverty in part because they barely turn out to vote. That common ground helps form the basis of an unlikely political alliance that could shape the 2018 race to determine the next governor of California."

The reporter quoted former Assembly Republican leader Rod Pacheco, my old boss and Antonio's mortal enemy, who knew Antonio's and my history as well as anybody. His reaction: "Are you kidding?"

Then Rod thought it over and had more to say. "After further reflection, Pacheco said the arrangement makes sense given the decline of the Republican Party in California and how the state's open primary is shaking up traditional partisan dynamics," the article continued, and quoted Rod: "Antonio Villaraigosa doesn't need a Latino consultant to tell him about Latinos. Mike's value is really as a Republican consultant, and he knows Republican politics very well."

We knew we had to message Latinos differently than anyone ever had in a statewide Democratic primary before. We had to talk about jobs and education reform as part of an aspirational middle-class agenda. We met these voters where they were and it wasn't what they were hearing from typical Democratic campaigns. But it was also 2018 and the first election after Trump took office. It was a time of Million Mom Marches and pink pussyhats. The shock of Trump sitting in the office Barack Obama had just left was still very fresh and Democrats, particularly white progressives, were in no mood for aspirational messages. They were in no mood to talk about a vision for working-class and poor voters. They weren't looking for answers or how better to solve problems. They wanted someone to fight Trump.

Through all the noise and fog of war in the Democratic primary, we stayed focused on messaging to middle-class and working-class voters. We prioritized economics, jobs, education, and health care in a way that was different than what they were hearing from Democratic leaders at the state and national levels. This wasn't the way Democrats ever talked to Latinos before—we would end up getting clobbered in the primary by white progressives who still dominate Democratic politics in California, but Antonio won both Black and Brown precincts in the state by respectfully engaging them in a way they had been wanting to hear. It was the first time I recognized that Black and Brown voters were increasingly the moderate voices in the Democratic Party, while white progressives were marching the party leftward.

It was a smart, novel, and necessary approach, but it was also one that reminded me of Republicans ignoring the same advice years prior, choosing, in effect, to emphasize the issues that resonated with their larger though shrinking white base while watching Latino voters grow more and more disaffected by the party. There's little evidence to suggest the Democratic Party will learn the lesson any faster than their Republican counterparts did. As recently as the primary in the 2024 Democratic race to succeed former U.S. senator Dianne Feinstein, the *Los Angeles Times* ran a story with numerous Latino voices saying that no Democrat in the race was showing up or conveying a message that resonated with them.

Like many "in the Central Valley, our communities often don't get a lot of focus and attention. A lot of the statewide candidates are focusing on large urban areas," said Luis Alejo, a former state legislator and one of Villaraigosa's earliest supporters, who is now the chair of the Monterey County Board of Supervisors. "Among all the top candidates, I have yet to see any of them have a direct message for Latino voters. . . . Unlike some of the past elections, I think they need to come out with a really working-class economic plan." A plan that includes addressing California's affordable housing crisis, which seeps far beyond the state's big cities.

Our focus on economics in Villaraigosa's campaign was working among the Black and Brown voters in the 2018 primary. While unsuccessful, that campaign laid bare a significant weakness in the Democratic coalition, namely that the "diploma divide" that is reshaping the contours of our country's political environment has strong correlation to the race and ethnicity of the emerging working class. Latinos and Blacks make up the lion's share of the shrinking blue-collar and non-college-educated voter base that the modern Democratic Party is rapidly losing a grip on. In February 2018, the headline on a George Skelton *Los Angeles Times* piece read "Latinos Lifting Villaraigosa in Tight Race for Governor." In a recent poll, Skelton reported, "Villaraigosa led Newsom among Latinos by 35 points. Among whites, Newsom led by 15. A whopping 67 percent of Latinos had a favorable opinion of Villaraigosa; 37 percent did of Newsom." The poll had the race at a statistical tie, with 23 percent of likely voters backing Newsom and 21 percent behind Antonio.

But by June, ahead of the primary, it was clear we were in a battle for second place behind front-runner Gavin Newsom, vying with Republican John Cox to see who would make it through to the November election. Cox, who claimed to be a one-time Jack Kemp Republican, went from having principles to desperately licking Trump's boots—and earned his endorsement. Under California's primary rules, the top two finishers move on to the general election, whatever their party affiliation. With four notable Democrats in the race and one Trump-backed candidate, simple math dictated there wasn't much of a path for Antonio.

Newsom ran away with it. He finished with more than a third of the primary vote—with more than 2.3 million votes. Cox predictably nabbed second by consolidating the white Trump vote, with nearly 1.7 million votes, and Antonio was well behind with less than a million votes. It was a joke: Cox had a zero shot against Newsom. He'd surged in the primary because of an endorsement from Trump, hugely unpopular in the state, which was going to drag him down in the general. Democrats outnumbered Republicans in the state two to one. "The idea that somehow wrapping yourself in the cloak of Donald Trump is going to help you win in California, I'm trying to be diplomatic here, it's peculiar at best," I told the Associated Press. Trump congratulated Cox on Twitter and added: "He can win." Not hardly. Newsom cleaned the floor with Cox, winning with more than 61 percent of the vote, 7.7 million to 4.7 million, one of the worst GOP showings in California history.

The numbers were never good for a Latino Democrat running on a platform of creating economic opportunity for working people, a pathway of upward mobility for the poor, and an overhaul of public education that would finally serve the Black and Brown kids our school system is currently failing. None of that was on the agenda of the Democratic California primary weighted heavily toward white progressive voters much more focused on cultural issues than addressing the economic concerns of those barely getting by.

I never for a second regretted working with Antonio. He was out there fighting, ready to go down swinging for the right issues, and he and I did that together. Up until then, I was still doing some contract work for the Republican Party in California, and when I started generating press for my work with Antonio, I got an awkward phone call from my good friend and Republican Party chairman Jim Brulte telling me that this was a bridge too far. Jim was right. He fired me right away and should have.

I made my choice. If it was working for Trump's party or working for a Democrat who was going to fight for poor people against the Republicans and his own party, I was with him. I'm not saying it wasn't hard. It was very difficult. We got our asses kicked. What I learned was that the more extreme and antagonistic and confrontational you are, the more voters love it—voters on both sides. I'm not making any false equivalencies here, but I've run big races on both sides of the aisle and I can tell you that Republican voters aren't the only ones who want to be lied to—so do a lot of Democratic voters.

Yes, Antonio ran as a Democrat, but one who was more concerned with leading and lifting people up, finding solutions and calming people down instead of angering them. Antonio and I get along because, while we don't agree on everything, deep down we care about the same things. We care about poor people. We care about Latinos. We care about the immigrant. We care about the voiceless. And as both of us found out that year, we were willing to make painful adjustments in our allegiances and alliances to try to work for change.

To me, I've always been consistent. You fight for those that aren't getting served. That's why I went into politics. I thought everybody went into politics for that reason. I was well into my forties before I learned how wrong I was about that.

The Lincoln Project

In the late fall of 2019, I got a direct message on Twitter from Reed Galen. He had been a Republican advance man in national campaigns, and he was an exceptional writer and fierce critic of Donald Trump. Reed's father, Rich Galen, had been an insider's insider in Republican politics during the heyday of the 1980s. Reed asked me if I would be interested in joining a handful of other Republican political consultants who were gathering for a singular mission: to defeat Donald Trump when he sought reelection in 2020.

"I'm in," I said before he even finished the pitch. "What's it called?" I asked.

"The Lincoln Project," he said.

Worked for me. From its inception, the Lincoln Project would be decidedly different from the hundreds of anti-Trump efforts quickly spawned during his tenure. We were a cadre of talented Republican operatives who had risen to the highest levels of Republican politics, only to arrive at the same painful conclusion: we must now work to burn down what our party had become. It was the first time—in my lifetime, or maybe ever in history—that a group of Republicans of consequence were willing to risk their livelihoods by going against the standard-bearer of our party and have that grow to what I called "fumigating the Republican Party rather than reforming it." Republicans simply didn't do this. We were instilled with Ronald Reagan's famous

"Eleventh Commandment," going all the way back to his 1966 campaign for California governor, "Thou shalt not speak ill of any fellow Republican."

This time was different. Dramatic action was called for. We didn't choose this. We didn't ask to see everything we held dear and important and honorable turned on its head. We were essentially drafted into action by events. The peculiar catalyst for the Lincoln Project was the abject failure of so many frontline Republican leaders who refused to stand up to Trumpist voices against hate, corruption, and vulgarity.

As an Associated Press story announcing the Lincoln Project's official launch in mid-December 2019 put it, "A small group of President Donald Trump's fiercest conservative critics, including the husband of the president's own chief adviser, is launching a super PAC designed to fight Trump's reelection and punish congressional Republicans deemed his 'enablers.'"

At the outset our group did indeed include George Conway, a brilliant man married to Kellyanne Conway, one of the few top-rate political operatives willing to work for Trump, and Rick Wilson, a top operative with a knack for stirring it up on social media. One thing I've always said about the Lincoln Project is: we said exactly what we were going to do, in detail, and then we went out and did it. That first AP article reported we'd already raised $1 million—but "hope to raise and spend much more to fund a months-long advertising campaign in a handful of 2020 battleground states to persuade disaffected Republican voters to break from Trump's GOP." That was pretty much it, though we'd be targeting our buys much, much more narrowly than "battleground states."

We launched the Lincoln Project the month after the first Trump impeachment hearings were dominating the news. Despite furious attempts by the Trump orbit to attack the credibility of the witnesses, many came across as solemn and serious and credible. I think, for example, of the son of Ukrainian immigrants, Lieutenant Colonel Alex-

ander Vindman—whom Trump would later fire, along with his twin
brother, just to be vindictive—declaring in his opening statement
before the committee and a live TV audience, "Dad, my sitting here
today, in the U.S. Capitol, talking to our elected officials, is proof that
you made the right decision forty years ago to leave the Soviet Union
and come here to the United States of America, in search of a better life
for our family. Do not worry—I will be fine for telling the truth." He
also said: "Here, right matters."

Before those hearings, a lot of people were still trying to figure out
what the hell was going on. How could so many people be falling in
line behind Trump? Was this actually real? How deep did it go? The
answer the hearings provided the country was: very, very deep. This
was a cultlike situation gripping the highest reaches of government.
We were off the grid, as we in the United States always understood the
grid. We'd entered the kind of fight for basic survival we associate more
with the dark corners of world history against the fascist threat of the
Second World War, but had never suffered through as a country since
the end of the Civil War.

There was no suspense about what had happened. A president was
being impeached for making a phone call leveraging a foreign leader
to come up with dirt on his political enemy—and Trump's voice
was captured clearly on tape, for all to hear, putting the squeeze on
Ukrainian president Volodymyr Zelensky. In terms of political crimes,
this was like running a red light and getting caught on camera, proving
you were behind the wheel.

Republican senators were blatant. They made no real attempt to appear to be honest brokers to determine during the impeachment trial
whether the president was indeed guilty. All they cared about was winning the political fight. They endorsed willful ignorance. They would
not allow evidence to be presented, since they didn't want to know.
And if you don't want to know in politics—it's because you know. They
weren't interested in having a fair trial. If you go to such great lengths

to suppress evidence, knowing how bad it will look, it's clear you think that evidence is quite damning and conclusive. The Republican senators showing a cultlike blind loyalty and willingness to desecrate the virtue of truth offered a kind of eerie premonition of what radicalized Republicans would do a year later on January 6.

Here's one point to remember about those callow Republican senators doing so much to defile democracy, putting their cowardice and more deficiencies on display in high definition: those senators were quite reflective of the Republican Party base. At the Lincoln Project, we were seeing in our own polling and analytic data, as well as anecdotal evidence rolling in, that the Republican base was bizarrely united on standing behind Trump no matter what. They were holding together even more cohesively than they had over the years on the tax issue, which for decades used to be the orthodoxy of the Republican Party. The one inviolate thing you could never do was raise taxes. But none of that mattered. You could do whatever you wanted—except dare to say the truth about Trump.

"The American presidency transcends the individuals who occupy the Oval Office," four of my Lincoln Project cofounders wrote in a *New York Times* article announcing our launch that December.

> Their personalities become part of our national character. Their actions become our actions, for which we all share responsibility. Their willingness to act in accordance with the law and our tradition dictates how current and future leaders will act. Their commitment to order, civility and decency is reflected in American society. . . . Mr. Trump and his enablers have abandoned conservatism and longstanding Republican principles and replaced them with Trumpism, an empty faith led by a bogus prophet. In a recent survey, a majority of Republican voters reported that they consider Mr. Trump a better president than Lincoln. Mr. Trump and his fellow travelers daily undermine the proposition we as a people have a responsibility and an

obligation to continually bend the arc of history toward justice. They mock our belief in America as something more meaningful than lines on a map.

It's a pretty scary state of affairs when a group of political consultants becomes the moral conscience of the Republican Party, but that's where we were. That was how morally bankrupt the party had become. We were not particularly interested in saving the Republican Party. We didn't give a shit, to be blunt. We saw how corrupt and hollowed out and beyond redemption it already was. Our interest was in saving the country—no matter what that might cost us personally.

For me, there was no obvious gain in joining the Lincoln Project, but there was an obvious downside to forsaking my life's work. I would argue that this lent the effort credibility. And clearly it did. We all had plenty to lose. There was no other conceivable rationale for us banding together than this: Donald Trump was an existential threat to the country, and we were the first Republicans of any stature willing to publicly say so and do something about it. That eight people would have the moral courage to stand up and hold a mirror up to the entire Republican industrial complex—lobbyists, consultants, officeholders—enraged those forced to rationalize their support of Trump.

As the Lincoln Project grew exponentially from its December 2019 launch, the attacks on Trump and all the Republicans who kneeled before him became more direct. The attacks against us individually would also become more direct, personal, and life-threatening than anything I had ever imagined could happen in America.

People who had begged me for jobs in previous years now began attacking my reputation. Republican consultants who had both profited from scapegoating immigrants and then switched to making money by creating Latino outreach organizations attacked my business. Right-wing gadflies who were animated by hating Latinos approached my children at their college apartments. Anonymous packages were sent to my house. Social media trolls cut and pasted my conversations to suggest I was a predator, grifter, pedophile, con artist, madman, turncoat, and whatever else you could think of. You would have thought we had opened the locked doors of those that had hidden their greed and corruption only to rage at having it exposed. We did.

One of the things we realized early with the Lincoln Project was that a sharp sense of humor could be one of our most important assets. This was a strategic reply to the very real sense of fear and intimidation the Trump cult generated in people. Humor is one of the best tools you can use to answer that, instead of letting fear become entrenched and paralyzing. You have to mock the aspiring dictator. You have to humiliate him. You have to make him look like a clown. When Trump held a campaign rally in Tulsa, Oklahoma, in June 2020, and attendance was paltry, we did an ad, "Shrinking," featuring a reference to that lackluster rally and a woman's voice saying: "You've probably heard this before, but it was *smaller* than we expected." Some of Rick Wilson's best work.

One spot called "P.O.W." contrasted shots of patriotic military service with Trump's disparaging remarks about the military, including a recent scoop at the time from the *Atlantic* reporting that, in 2018, Trump had refused to visit U.S. war dead in France and called them "suckers." Another much talked about spot was "Flag of Treason," showing the Confederate flag. Not pulling a lot of punches.

The Lincoln Project would grow to become the most successful political action committee (PAC) in American history. It would achieve a number of things no other political organization had, including raising nearly $100 million, largely through small donations; spilling over into pop culture, supplying much material to late-night comedians, etc.; forcing the firing of Trump's campaign manager, Brad Parscale; and, last but not least, completely occupying the focus and attention of the president of the United States.

We knew Trump was watching. He couldn't not watch us. We were in a sense beating him at his own game and he was both fascinated and horrified. Trump was used to being the one willing to be cruder and coarser and nastier than anyone around. Guess what, so were we. Did Trump think he invented personal attacks in politics? We were all Republican operatives with decades in the trenches. We'd seen it all, done it all, or almost. He wanted to go into the gutter? We built that gutter! We were all too happy to roll up our sleeves and get just as down and dirty as we wanted. And we were able to do it at a base, guttural level that the Biden campaign and other Democrats shied away from, worried they'd be criticized for talking like Trump. We didn't care. We weren't running for anything.

We beat Trump at his own game in another sense: He couldn't attack us without making us stronger. And yet, he couldn't *not* attack us. Discipline and self-restraint were never his strengths. Once he started engaging us, that just multiplied the attention we were getting. Everyone started focusing on us. Every new insult or swipe he took at us only made us more powerful. He was damned if he did, damned if he didn't. All that mockery added up. Trump was right to want to slow us down, but nothing could do that. We were making him so toxic, such a joke, albeit a dangerous joke, we started to make inroads with country-club Republicans who found themselves increasingly embarrassed to be Republicans. Shame and ostracization weren't present in most Republicans anymore, but we were betting that there were just enough left for Joe Biden to win.

~

One of the strange things about the arrival of Donald Trump on the national political stage was the fact that he came surrounded by such a third-string collection of advisers. It was amateur hour all the way, and they were clearly winging it in the 2016 campaign. Real campaign professionals are a little like generals or baseball managers; it's a small world, many of us know each other personally or at least know each other's personalities and tendencies and tactics. You get a massive leg up if you know going in your opponent's strategic approach and objectives. If you understand that, you have a very decided advantage, because remember, these campaigns are not so much about the candidates. They're mostly about the consultants plotting and executing strategy. A lot of people watching politics from afar think it's all about which candidate you'd want to sit down with to drink a beer and hang out—but that's not it. That's an easy, consumable, digestible way for people to understand the narrative and the tactics that have been executed. You have to build your approach around your candidate's skills and strengths, but you're still the one doing the building.

The team of D-minus operatives around Trump in 2016 had no track record. The lack of political talent around Trump created a massive opening for this underclass to come in and run this operation. Better people came along later. Kellyanne Conway has to be one of the most talented operatives I've ever worked with, man or woman; she's damn good at what she does. Early on she was working with the Ted Cruz 2016 campaign, but fell into line, as is common for campaign professionals as the eventual nominee becomes clearer. I met Kellyanne in the mid-nineties when she had carved out a place in the party as a pollster with a particularly keen insight into women voters. I admired her work and could relate to her as someone else who was a "non-white guy" in the GOP. As political director of the California Republican Party I wanted her voice heard, so I made sure she was invited to present at one of our biannual conventions. As much as I disliked what Kellyanne was doing for Trump, I respected her abilities and took them seriously.

We knew the Trump team's weaknesses better than they did and were able to blow them up, which was what we did with Brad Parscale—Brad's a big guy, given to bombast, given to puffing out his chest, and we did a Lincoln Project ad glorifying him as "the man Trump can't win without." Pretty slick, right? That ad, predictably, led to Trump exploding at Parscale for daring to think he was bigger than the Big Man himself—and dropping him. That was how effective the Lincoln Project was. It was not important in terms of grand strategy, but if you can knock out the number one general on the other side, you're usually helping your cause.

When the name Steve Bannon started popping up, we were like everyone else, reading press accounts to try to get some handle on someone about whom so little was known. This is a basic part of politics, again, as in the military or sports: Scout the opposition. Know thy enemy. Do they get shaken? What's their weak point? How do you attack the weak point? What are their strengths? What issues do they want to avoid?

Bannon was a peculiar guy who came up through Hollywood, after stops as a U.S. Navy officer and a Goldman Sachs investment broker. Bannon was making money off *Seinfeld* residuals, and in 2007 cofounded the far-right disinformation website Breitbart, which even Bannon himself called "alt-right." I read more and found out he was a conservative Catholic, as in extreme-conservative Catholic, tapped into some murky global Catholic right-wing organizations for which he did who knew what. Not my brand of Catholicism, but it was information that gave me insight looking into this guy's brain.

Bannon turned out to be a surprisingly intelligent and resourceful thinker, which made him very dangerous, and he was also a Leninist—and would tell you so. Bannon emulated figures like Russian revolutionary Vladimir Lenin, adopting his frame of reference, in seeking to undermine any and all institutions; destruction that ultimately allows for the rise of dictatorship, of authoritarians, which Bannon sought to promote so that he could gain power for himself. You attack the media. You attack academia. You attack science. You attack the government. You attack all these as enemies of the people. And when you execute that strategy to the point that you have eroded public confidence to a certain threshold, like after an earthquake, you march into the rubble and boldly declare, "Only I can fix this!" The strong man is stronger when everything else is weaker. That was the whole philosophy behind it, and if you don't believe me, ask Steve Bannon himself.

"I'm a Leninist—Lenin . . . wanted to destroy the state, and that's my goal, too," Bannon told author Ronald Radosh in 2013. "I want to bring everything crashing down, and destroy all of today's establishment."

Starting with the Republican Party. Bannon had clearly studied his Lenin, for example these lines from Lenin's 1902 pamphlet, *What Is to Be Done?* "If you can't build a party, paralyze the party; circumvent it; and take it over," Lenin wrote. "Before you become the de jure leaders of the party, make sure all its institutions are crippled."

Author Anastasia Edel, born in the Soviet Union, wrote in January 2017 just after Trump was elected—presciently, as it turns out: "It is something akin to what the Russians experienced 100 years ago when they woke up to the news that the legitimate provisional government had been disbanded by the Bolsheviks, whose stated agenda was the destruction of the Russian state and building a completely different— Soviet—entity in its stead. Indeed, the president's chief strategist, Steve Bannon, has himself cited Lenin as an influence."

Bannon had a very Leninesque conception that you only had to focus on one-third of the population. You did not need a majority, the way one does in a democracy; with one-third of the populace committed to destroying institutions, you will eventually be successful. The goal is not to govern. The goal is not to do the difficult work of providing alternative solutions. The goal is simply to destroy confidence in the institution, so that increasingly it's no longer viewed as a viable alternative. It has been so degraded and so corrupted in the minds of the populace that a small, committed minority can tear it down, run in, and take over. That was how Lenin rose to power, and that was how Hitler rose to power. It's a very common tactic of the dictator or the authoritarian.

- 9 -

The Bannon Line and the New Southern Strategy

The Bannon program represented a frontal assault on everything I'd been raised to believe was important. This was weaponized tribalism seeking to impose its will on the majority and rob that majority of its rights, checkmating anyone who sought a pluralistic society in which differences make us stronger and bring us together, rather than being used as fodder to manipulate and foment hatred and resentment. In my work on the Lincoln Project I came to see that my longer-term goal to have Latino voters represented would require a pivot to defeating Trumpism by shifting the votes of college-educated women in the suburbs.

We threw a very small amount of money—roughly $20,000—into ad buys directed at Cubans and Puerto Ricans in Florida, but just enough to keep Trump focused on Florida while we pulled the bulk of our ad money out of there and shifted it to Georgia. We knew Florida was out of reach and we knew Georgia was in the hunt. Trump was getting dramatic overperformance among Latino voters in Florida that was locking up the state for him. Our bet was that Trump's team was paying more attention to Hispanics in Miami-Dade County than they were to Republicans in Gwinnett and DeKalb Counties in Georgia. We were right.

Everything we did targeting Latinos for the Lincoln Project was what we call a "show buy," a way to trick your opponents into concentrating money and resources in a place where you're not actually competing. The Lincoln Project was perfectly positioned for this because everything we did got national attention and Trump's team would have to respond.

We also used the novel technique of running ads targeting Puerto Rican voters in the Interstate 4 (I-4) corridor in Florida by running ads in Spanish in Puerto Rico. Why? Because even though we were targeting Puerto Ricans in Florida we could get ads placed cheaply in Puerto Rico and we knew families talked and shared ads on Facebook, so we wanted to try something new.

I read an interview Bannon did with the Associated Press in early 2020 where he talked about the dynamics of the November 2020 election and spelled out what was already clear to me: the Lincoln Project could not shift a large percentage of Republican voters away from Trump. But that was not necessary. All that was necessary was a thin slice, a very thin slice, probably 3 to 4 percent.

Bannon was up to something in talking to the Associated Press, and I knew just what it was: he was sending a message to Trump, call it smoke signals. Bannon understood Trumpism, from the inside out, better than anyone. He saw its weak points and had the acumen of a top strategist despite never working on a high-level campaign before. He understood the architecture of the right-wing media better than anyone and that's really all that's required of a Republican campaign anymore. Control the bullhorn and direct the hate where you want it to go and there's a very high likelihood you'll win the nomination. Bannon was trying to legitimize himself back into the good graces of the campaign after a steep fall. Bannon's role as one of the early generals of Trump's operation came to a screeching halt in August 2017 after infighting with Jared Kushner and regular media leaks were traced back to him. Bannon's greatest offense however was taking credit for Trump's come-from-behind victory.

"Steve Bannon has nothing to do with me or my Presidency. When he was fired, he not only lost his job he lost his mind," President Trump said in a statement at the time. But Bannon knew tactics and he also had the larger point of trying to shake a little sense into Trump supporters, stuck inside their own media bubble and used to a steady diet of reading their own press releases. Trump won by the smallest fraction in 2016 and his position was not getting stronger. Bannon was saying everything that I was seeing tactically—and he gave me an idea.

~

The Lincoln Project viral videos were cool, deviously smart, and on target, and the creative guys did their best work ever on the ads they were cranking out. And those spots will be how the Lincoln Project will be remembered by many, I'm sure. But in terms of swinging the 2020 election, actually breaking it down like a pro, swing state by swing state and district by district, the analytics work the Lincoln Project data operation did was as decisive, or more, in determining the outcome of the 2020 election as the ads everyone talked about. I'm proud to have headed up that data operation.

For the most part we ignored the traditional polling that has come to dominate American politics. While polling is a necessary and useful tool for any campaign, for us it didn't make much sense. We were focused on such small groups of voters that most polling wouldn't have been helpful, tempting as it was to launch into deep data dives on our most coveted swing demographic—*college-educated suburban white women.* We did such a good job with our message discipline that it became common for reporters and journalists to start referring to Republican defectors from Trump as "Lincoln Project Republicans."

We quickly recognized we were better off using a more dynamic method of tracking the messages we were putting out to guide our ad placement. We relied almost entirely on analytics and viewer response

to our social media ads, as well as some of the viral videos that captured the imagination of the country. This technique is now known as
"social listening."

Most political organizations start their efforts with polling and
focus groups to develop their message to voters. We did the exact opposite, to greater effect. We had so many ads and ad variations we were
running daily that the analytics the data team was getting far surpassed
any data we could get from traditional polling and also made focus
groups a relic. The Lincoln Project redefined the way media works in
modern campaigns—you don't need polling, focus groups, or that one
"killer ad" that campaigns were always looking for in the past. That's
all irrelevant now. Quantity and speed were becoming as important—
oftentimes more important—than quality, and our analytic results
were proving it. The Lincoln Project's speed mattered as much as the
message. Coupled with a country desperately waiting for our response
to Trump's daily antics, it's not difficult to see how we were doing
something unique in American politics.

Critics of the Lincoln Project complained that the now famous online videos we created did not work to move Republican voters. Some
progressive groups spent critical campaign dollars running our ads in
front of Republican voters to test their efficacy. Can you believe it? Instead of spending money to defeat Donald Trump, they were spending
thousands of dollars to prove that the Lincoln Project ads didn't sway
Republican voters.

There was only one small problem with this criticism: none of
those ads were designed to sway Republican voters. In fact, most of
the ads we were running to move the critical voters we needed in Arizona, Georgia, Pennsylvania, Wisconsin, and Michigan weren't ever
seen by the American public on Twitter or cable news. Why? Because
they weren't the intended audience.

The ads we developed were tailored to small, niche-specific GOP
audiences that would move just the right number of voters, in the right

precincts, in the right counties in the right states to win the race. Voters are very stratified. There is incredibly little movement happening with voters, like a single-digit variation at the most. My job as the data guy is to go in and find out where those potential slivers are and focus like a laser beam. You need them in swing states, in the right precincts, with the right message to move them over.

According to Pew Research, approximately 158 million ballots were cast in the 2020 election. I was targeting less than a million voters across a dozen states. I had to find these tiny niche audiences of people that were truly open-minded and then message them to vote for Biden.

When we flipped the traditional model on its head, it allowed Republican voters to tell us what they were interested in. The Lincoln Project was producing so many videos daily that we could easily slide the ads into targeted universes and determine which ones were the most effective with the audiences we needed. This was revolutionary and no one had done it before—the fact is, no campaign is doing this today.

This process allowed us to recognize that cultural issues like the extremism among Christian religious adherents and defending Southern monuments as symbols of white supremacy were becoming more repellant to suburban college-educated Republican women than "economic" issues were attracting them. This was the first time in thirty years of professional campaigns that I had seen this happen.

I recall in one final campaign strategy meeting, Stuart Stevens, the legendary GOP ad man who came later into the Lincoln Project, asked me the question: "If you had to run one ad for the rest of the campaign, would it focus on cultural issues or economic issues?"

"Cultural issues," I responded immediately, completely aware as I said it that I would never have answered like this before. College-educated Republican voters were overwhelmingly economic voters—"country-club Republicans," we called them. These voters were concerned about lower taxes, the S&P 500, and capital gains tax cuts. They were willing to tolerate attacks on cultural issues they did care about—primarily abortion rights for women—as a political platitude, never believing that anyone would take them away. Voting in coalition with the "church-going" crowd was something they did as they held their noses to win elections.

The analytics showed how this was changing. In states like Arizona, Georgia, Wisconsin, and Pennsylvania, we were moving college-educated voters away from Trump at the level we needed to carry those states. These voters were responding to the shame and ostracization of being associated with a party that was obsessing over Confederate monuments, attacking George Floyd, and glorifying a president who held up a Bible as an enforcement authority during protests in front of the White House. For a tiny subset of Republicans, no increase in their bottom line was worth losing their country or their soul. We were moving their votes.

Shame was becoming the strategic objective with higher-educated voters. We recognized that people who were denying science, believing obvious lies, and changing their core beliefs at the direction of a con man were not going to be persuaded out of their own bias bubble. The future of the republic lay squarely on the votes of thirty thousand or so college-educated women across three states who were so ashamed of being associated with Trump and the party of a resurrected confederacy that they were too embarrassed to say they were Trump supporters at the soccer field on Saturday morning. Those women were our target and we homed in on them and used every ounce of our familiarity with their Republican language and thinking to shame them out of voting for what they knew deep down was horrible for their children and the country. We began our summer assault on Trump on June 1 with a devastating ad called "Flag of Treason" that squarely addressed the fracas Trump created for himself by defending the Confederate flag. Later, we launched "Girl in the Mirror," an iconic ad that showed the world through the eyes of a young girl hearing the horrific words of

Donald Trump demeaning women. For the first time we were showing that Republicans could lose a culture-war campaign. Culture wars had been where Democrats went to die since the 1990s, but in 2020 the Lincoln Project was turning the cannons inside the ship and peeling off the exact same voters we had spent years focusing on keeping in the Republican camp. This dynamic was part of a larger split among coalitions in both parties that were now divided by education and cultural issues. College-educated voters were ditching a party that had shifted its focus to restricting abortion access, was openly hostile to minorities and gays, and openly defended Confederate statues. These defectors were led by female voters.

History will remember the Trump era for many things, but for political data nerds, it may well be remembered for how resilient the Republican base remained in steadfast support of such an obviously flawed human being who stood diametrically opposed to every value and core belief they claimed they stood for. While I'm certain future studies will seek to determine how millions of people could ignore and excuse incompetence, corruption, and the moral failures of their leader, my job didn't provide me much time to consider such grand notions. I had to figure out how many Republicans we could move to the Democrats, and in which critical states this would have to happen to keep Trump under 270 electoral votes. We also had to determine which regions we had to target and what messages we needed to create. Trump's support levels among Republican voters were at a historically high range, a reflection of strongly partisan voters and stratified news bubbles that define today's American political landscape. Biden could not win the campaign without the defection of something like 5 percent of Republican voters and there was no group in the country better prepared to accomplish that task than the Lincoln Project.

As we said in the campaign war room: *Never send a Democrat to do a Republican's job!* We had to focus on peeling off just enough

Republicans while Democrats consolidated their base vote by generating turnout among minority communities to put them over the top. It would only work if the Lincoln Project was successful in moving enough Republicans and if the Democrats were successful in getting high turnout and large margins among Black and Brown base voters. If we could pull all that off, this would be an effort unlike any in modern presidential history.

The challenge for us was that Republican voters were very dug in. Say what you will about the cowardice and complicity of the Senate and House Republican members of the Congress, but they reflected the will of the Republican voters. What worked in our favor was that in a highly stratified environment, small movements on the margins can have a tectonic impact in elections. The analytics on our ads showed that we could consistently move 4 to 6 percent of Republican voters in key states, and in the tightest races it would be enough to win the election.

The expectations of the Lincoln Project were high and getting higher as we soared in popularity and began to dominate the media narrative of the 2020 campaign. I began to publicly message that 4 to 6 percent number to dampen rising expectations. The Lincoln Project was not fighting for the heart and soul of the Republican Party—we were fighting for the heart and soul of the country and trying to keep democracy alive. That meant being smart, disciplined, and focused.

I remember seeing what Steve Bannon had told the AP in January 2020 and doing a call with my political director, Zack Czajkowski. I was in an old Victorian in Sacramento, pacing as I talked the way I usually did on this kind of call, and told Zack we were going to make the most of what Bannon had given us.

"We're going to start referencing this as the 'Bannon Line' whenever we can," I said. "This is what the Lincoln Project is trying to do."

It was great to make snappy commercials and viral moments, all necessary tactics to get where we needed to get. As I told Zack, we would reference the famous "Mendoza Line" in baseball—if you were below it, below .200, you sucked—and brand this as coming from the Trump inner circle. We were going to win this race by getting above this Bannon Line, also a gauge of success or failure.

It was one of the better ideas I've ever had. Or at least it played out that way. Before then, we had a problem with expectations. The Lincoln Project was such a hit, culturally and otherwise, it generated unreasonable assumptions about what we could and could not accomplish. We were getting hammered for lifting hope beyond what we could deliver. And in a way, that was right—not about us raising hope, but about the limitations on what we could deliver. We were fighting a cult! Its adherents were not easy to deprogram. But the Bannon Line, yes, this was a threshold we could hit.

We started to message "The Bannon Line" and it took off immediately. On August 13, 2020, I tweeted: "Ever heard of 'The Bannon Line'? It's the percentage of Republican vote that Steve Bannon and I agree @ProjectLincoln needs to assure Trump's defeat."

One thing I knew was that Bannon was listening to our podcast. He was listening to my strategy. He was paying very close attention to what we were doing because he didn't view the Biden campaign as the biggest threat. He viewed Republican defections as the biggest threat—as he should have. That was exactly the biggest problem that the Trump reelection faced.

One of the great things about working on this campaign was that it allowed me to be 100 percent transparent about our entire strategic and tactical objectives. I was telling the whole world what we were doing, down to the last detail: here's where we're buying, here's where we're targeting, here's the messages, here's what works, here's what doesn't work, here's why we're going here, and here's what we're trying to accomplish.

I was telling millions of people every week on the podcast just what we were thinking and what we were doing. I was hiding nothing in our strategy because, first, I was confident, and confidence rubs off, and two, I wanted The Bannon Line to become the center of discussion and debate, which it ultimately became.

By framing it as "The Bannon Line," we shielded ourselves from criticism of low expectations, since we could deflect any such thinking by pointing out this was how Trump's advisers themselves were assessing the blunt realities of the race. Know thy enemy, and all that. It worked like a charm. "The Bannon Line" became a ubiquitous part of the 2020 campaign narrative.

Even Bannon himself started talking about "The Bannon Line" and even picked up that it was a reference to the Mendoza Line in baseball—I didn't know Steve was a baseball fan, but okay, cool. In August 2020, Bannon launched an extended discussion of our thinking on his *War Room* podcast on Newsmax.

"Remember, these are the hardest core of the Trump haters that nobody should dismiss, these are smart, tough guys," Bannon said with the ocean in the background. "They just hate Trump and they actually hate Trumpism. Remember, the key to the Lincoln Project, they say, 'We don't want to defeat Trump, we want to defeat Trumpism.' What they mean by that is populism and nationalism."

He was on target so far. "These are old-school RINOs that are globalists, okay?" he continued. "And they've now applied this in I think a very sophisticated and smart way. They're just trying to peel off—you know, they call it the Bannon Line, kind of like the old Mendoza Line, if you're a baseball fan, right? I think Mendoza hit .215. The Bannon Line was about 4 percent. And if they can peel off those voters, it's going to be trouble."

I was living rent-free in Steve Bannon's head.

One day later, Bannon was hauled off the yacht of a sketchy Chinese billionaire, where he'd recorded those remarks, and arrested in New York City on fraud charges for absconding with much of the money he raised through his "We Build the Wall" con.

~

Beyond the Bannon Line strategy, my data team bore down to look closely at how the traditional road map to 270 electoral votes was changing along with the demography of the country. The analytics showed white non-college-educated voters shifting further toward the Republican Party, and white college-educated voters shifting more to the Democrats. That's important because if you look state by state you notice states like New Hampshire, Ohio, and Maine becoming more Republican. What do they have in common? Fewer white college-educated voters.

We said: *Wait a second, this education divide is shifting these states. Let's follow that. Let's invest money where there are enough college-educated voters to make a difference and double down on the shame and ostracization some of these voters were feeling.* This turned out to be very effective. There were more fish in that barrel, so let's go fishing there as opposed to trying to convince people in Ohio that the Confederacy was bad. Neither Ohio nor Florida were really winnable states for Democrats in 2020. That was the reality. So we would just have to find votes elsewhere.

I knew as a Republican who had made a career of winning just enough votes for GOP candidates that the Latino vote wasn't as reliable as Democratic Party strategists assumed. For the first time in my life, I was working against the election of a Republican president, and I began to wonder, often publicly, if the Democrats realized their Latino base wasn't nearly as solid as they thought.

Despite being fully funded to accomplish the goal of moving 4 to 6 percent of Republicans, we were going toe-to-toe with what Trump's campaign manager, Brad Parscale, described as the Death Star. Tens of millions of dollars and years of data accrual and refinement had built a formidable machine. Dozens of staffers manned the data operation at Trump's headquarters. My team consisted of just a handful of research

assistants, data analytics professionals, and some really willing and ambitious, but inexperienced, staffers.

I knew we would have to do things differently than any campaign I
had worked on before and that we'd have to round out our team with
people who could look at data differently. In spring of 2020, COVID
was in full raging force and Major League Baseball had shut the season
down. That meant a lot of data analysts were sitting at home with the
rest of the country watching *Tiger King* and ordering Postmates. I had a
long discussion with Zack Czajkowski about the need to shake it up and
be bold and innovative in our data work. We didn't have the resources
of Trump's Death Star, so we'd have to do what the rebels did and out-
maneuver them. Outflank them. Outthink them. We needed to get
away from the tried and true and think cutting edge. Zack and my team
knew that I didn't think very highly of political data guys. The reason is
most of them really suck at campaigns. They can tell you everything you
need to know about a congressional district except who is going to win.
Remember, politics requires a balance between art and science and data
guys are focused so much on the science that they know very little about
the art of politics and campaigns. At a time when there's so much data
available, political data guys aren't nearly as useful as actual campaign
operatives. Zack heard me out, thought it over—and suggested we hire
a college friend of his, Spencer Harrison.

Spencer was a great hire. He turned out to be one of the best-kept
secrets of the Lincoln Project data operation. Spencer has the calmest,
clinical, stoic demeanor of any human being I have ever met. You could
be forgiven for thinking he just walked off a *Star Trek* set. Try to imagine if Spock and Data had a baby. That would be Spencer. He had been
working for the New York Mets baseball operations department on
baseball analytics before we hired him. Perfect. Spencer cared about
baseball. He had only a passing interest in politics. So he came with a
fresh eye to political data challenges we'd all been staring at for years. I
wanted a real data guy, not a political guy. I could handle the politics. I

wanted Spencer to look at what we were doing differently because we were doing something different.

He quickly identified a curious pattern in public opinion. As we watched daily analytical data come in alongside public-opinion polling in battleground states, a sharp downward movement would occur for Republican governors, senators, and Trump as COVID would rage through red states. It was hard to find good information on the COVID virus at this time. Trump was shutting down CDC data so no one would know the deadly impact of the virus. Spencer surmised that if we could find an accurate data source on COVID movement and match it to where there were especially susceptible populations—for example: older, white conservatives who refused to take the vaccine because of misinformation from the president and Fox News—we could literally spend money on advertisements to Republicans impacted by the virus. We believed that could give us the edge we needed.

We would "Buy into the Spike" and leverage GOP voters getting sick, hospitalized, and having family members die because the president was lying to them. Ultimately, we secured a reliable private data source from a vendor that worked in the health-care space that allowed us to track the movement of the virus and we would message into the life cycle of what COVID was doing to communities.

Spencer flagged a data correlation that was very interesting to me. If we identified areas where hospitals reported an increase in calls relating to COVID symptoms, and where Google searches on COVID and related symptoms started to increase above the national average, we would shortly thereafter see spikes in COVID infections.

We were learning about the life cycle of the virus. First you would see the numbers of infections go up, and then it would take about two weeks before you started seeing really bad symptoms and people going to the hospital. And then you would start seeing hospitals overflow. So there was about a three- or four-week cycle of the virus dramatically changing. We would look for that first spike above the national average and then we would start buying ads, especially targeting older Republican voters.

The ads were about COVID. The idea was to burst through the Fox News bubble that older people were watching and bust through the right-wing media. We would start by warning that COVID is coming to your local city or town and the hospitals are going to be overflowing, and we would just deluge these demographics for a week while the coronavirus was settling in. And after a week or two, lo and behold, the hospitals would start overflowing. And when that started happening, we started messaging again, saying that deaths were coming.

This was certainly not the type of tactic that makes your mother proud, but it was devastatingly effective. We would see massive drops among Republicans supporting Trump in key states, DeSantis in Florida, Doug Ducey in Arizona, and Ron Johnson in Wisconsin. While it may have been macabre, it would have been political malpractice not to attack the president's utter lack of concern for his countrymen and voters. We were finding that, even among older voters in red states, it was possible to lower Republican support levels for Trump. Sadly, many would have to see their friends, family, and spouses die before they realized they had been lied to.

To this day, I remain convinced that had Trump simply told the country to wear a mask, he would have handily won reelection. His stubborn shortsightedness cost him the election and we were all about seizing the opportunity to help make it happen. It went down to the wire. One of the things that most people don't realize is Wisconsin had a huge surge of COVID going into the last couple of weeks of the election. If that surge had not happened, there was a very good chance that Trump would have won Wisconsin in 2020. Think about that.

Another strategy we used was called: the New Southern Strategy. Central to this strategy was the reliance on a mix of a high number of college-educated white voters and a growing number of Latino voters in states like Arizona and Georgia, but also Texas and Florida.

While the polling numbers I was seeing in Arizona and Georgia made those two states possible to push into the 270 map, Texas and Florida were looking more Republican than recent history would suggest they should be. Where Arizona and Georgia Latino voters were polling in a typical range in favor of the Democrats for a large number of Mexican and Central American voters, Florida and Texas were breaking away for the Republican Party in significant numbers—big enough that the Biden campaign's dismissal of the movement as "polling error" wasn't cutting it. Latino numbers were moving rightward, and denying it signified a bigger problem. It told me that neither the Democrats nor the Biden campaign had an answer for it, so they were trying to stop the media narrative by arguing it wasn't happening. This was a huge red flag.

While Biden's team was arguing the shift wasn't happening, Trump's team was brazenly and openly stating that they were going to win a record number of Latino votes. Jason Miller, one of the senior advisers to the Trump campaign, publicly stated that they fully expected to win half of the Latino vote. Now, campaigns often bluster and make pronouncements to throw the opposition off track, but this was a very ambitious statement. While I never believed that a Republican like Trump could win half of the national Latino vote, it was Miller's pronouncement that made me realize they were resourcing the effort to try to get there, or at least as close as they possibly could. Trump's data team was seeing the same thing I was seeing and Biden's team was saying it wasn't happening. The truth was, for Republicans trying to get 270 electoral votes, it was necessary to dramatically overperform their 2016 numbers with Hispanic voters, and going forward, it would be even more important. There is no longer a sustainable road map to victory for Republicans to win a national campaign without a Latino strategy that gets them near 40 percent of the Latino vote—and it's getting tougher every year.

By the summer of 2020, it was clear that the Biden campaign had a serious problem with Latino voters. The pronouncements from his campaign team were not inspiring confidence. Many on the Biden Latino team were the same people who had missed a million red flags on the Hillary Clinton campaign in 2016. Generational differences and geographic variations were becoming easily evident among Latino voters and the response was to just double down on more of the same stereotypical campaign activities, if they even acknowledged them at all.

All the public polling showed a significant shift rightward among Latino voters. The rightward shift was most pronounced among non-college-educated, U.S.-born, English-speaking men. The shift was glaring and evident, nothing subtle about it, and yet all that was coming from the Biden campaign was denial or attacks on the methodology of the polling. Where Hillary Clinton had demonstrated a serious intensity problem due to likability issues with Latino voters and failed to get the expected turnout numbers in key states in 2016, Biden was risking actual defections on an unprecedented scale. For my entire career I had been suggesting that Democrats' turnout problems were a sign of lackluster support that could be exploited by Republicans, and it looked like Trump's team had figured this out.

This was the first time since 2004 that I had seen a Republican presidential campaign moving measurable numbers of Latino voters toward the GOP and, of course, there was a lot of consternation and disbelief that it was happening for Trump. I was not surprised in the least, but I was also helpless to assist because the Lincoln Project was an independent campaign, legally prohibited from any contact with the campaign.

The only thing I was certain of was the inability of the Biden campaign to respond to the coming shift. If Biden's campaign was capable of fixing the problem, they never would have *had* the problem in the first place. Of greater concern was, if Biden lost too many Latino voters to Trump it could more than offset all the work the Lincoln Project was doing to move white, college-educated Republicans to Biden. This was the first time we started to see what I believe will be the biggest shifts in partisan voting behavior over the next decade—white, college-educated Republican women in the suburbs voting for Democrats and Latino U.S.-born, college-educated, English-speaking men voting for Republicans.

I couldn't directly communicate with the Biden campaign, but I could sound the alarm bells! We had built the loudest bullhorn in American politics with the platform that I had on the Lincoln Project, and I intended to use it to force the Biden campaign to start taking the Latino problem they had seriously. The first thing I did was begin to communicate with political reporters covering the race and walk them through the data and history to inform them that the problem Democrats were looking at with Latinos wasn't some polling error, despite what the Biden team was telling them. Nor was it a head fake from Team Trump. The problem was real, and if they did not address it they would certainly lose Cubans in Florida by a record margin, but the problem was leaking into the Mexican American vote, too.

But we did something more significant. The Lincoln Project had immense credibility to convene groups from across the aisle in an unprecedented way and I was determined to use that position to break the Democrats out of their political power structures far removed from the community and make them realize that they were in real trouble of losing the White House. The Lincoln Project Hispanic Summit was launched to start reasserting the narrative that anti-Trump Latino organizations weren't going to cede ground. Just as I had done in the late 1990s with the Hispanic Summit for California Republicans, I could get national media attention by gathering Latino celebrities and political leaders from both parties and drive the message that Latinos were a bloc that needed attention.

My concerns about Biden's sliding support were widespread, as *Newsweek* reported in a mid-September run-up to the planned summit. "There's a sense of urgency, and to a large extent, a feeling that the Biden campaign is lackluster in reaching out to the Latino community," said Domingo Garcia, president of the League of United Latin American Citizens (LULAC), a longtime national Hispanic group, "so we're having to go to third parties like The Lincoln Project to activate the Latino community, because the Biden campaign has been so unresponsive to Latino organizations."

I had no confidence in Biden's Latino consulting team. I was horrified at the thought that this team was in control of moving Latinos off Trump, and so I used the profile of the Lincoln Project to organize Democrats outside of the Biden campaign. We were able to corral some of the best people in the business to help rally Latino organizations to signal that Biden had a Latino problem. Celebrity actor John Leguizamo, political analyst Maria Cardona, Bernie Sanders campaign adviser Chuck Rocha, former U.S. treasurer Rosario Marin—and many others.

Ultimately, it wasn't enough. We won the race, of course, and our Republican voter strategy paid off perfectly, just as we had publicly predicted. All our targeting and ad spend was overlaid perfectly with the biggest shifts in Maricopa County, Arizona; Gwinnett and DeKalb Counties in Georgia; and targets in Wisconsin, Michigan, and Pennsylvania. Early spends in Florida and North Carolina, while tactically wise, also gave us the analytical data to show we weren't gonna get there in those two states.

My heart sank when the first Latino numbers came in and all of my public warnings came true. The Latino shift rightward I had been shooting up warning flares about happened and it was significant. Biden slipped further against Trump, who would increase his support from 2016 levels of 28 percent to 37 percent in 2020. It was a warning of how isolated and removed Latino campaign advisers can become when they are looking only to reinforce their own positions in the Democratic Party and incorrectly assume that any single political party speaks for Latinos. It was the most important and consequential campaign of my career, and it required expertise on two of my specialties, as my former boss Assembly Republican leader Rod Pacheco had put it when I went to work for Antonio Villaraigosa—Republican voters and Latino voters. My job was to focus on moving Republicans, and we did. But Latino voters had slipped away significantly. My only lingering regret was that I wasn't able to do more on the Latino vote in 2020.

- 10 -

The Latino Voter

The study of my ethnic group and of Latinos as a diverse community has been my life's work. It began when my personal cultural experience challenged my assumptions about America and highlighted my ethnic differences with our country's children of privilege. Where did I fit in? Where did Latinos fit in America? It's been a question that has marked my life and, I would argue, has marked the lives of a majority of Latinos in America.

I continued to search for answers in the place I found comfort—in the data. I became consumed with trying to take the cultural alienation I felt and quantify it through data and research. I hoped that if I could find answers, I could explain this transformation to the country. As a young man, my professors at Georgetown urged me to work with Latin American professors at the School of Foreign Service. My thesis examined the importance of Latino voters in the Southwest to the U.S. electoral future and a demographic transformation of our country driven by Latinos. Looking back, I shake my head at this lack of intellectual curiosity from my academic leaders. Sad, truly sad. I was relegated to the international department. The thesis I would write at Georgetown ultimately ended up being the framework for my thirty-year career— and, I expect, for whatever comes next.

I buried myself in the basement of Lauinger Library on Georgetown's campus, at a time before the internet when most research was done on microfiche and by thumbing through old newspaper clippings and academic works. In the mid-1990s, most public opinion surveys of Latino political attitudes were confined to California, Texas, Florida, and New York. And even in these states, the size of the Latino electorate was in the single digits or low teens. That was not enough for news operations to invest in detailed surveys of Latinos. Sometimes I found academic research on Latino subgroups—for example, Puerto Ricans in New York—but those were the exceptions. Without the benefit of a national organization like Pew Research, which is the gold standard of polling today, we had to rely on Associated Press exit polling data. AP commissions exit interviews at polling places and demographically valid samples of absentee voters by mail, to ask voters for whom they voted on Election Day. Once they are able to get a statistically valid sample they are confident in, they use this data to "call" a race, which is why we are able to have winners announced on Election Night. AP exit polling has been criticized for not accurately reflecting the actual precinct-level data that sometimes comes months after an election, when results can tell a very different narrative, but the Associated Press freely acknowledges its data is used only to determine a winner on Election Night.

The data that emerges from exit polling has severe limitations, but in the way of self-fulfilling prophesies, the trend is for polling data to become fact. It may or may not be as accurate as we would like for research, but for the vast majority of the population it doesn't matter. Once a news story is written and the narrative is set, no amount of post-election analysis can change the history of the exit polling. What began as a niche effort by exit pollsters in the 1980s and '90s has grown into the baseline upon which consultants and analysts rely for historical performance metrics. The only way to compare the performance of Latino voters from Ronald Reagan to Bob Dole to Donald Trump is through AP exit data.

There were just a couple of Latino pollsters in the country in the

1990s and before, most notably Sergio Bendixen. A Peruvian, he was not only the first Latino to run a presidential campaign (for Jimmy Carter) but he also chronicled the rise of Republican Cuban Americans and pioneered efforts to poll Latinos through multilingual and nationality differences to better gauge opinions in the community.

As an undergraduate at Georgetown, I was certainly no polling expert, but I had learned the basics talking to Arthur Finkelstein on the Gallegly campaign and dozens of pollsters since then. I was pulling together every poll of Latino political opinion I could find and learning as I went. Nearly everything from news sources had a major methodological problem: the sample sizes of Latinos were too small to get an accurate assessment of the community, a problem that exists to this day, especially in national surveys.

Polls, properly constructed, represent the community being interviewed with as much demographic criteria as possible, including age, gender, partisan affiliation, education levels, income levels, geographic distribution and, of course, race and ethnicity. A poll should reflect the balance of all these considerations in a manner that is representative of the population being polled. For example, roughly half of the country is female and half is male, so the respondents should match those criteria. If we were polling just women, we would not include men in the survey.

In 2020, for the first time, Latinos surpassed Black voters as the largest ethnic group in the country, constituting about 11 percent of all voters. This means that to get an accurate reflection of the country's opinion, 11 percent of poll respondents need to be Latino—but often the 11 percent sampled do not offer an accurate reflection of the overall Latino community. In a poll with eight hundred respondents, 11 percent amounted to only eighty-eight people, far too small a sample size to yield reliable results. Most pollsters will tell you that any sample size under one hundred is useless for a community the size of the U.S. Latino electorate. Really, in my experience, until you're surveying a minimum of four hundred Latinos, you're not examining anything reliable.

A "Latino Mirage" is created with small sample sizes pulled from larger polling instruments. That's what I've come to call it over decades of watching news services, pundits, and political consultants wrongly using these numbers. Polling based on insufficient sample size tends to be wrong, sometimes dramatically wrong. The results usually skew more right-leaning than actual voter sentiment, giving such polls a more "conservative" or "Republican" bias. This occurs for a number of reasons, but generally it almost always includes a bigger tilt toward generations of Latinos that have been in the country longer. More recently migrated Latinos are often more difficult to reach, are more transient and mobile, less likely to be a homeowner and have a voting history, and change place of registration more often. Republicans often think they're more competitive than they are, creating significant surprises on Election Day. That's the "mirage."

This was very much the case during the recall election of California governor Gavin Newsom in 2021. Most public opinion polls showed Latinos as the ethnic group most favorable toward recalling the Democratic governor. A number of Republican consultants gleefully appeared on television, confidently predicting that Governor Newsom would be recalled and Latino voters would seal his fate. On Election Day these predictions would prove wildly incorrect, with Republican consultants continuing their three-decade habit of misunderstanding Latino voters, who would ultimately serve as the greatest base of Newsom's support in defeating the recall. Latinos would oppose the Republican efforts by a 75-to-25 margin, an almost exact partisan outcome consistent with twenty-five years of voting behavior in the state.

One of the biggest mistakes pollsters make is weighting incorrectly for language. The more Spanish-speaking respondents a poll has, the more likely it is for the responses to skew leftward because Spanish-dominant audiences are more recently migrated and tend to be poorer and have less assimilated political beliefs. It is therefore not uncommon for Democratic partisans unhappy with public polling results to complain that the poll did not include enough Spanish speakers. However, an increased sample size of Spanish-speaking individuals leads the poll to become skewed leftward instead of providing an accurate snapshot of the electorate.

If one has to err in one direction or the other, it is far more accurate to oversample English-language-dominant Latino voters than Spanish-speaking respondents, and this is why most credible pollsters have more accurate results than partisan pollsters looking to develop narratives rather than scientific results. Generally, the more partisan the firm, the greater the sample of Spanish speakers has grown over the years, leading Democratic firms to miss both the rightward shift occurring in the country and the turnout rates they've needed in recent elections. Latino turnout estimates from some prominent Democratic firms were considerably off in both the 2014 midterms and the 2016 presidential race.

In 2014, a Democratic firm comprised entirely of academics began to issue polling results with remarkably different claims on Latino public opinion than anything political professionals had ever seen. The firm, Latino Decisions, cleverly occupied a void in the media's understanding of the emerging Latino vote and began making data publicly available that showed a dramatic leftward lean on public policy issues never identified before by nationally recognized pollsters with strict methodological standards for their research.

In polling conducted for an organization called America's Voice, an immigration reform organization pushing the Obama administration and Congress to change the nation's immigration laws, Latino Decisions made the unconventional proclamation that comprehensive immigration reform was the most important issue on the minds of Latino voters. In thirty years of polling, this had never come close to being the case, and yet, here were findings suggesting something completely new had not only emerged among Latino voters but was dominating their list of concerns. In their 2014 Latino Election Eve Poll findings presented at the National Press Club, Latino Decisions made the claim that 67 percent of Latinos agreed that the issue of immigration was either "the most important" or "one of the most important" issues in that election. This was astonishing because no respected pollster examining Latino public opinion had ever found that to be true of immigration—nor had it found that to be true of any issue polled. This level of intensity would invariably result in record-high Latino turnout regardless of congressional action or inaction or presidential executive action. But the exact opposite happened; Latino turnout was indeed historic in the 2014 midterms—but historically low.

The issues matrix that some of the most notable national Latino organizations had relied on was wrong, wildly wrong. Groups like the National Council of La Raza (UnidosUS), Mi Familia Vota, the National Association of Latino Elected and Appointed Officials (NALEO), and even traditional Democratic organizations like the AFL-CIO had been led to believe that the focus on key policy issues of immigration and the environment would help raise Latino turnout in the midterms. Beyond the intense and misguided focus on immigration, it was advised that "protecting the environment, addressing climate change, and conservation of land and waterways are a top priority for Latino voters." While these were clearly the priorities of key interests in the Democratic Party, no credible researcher has ever found them to be prime motivators for Latino voters.

So how could this have happened? Well, to be this far off requires a lot of misunderstanding and error, but the methodology used in the press club presentation provides one important clue. Latino Decisions "completed 4,200 interviews with Latinos who had already voted early, or were certain to vote in the November 4, 2014 general election. . . . Overall, 66 percent of interviews were completed in English and 34 percent in Spanish." That's an extraordinary flaw—34 percent of interviews conducted in Spanish is nowhere near a representative sample of any Latino electorate outside of the island of Puerto Rico or very dense Hispanic precincts in Miami-Dade County, Florida, or East Los Angeles in California. It is certainly not representative of a national or statewide survey of Latino voters. This number is double what a representative sample would be from nearly every credible poll of Latino voters.

There seems to be a partisan bias growing in some Democratic research firms that is regularly missing the rightward shift happening with Latino voters. In an October 2016 news article for Univision News titled "Do Polls Underestimate the Democratic Party's Latino Vote?" one of the partners of Latino Decisions, University of New Mexico professor Gabriel Sanchez, was cited as saying, "The polls also target the 'wrong Latinos,'" making their sample unrepresentative of eligible voters. By not offering interviews in Spanish and relying on interviews via internet and fixed home phone lines, they end up with a biased sample of more assimilated, native-born, higher-income, and higher-educated voters, according to internal poll research conducted by Latino Decisions. First-generation Hispanics speak less English, rely more on cell phones, and often don't have internet, he noted.

While Gabriel Sanchez was not employed by the Hillary Clinton campaign team, at least some of his colleagues were working directly for her campaign, as noted in the article. Sanchez was clearly using the wrong methodology and it may well have cost Hillary Clinton Florida and other states like Pennsylvania and Wisconsin with measurable Latino voting populations. While it would not be appropriate for Sanchez to have shared information with the campaign team, it's not a big stretch to assume they use the same methodology. This would explain not only the wild miss in 2014, but also the miss in 2016, and again, very likely 2020, as well as the higher sustained levels of Latino support for Republicans in 2022. While we will never be privy to the internal polling of these campaigns, the public information we do have clearly demonstrates flaws in four of the five most recent election cycles where Democrats have dramatically missed the mark.

According to Pew Research and Edison exit polling data in Florida, Cubans were about twice as likely as non-Cuban Latinos to vote for Donald Trump in 2016. More than half (54 percent) supported Trump, compared with a quarter of non-Cuban Latinos. Overall, 35 percent of Florida Latinos supported Trump, and while that share was down from 2012, when Mitt Romney won 39 percent of their vote—it was higher than both Republicans and Democrats had planned on and confidently predicted. A Politico headline screamed just five days before the 2016 election, "Clinton's 30-Point Lead in Florida Hispanic Poll Is 'Terrifying' to GOP Nationwide," citing a Univision poll conducted by the Republican-leaning Tarrance Group and Democratic firm Bendixen & Amandi International.

"These Florida numbers are not only ominous for Donald Trump—they're downright terrifying for Republicans nationwide," said Fernand Amandi, Bendixen & Amandi pollster, who called Clinton's thirty-point margin "historic." That margin, of course, never materialized, and Trump performed five points better among Hispanics than the poll predicted, winning Florida that year by about 1.2 points.

"The share of the Hispanic vote is growing every election cycle and this will be the third presidential election in Florida where Hispanics trend heavily against the GOP," Amandi said. "And if that continues, it could turn Florida into the next California in future presidential elections, a blue anchor state."

In fact, the exact opposite has happened.

Trump drastically improved his standing four years later in Cuban-dense Miami-Dade County, going from 333,999 votes in 2016 to at least 529,160 votes in 2020, and moved his statewide support among Florida Latinos from 35 percent to 55 percent—a massive twenty-point shift. In 2022, just two years later, Republican governor Ron DeSantis made even further gains with Latinos in the state, commanding a jaw-dropping 57 percent of the Latino vote, according to CNN exit polls, showing significant Latino support growth for the Republican well beyond the Cuban American diaspora, most notably breaking 50 percent of the Puerto Rican vote, which is traditionally a reliable Democratic constituency.

The New York Times/Siena poll, one of the largest nonpartisan surveys of Latino voters conducted since the 2020 election, reflected nuances of both language and generational variation, as reporting on Latino voters has become more sophisticated. Identifying Spanish-speaking respondents was done through a highly effective screen. Given a choice of language—asked directly in Spanish or English—only 14 percent of 522 self-identified Latino voters chose to have the interview conducted in Spanish. While there have been numerous criticisms over the years about the likelihood of Spanish speakers "feeling comfortable" after being approached in English or refusing to talk to pollsters altogether, most credible nonpartisan polling organizations have found the range of Spanish-speaking respondents to be in the mid-teens range.

To be accurate, polling must also account for generational differences, and differentiate answers based on naturalized immigrants (first generation), the sons and daughters of immigrants (second generation), the grandchildren of immigrants (third generation), and beyond. Polling organizations like the Texas Hispanic Policy Foundation and the New York Times/Siena poll have done this to great effect and have benefited accordingly from highly accurate results. They therefore provide keener insight into public policy issues and the assimilative affect with which Latinos approach these policy differences.

Prior to the great migratory wave of Mexican Americans arriving in the Southwest in the late 1980s and '90s, the Latino population—less recently migrated—had begun to take on the voting characteristics of the dominant non-Hispanic white voter and reflected a rightward shift not unlike previous generational assimilation of European immigrant groups of the past. This dynamic explains why many Republicans performed strongly with Latinos in the 1980s and prior to that. In 1984, Ronald Reagan polled at 37 percent. Senator John McCain often won up to 60 percent of the Latino vote in Arizona. The same dynamic helps explain the rightward shift of Latinos in the 2020 election and the 2022 midterms.

The battle to define who is Latino and what generational differences exist is essential for partisans on both sides to lay claim to the validity of their policy positions. If Democrats want to push for a more ambitious immigration reform proposal, they have a vested interest in oversampling Latinos closer to the immigrant experience. Conversely, if Republicans are polling border security, they can oversample third- and fourth-generation Latinos. As a practical matter this can pose a significant challenge for professional campaign consultants trying to target different messages to multigenerational Latino households, which are common in Latino families. Elderly Latino grandparents who predominantly speak Spanish and hold more socially conservative views have a much different political perspective than their bilingual adult children and far different than their English-language-exclusive grandchildren who are growing up in the most culturally progressive generation of Americans in history.

Democrats in particular have been led astray by resorting to a highly questionable methodology for political campaigns—population density—which has shown to be a disaster. In a nutshell, population density overweighs interview samples from neighborhoods where there are more Latinos. While this may provide accurate assessment of Latino public opinion overall—it grossly exaggerates Latino *voter* opinion in the opposite direction in which it's moving. More Latino-dense communities, like most ethnically dense communities, especially those of immigrants, have a decidedly different political perspective than less dense neighborhoods. The idea of using an ethnic population's "density" to weigh opinion for political purposes leads to a significant problem where opinion is skewed toward a more recently migrated, poor, non-college-educated, non-homeowning, and Spanish-language-dominant voter. Not only does this lead to inaccurate polling results, but it also drives a false stereotype about Latinos. It is precisely those Latino voters who do not live in Hispanic-dense precincts that are the most likely to hold opinions consistent with an assimilative generational pattern. Combined with the significant over-sampling of Spanish-speaking voters, it is the additional reliance on this technique that led Democrats to miss the rightward shift that began at the national level after the 2012 election.

With few exceptions, Democrats have miscalculated both Latino voter sentiment and turnout since Obama's high-watermark reelection campaign in 2012. Speaking of Obama, what was driving the success of his outreach with Latino voters? Could it have been his eloquence, charisma, and personality that defined him as one of the great politicians of his generation? Very likely that played a factor. But was that so much stronger than the policy positions he took, especially those on undocumented immigration that led Latino advocacy organizations to dub him the "Deporter in Chief"?

At least some of the answers lie in simple demographics. Pew Research found that among voting-age adults, the share of U.S.-born Latinos increased from 45 percent in 2007 to 55.2 percent in 2019. This means that over 10 percent of the entire Latino voting-age population had changed from Obama's first election to Joe Biden's first election in the direction of a more assimilated English-language-dominant U.S.-born voter—at precisely the same time leading Latino Democratic pollsters were advising their presidential candidate to move in the opposite direction. The Latino voter is changing empirically in exactly the opposite direction of where the Democratic Party is being advised to focus. Is it any wonder they've been taken completely by surprise?

Strikingly enough, Latino voter registration rates are lower than virtually every other group, and it's not even close. Does that sound confusing? Or contradictory to conventional wisdom about Latino voters in recent elections? The answer is that miserable Latino registration numbers are neither confusing nor contradictory to the few people paying attention to the data rather than to the partisan talking points or lazy journalistic analysis.

In the 2020 election, Latinos had the lowest voter registration among racial and ethnic groups at 61.1 percent. This is more than ten percentage points below the 72.7 percent registration rate among all voters. In my home state of California, Latinos have the lowest registration of all voters at just above 60 percent, even lower than the national average. Think about it: at the national level and in California, the state with the highest numbers of Latinos, close to 40 percent of potential Latino voters are not registered to vote. How messed up is that?

It is very problematic that Latinos have the lowest voter turnout rate among the top four racial and ethnic groups in California despite being the largest ethnic group in the population. California has the most progressive and robust methods of voting among any state in the country, while also having some of the lowest voter participation rates anywhere. It's time to be honest, folks. This is not about apathy and it's not about voting processes. The reality is Latinos don't have a compelling reason to support either party in a meaningful way, and decades of election results exist to prove it. In fact, since the initial burst of Latino voters after the catalyst of California's Proposition 187, Latino voter turnout essentially flatlined in the most populous Latino state for twenty years, returning to higher levels during the Trump era, but still lower than any other group in California.

Declining confidence in the U.S. economy among Latinos largely, though not entirely, explains why this working-class group has shifted rightward in the 2020 and 2022 election cycles. The Hispanic Consumer Sentiment Index, conducted by Florida Atlantic University in the closing days of the 2022 midterms, showed a drop to 74.3 percent from 78.3 percent in the second quarter and 92 percent for the first quarter. Only 44 percent of the 454 respondents said they were better off financially than a year before, down from 56 percent in the second quarter and 65 percent in the first quarter. In addition, a smaller percentage of respondents said they were optimistic about their financial futures. Latinos are much more price-sensitive to inflation and cost-of-living issues. As the globalization of the marketplace shifts into higher gear, the loss of manufacturing jobs and the loss of economic mobility and opportunity compound the differences Latino workers—like their non-Hispanic, white, non-college-educated counterparts—feel with "new economy" workers.

Latino, Black, and immigrant workers of all backgrounds were also a large share of what we called "essential workers" during the COVID pandemic. This was a term used to make us feel better about throwing a certain segment of our society into the petri dish of the coronavirus so that the rest of us could ride it out in the comfort of our own homes. Latinos were infected with the coronavirus at very high rates, in part because they were exposed to it more frequently. In fact, a March 2021 article by the Center for American Progress reported that Hispanics were 1.7 times more likely to contract COVID-19 than their non-Hispanic white counterparts, as well as 4.1 times more likely to be hospitalized from COVID-19 and 2.8 times more likely to die from the virus. According to Pew Research, 45 percent of Hispanic adults worked at jobs that required them to work outside the home since the pandemic began in February 2020. About half of Hispanics (54 percent) who have worked outside their home during the pandemic in a job that involves frequent contact with others say they have experienced a job or wage loss since the start of the pandemic. So, if you're forced to work in dangerous conditions, often at reduced hours or under conditions that limit your ability to earn more, why are we surprised that Latinos voted in greater numbers than ever for a party looking to open up the economy?

– 11 –

Beyond the Politics of Immigration

While no issue is more closely associated with Latino voters than immigration, in fact it rarely shows up among the top five topics of concern to Latinos. As for their actual views on immigration, Latinos broadly agree that the U.S. immigration system needs an overhaul, with large shares saying it either requires major changes (53 percent) or needs to be completely rebuilt (29 percent). Only 17 percent say the immigration system needs no or only minor changes, according to a March 2021 Pew Research Center survey of Hispanic adults. The year 2021 marked a time of an increasing number of apprehensions along the border and this coincided with a significant number of Hispanics in the Pew survey who said that increasing border security is an important policy goal (42 percent), while only 18 percent say increasing deportations is a very important goal. In another strong sign of merging views on border control issues, a similar share of Hispanics (44 percent) and U.S. adults overall (48 percent) say illegal immigration is a very big problem in the country today, an increase of more than 15 percent among both groups since June 2020. Perhaps more than any other data point, this merging of Latino views on border security will challenge Democrats, balancing the demands of advocacy groups with the shifting views of Latino voters toward a more centrist view.

Perhaps even more interesting, Pew found considerable divisions by political party among Latinos in the same survey. Latino partisans tend to reflect the major parties' polarization on the issues, while Latino voters overall reflect an almost perfect split on some of the most polarizing issues related to the border and immigration. Latinos who identify as Democrats are more likely than those who lean Republican to say it is a very important goal to allow immigrants who came into the U.S. illegally as children to stay in the country and apply for legal status (61 percent to 36 percent, but 52 percent with Latino voters overall). A similar split shows when asked if it is very important to establish a way for most immigrants in the country illegally to stay in the country legally (59 percent to 33 percent, but 51 percent with Latino voters overall).

There has always been a wide swath of Latinos who support significant, sometimes severe restrictions and penalties on undocumented immigrants. More than 30 percent of Latinos actually supported Proposition 187, the polarizing California ballot measure that catalyzed a generation of Latino politicians and activists to become more civically engaged. Some of the most anti-immigrant sentiments come from those Latinos who themselves previously endured the long and arduous process of legal migration. Growing concerns about illegal immigration are showing up in polling among Hispanics in Texas and account for at least some of the state's Hispanic movement rightward. This is especially true in communities along the Mexican border in southwestern states where the recent rightward shift in voting patterns has been most pronounced. As recently as 2020, a poll conducted by the Texas Hispanic Policy Foundation found that "[t]wice as many Texas Hispanics support (51 percent) than oppose (25 percent) the Texas policy of having Department of Public Safety (DPS) officers and local law enforcement arrest immigrants who cross the U.S.-Mexico border illegally." Far more Hispanics supported dispatching DPS officers (48 percent) and Texas National Guard soldiers (46 percent) to patrol along the border than opposed these policies (30 percent and 32 percent).

Nationally, Latinos overall are less likely than a decade ago to say that the U.S. has too many immigrants. They are more willing than the general public to favor granting legal status to unauthorized immigrants brought to the U.S. as children. And they are more likely than the general public to oppose expanding the U.S.-Mexico border wall.

Nevertheless, Latinos appear to reflect overall public attitudes on increasing border security as illegal crossings grow in number. In April 2021, Pew reported some illuminating details, amid a growing number of apprehensions at the U.S.-Mexico border that have reached levels last seen in 2006: 42 percent of Latinos said increasing border security is a very important immigration policy goal, while only 18 percent said increasing deportations is a very important goal. The vast majority of Hispanics in the U.S. said they have heard a lot (52 percent) or a little (39 percent) about the increase in children and families seeking asylum at the U.S.-Mexico border. However, relatively few Hispanics said the U.S. government has done a very good (5 percent) or somewhat good (31 percent) job of dealing with the influx.

Joe Biden's change in policy on constructing a border wall and focusing resources on border security certainly reflects a change in his and his party's public messaging. At the time of this writing, Biden's policies also certainly reflect the changing attitudes of Latino voters on this policy issue. Mexican American voters along the border communities in the Rio Grande Valley and in southern New Mexico reflect a new reality about border politics that will require Democratic presidents and policymakers to move to the center. Curiously, Biden may find more resistance from college-educated white progressives and professional Latino advocacy voices on this change in policy than he will from the growing number of Latino voters.

Latinx

Many Latinos find it increasingly difficult to relate to what they see as a white, educated, progressive Democratic Party, a cultural drift probably best summed up with one word: "Latinx." The term, whose etymology is not known with certainty, symbolizes the cultural alienation of institutions far removed from the realities of life for an overwhelming number of working-class Hispanics.

Like the term "Chicano" back in my father's day, the term is used largely by a politicized minority. While the term is intended to be inclusive, Latinx is barely known within the community it seeks to describe. Commonly used by media, political, and academic elites as a self-congratulating sign of gender inclusivity, an August 2020 Pew Research survey found that only 3 percent of Latino adults used the phrase, while 9 percent of white liberals think it is the most appropriate term to use. In fact, only 14 percent of Latinos with a high school degree or less had even heard of "Latinx."

One of the ironies of this phrase is that it is gender neutral, while in the Spanish language, masculine nouns end with the letter *o* and feminine nouns end with the letter *a*. Some advocates have declared that it is unfair and inaccurate to suggest that "Latinx" is, in fact, a creation of white progressives. Fair enough, but there is an increasing problem of leftward cultural drift that is developing as the Democratic Party continues to consolidate white, college-educated, progressive voters. "Latinx" is very likely to go the way of "Chicano," never finding mainstream adaptation, but engendering strong feelings against it among a wide swath of the community. It's a political term, not a community term.

Democrats are increasingly a college-educated constituency, but to many Latinos, cultural designations hatched on college campuses are not relatable to the average experience of everyday working-class, blue-collar Latino voters. The education divide is a cultural divide, but it's also a racial and ethnic divide that is cutting into Democratic vote margins. Whether it's critical race theory or the term "Latinx" or gender studies, the messengers of these ideas are too often higher-income progressive thinkers who are trying to address society's cultural problems. Meanwhile, many Latinos are more worried about paying for groceries, filling their gas tanks, and making rent payments. Democrats are becoming less relatable to Latinos as the culture and diploma divides widen.

To be sure, there are Democratic campaign professionals that have been sounding alarms over research showing that Republican attacks on culture-war issues are working, particularly with center-left, Latino, Black, Asian, immigrant, and independent voters. Democrats now understand that they are losing support among Hispanics on culture as well as pocketbook issues, leaving little in the message arsenal for the party's candidates to stanch what appears to be emerging as a small but consistent long-term bleed.

The Catholic Question

The abstract discussion of abortion became very real in the wake of the *Dobbs* Supreme Court decision in 2022 that effectively overturned *Roe v. Wade*. The electoral earthquake that resulted post-*Dobbs* had a discernible effect in limiting Republican gains in the 2022 midterms in large part due to the increased turnout of women and the fact that Latinas who may have been tepid about Democrats' performance rushed back to the party in response to the potential loss of rights. From an electoral perspective, Hispanic women were voting as we have come to politically define "women" and "women's issues" more than they were following Catholic doctrine.

The Latinos most likely to identify as pro-life are those who have most recently migrated, and therefore tend to reflect the conservative Catholic cultural values of their country of origin or are part of the growing evangelical movement among Latinos. However, the tendency to stereotype these voters as representative of the entire Latino electorate has stifled the discussion and understanding of what is developing in Latino communities on the abortion issue. As the Latino electorate grows into second, third, and fourth generations, their political opinions begin to mirror the dominant culture's views. From immigration to abortion, the stereotype of issues falls away and we start to see an emerging voter group driven more by traditional demographic data points—age, economic class, education levels, and gender—than by race or ethnicity. Assimilating political views don't just benefit Republicans, it would appear.

Pew Research Center data published in September 2022 suggests Democrats' hold on the Latino community may continue to be surprisingly durable, with most of its voters viewing the party favorably. One possible explanation? Ironically it is the exact opposite of the stereotype political pundits have been promulgating for years: the rising importance of abortion rights, which a majority of Latinos support, according to the findings. In fact, abortion now outranks immigration, climate change, and the Supreme Court in importance to Latinos, climbing from the fifteenth spot in a March 2022 survey to the seventh spot that August. A majority—57 percent—of Latinos say abortion should be a legal option, including 39 percent of Latino Republicans.

Hispanic evangelicals, who make up about 15 percent of the U.S. Hispanic population, are one of the most conservative religious groups on the issue of abortion, and overall Latinos are more likely (23 percent) than the general population (15 percent) to think abortion should be illegal in all cases, and less likely (19 percent) than all Americans (23 percent) to think it should be legal in all cases. The largest divide is by place of birth. A majority (57 percent) of Latinos born in the U.S. believe abortion should be legal in most or all cases, compared to 36 percent who say it should be illegal in most or all cases. Among Latinos born in Puerto Rico, 41 percent support abortion legality, compared to 53 percent who say it should be illegal in most or all cases. By contrast, only 33 percent of Latinos born outside of the U.S. say abortion should be legal in most or all cases, while nearly six in ten (59 percent) say it should be illegal in most or all cases.

Place of birth also stratified age groups. More than six in ten (63 percent) of young Latinos aged eighteen to twenty-nine born in the United States support abortion, compared to just 38 percent of young Latinos born outside of the United States. Among seniors aged sixty-five and over, 44 percent of U.S.-born Latinos favor abortion legality, compared to just under one in three (31 percent) foreign-born Hispanic seniors.

The abortion question has changed as the Latino electorate has changed, and the post-*Dobbs* era is demonstrating that as the climate for abortion rights becomes more charged, the changes that have occurred are likely to continue. Early polling in the 1980s showed that Latinos were demonstrably more opposed to abortion than the general public. The Latino electorate at the time was both more Catholic and religious (as was the rest of the U.S. population), less partisan, and less recently migrated. Given the changing composition of the Latino electorate, especially with the rapid growth of second- and third-generation U.S.-born women composing a growing segment of the Latino vote, abortion rights should continue to be a winning issue for Democrats. The *Dobbs* ruling, in short, may have saved Democrats with Latino voters—at least for a few years. Even among Catholic Latinos, 59 percent said they would prefer to vote for a Democratic candidate for the House of Representatives in the 2022 midterm elections, according to Pew.

Evangelical churches have proven to be a good recruiting ground for Latino Republicans. They are far more animated in their faith than Catholics, who are best described as ambivalent. The growing numbers of evangelical churches are illustrative of changing religious beliefs among Latinos but, in a bigger sign of changing religious views, most Latinos who are leaving the Catholic faith aren't becoming evangelical, they're losing their religious faith altogether—another assimilative characteristic that reflects American society. That trend line is accelerating as more Latinos are U.S. born and reflect their white peers. Republicans have likely reached their ceiling with Latino religious voters. The stereotype of Latino Catholics being motivated by social issues has never been backed up by hard data or electoral results. This will be a hard one because Republicans are addicted to faith voters at a time when more people are losing touch with organized religion. It is easier for Republicans to try to tie their white evangelical Christian base to the stereotype of the Catholic Latino voter—but this is an extraordinary mistake—one that they have been making since at least the 1980s. In fact, in light of current religious trends, it is more likely that Republicans are turning off two Latino voters who are not religiously aligned for every one evangelical they are recruiting with socially conservative messaging.

Guns

A 2014 Pew Research Center survey asked U.S. adults what is more important—protecting the right of Americans to own guns or controlling gun ownership. Latino registered voters nationally said they prefer gun control over the rights of owners by 62 percent to 36 percent, as do Black registered voters by a margin of 71 to 26. By contrast, white registered voters choose gun owners' rights over gun control by a margin of 59 percent to 39 percent. Like many issues, gun control changes generationally, depending on how far removed Latinos are from the immigrant experience. Where fully 82 percent of Latino immigrants think that gun control is more important than protecting individual rights, nearly 40 percent of gun retailers saw an increase of U.S. Latinos purchasing firearms in 2021, according to a survey by the National Shooting Sports Foundation, the firearm industry trade association. Latinos purchased firearms in 2020 at a 49 percent higher rate than they did in 2019.

In rural communities the sentiment for gun ownership may be even stronger among Latinos. In Uvalde County, Texas, with a population that is over 80 percent Latino and home to the horrific school shooting that rocked the nation just months prior to the 2022 midterms, conservative politicians performed stronger than expected despite opposing almost every piece of gun control legislation. According to official results, 60.18 percent of Uvalde County residents voted for Republican governor Greg Abbott compared to 38.32 percent who voted for Democrat Beto O'Rourke, a gun control advocate.

Affirmative Action

Latino attitudes on race-based preferences tend to match their blended ethnic and racial perception of themselves in relation to other groups in the United States, but perhaps more important, the political environment of the times. Not being fully white, but also not being fully non-white, is an ethnic characteristic that shows up in both polling on the affirmative action issue as well as in voting results. In an April 2022 poll examining racial attitudes toward race-based admissions decisions, Pew found that "majorities of Americans across racial and ethnic and partisan groups say race or ethnicity should *not* be factored into college acceptance decisions," but "there are variations in how widely this view is held."

"About eight-in-ten white adults (79 percent) say race or ethnicity should not factor into admission decisions," Pew reported. "By comparison, 68 percent of Hispanic adults say this, as do about six in ten Asian American (63 percent) and Black (59 percent) adults. And while 87 percent of Republicans say race or ethnicity should not be a factor in admissions, that share falls to 62 percent among Democrats. While three-quarters of Americans say having a relative who attended the school should *not* factor into decisions, white adults (80 percent) are more likely than Hispanic (67 percent), Black (62 percent), and Asian American (59 percent) adults to say this."

Climate Change

Latinos often report significant concerns about the environment, climate change, and pollution, but these concerns have yet to be effectively transformed into a significant political motivator in the Latino community beyond regional issues. Working-class Latinos consistently rate jobs and the economy as top-tier issues and environmental concerns much lower, demonstrative of the tension that the pillars of the Democratic Party face and will increasingly face in the future. The building and construction trades, a central part of organized labor unions that make up the heart of the Democratic Party, are regularly in conflict with the environmental organizations that also make up the Democratic coalition. That building trade unions are increasingly diverse and represent more and more Latino members every day while environmental activism and membership organizations remain overwhelmingly white illustrates the growing demographic split among the coalitions of the left. As I regularly counseled clients, "The only organization more white than the Republican Party is the Sierra Club."

Climate change is regularly cited as a priority issue among wealthier white progressives who don't face the crushing economic concerns of blue-collar working-class voters. Conversely, it is Latinos that often have to live and work in some of the most environmentally degraded parts of the country. In the near future, Latino voters will increasingly be faced with these two dire threats to their quality of life: the need to make a sufficient income to support their families or pursue policies that may harm that income potential while cleaning up the communities in which they live. For those who suggest this is a false choice, the burden is on policymakers to prove this to working-class Latinos who are coming to believe it more and more every election cycle.

- 12 -

The Flip Slide of Machismo

Respect for women leadership roles runs deep in Latino culture generally, and in the Mexican culture, specifically, very deep. People of Mexican heritage are very focused on the maternal, on birth and birthing, on Mother Earth in all her glory, and the continuity of birth and death and birth. We are living representatives of the Indigenous people who make up half of our bloodline, and reverence for the mother was an important part of our ancestors' culture. Feminine power was celebrated and revered. For agrarian cultures, going back, you survived as a tribe, as a community, as part of a larger cluster, and for us culturally the idea of needing to be interdependent through village and beyond comes through in our mythology of ourselves, the narrative that we as Mexicans—and Central Americans as well—were taught as children.

Latinos often don't see holding political office as a necessary or even desirable step toward bringing political change, and much of that has to do with the influence of women. When I look at the number of women in elected office in California and break down their backgrounds, a huge amount of them come from nonprofits. When they see a social problem, they go out and do something about it. They don't think that it's necessarily a government solution. That doesn't make them anti-government. The mindset is: *Hey, there are some environmental problems in the riverbed. Let's go fix that. How do we go about getting that done?*

Latinos generally, and Mexican Americans specifically, have long looked to women as catalysts for political action. The very origins of Mexican national and political identity are intertwined with the emergence of the cult of La Virgen de Guadalupe, the brown-skinned mother of God. As any Mexican Catholic will tell you, La Virgen is more venerated than Jesus. For us she is *the* symbol of the Catholic Church, that colonial religion that was imposed by the sword, but remains so culturally and spiritually revered by so many of us. Over the centuries Catholicism was a function of its malleability and ability to adapt to preexisting religion and spirituality. That's where relying on the feminine is such a big part of it, to the point where the Virgin of Guadalupe is revered as essentially a goddess. She's also the symbol of Mexico and of Latin America, deeply entwined with our sense of national identity, and to have the same iconography be both a symbol of the oppressor and of the revolutionary movement to cast off the yoke of that oppression—that really captures Mexican identity in a way that few things can. It is both. She is both the oppressor and the call to arms against it.

It's just a split personality. We're not just mixed-race people by blood and biology. We are truly a mixed culture. There's an oppressed element, but there's a revolutionary element, too, and it runs right through national ideas of the power of women. When you understand the Virgin of Guadalupe and what she means to Mexicans, then you can understand the Mexican view of the world.

Another iconic figure for us is La Malinche. Talk about your complicated legacies! She was born in 1500 or soon after in a Nahuatl village along the Coatzacoalcos River in what is now the Veracruz state to a family with ties to local rulers. Taken young as a slave, she became famous as a translator to Hernán Cortés before and during the fall of the Aztec empire. She was also an adviser to Cortés and became his lover. Historically, she's been viewed as the traitor to her people because she told Cortés and the Spaniards where to find Moctezuma so they could kill him, but she also gave birth to the first mixed-race child, her son with Cortés, which makes her our mother. Think about that. When your mother is a traitor to your people, the psychology of that is fascinating. But there has been a shift in how people think of La Malinche. More and more she's celebrated for her strength and her resourcefulness. That view is gaining greater traction as people are examining Indigenous nationality and what it takes to survive.

These myths are very important in building a sense of Mexican identity that resonates. Biology alone is not enough to create a nation. The Virgin of Guadalupe and La Malinche present a very significant perspective because each is viewed as the political leader, the nationalist leader, the revolutionary leader, the mother of the Americas, from a spiritual, ideological, emotional place that is necessary to create a nation, right? The Virgin provides that in a very uniquely Mexican way. La Malinche provides that in a very biological way. As the mother of our mixed race, of our *raza cosmica*, our mestizo people, old and new worlds together, she brings forth the first new "race." And these two provide the entire framework and narrative of who we are biologically, spiritually, and politically.

The Virgin of Guadalupe is undeniably a political symbol and a strong one, a symbol of nationalism. That is very foreign to non-Hispanic whites to have a female iconography of such profound importance. The Statue of Liberty might be as close as we come, but let's remember Lady Liberty was presented by the French as a gift in 1886, more than a century after the founding, so as a symbol she represents more of a Lincoln-like reminder of who we needed to be instead of a Jeffersonian goal of who we were trying to be.

For all the attention Americans give to Latino machismo, few consider how matriarchal Mexican culture is. Anybody who understands Mexican identity would say it is women who are more often than not our leaders in the home, in politics, and certainly with social movements and social change. And as Latinos grow more numerous in the

United States, it follows that a slow cultural shift toward greater influence and power for women will continue to move forward.

In 2022, of 7,383 state legislators in the United States, 2,259 (or 31 percent) were women, according to the National Conference of State Legislatures. But among the exploding numbers of Hispanic elected officials, the numbers of women were considerably higher. Of the 451 Hispanic state legislators, 195 were women—43 percent—the most recent data found. Those were record-breaking numbers, according to a recent report by the National Hispanic Caucus of State Legislators.

As of June 2022, there were 122 women in the U.S. House of Representatives (plus four female nonvoting delegates), making women 27.9 percent of the total. Of the forty-three Hispanic members serving in the House, twenty-nine were men and fourteen were women—a slight but measurably better 33 percent of Latino members were women. Perhaps more important, as a barometer of the near future, more Latinas ran for Congress than ever before in 2020 with at least seventy-five candidates. This was more than four times the number in 2010, when seventeen Latinas ran. (In 2022, according to the UCLA Latino Policy & Politics Institute, forty Latinas ran for House seats.)

In California, home to the country's largest Latino population, fully 60 percent of Hispanic state legislators are women—nineteen women to thirteen men. In red Texas, the country's second largest Hispanic state, twenty-three men and eighteen women serve in the state legislature, meaning 44 percent of Hispanic lawmakers are women. But it's not just Mexican Americans in southwestern states. Nationally, of 425 Hispanic state legislators, 166 or 39 percent are women according to the National Hispanic Caucus of State Legislators. For all women in state legislative offices, the number is 33 percent.

This is all unfolding evidence that the Latinization of America will result in considerably greater female representation in our government. What non-Hispanic white women have been struggling to achieve over a century since suffrage, Hispanic women seem to be rapidly accomplishing in a fraction of that time. NALEO, the National Association of Latino Elected and Appointed Officials, the membership organization representing the rapidly expanding roles of Hispanic elected officials, has conducted research concluding that the engagement of the female head of Hispanic households had a cascading effect on men and voting-age adults in the family. Hispanic women are truly the drivers of civic engagement and voting behavior, and are increasingly running for office.

The growing trend of female elected representation includes a wide diversity of ideology, nationality, generational status, and geography. Like the community itself, Latina elected officials are not monolithic. Where the progressive Boston University alumna Representative Alexandria Ocasio-Cortez—of Puerto Rican descent—represents an urban district and has ushered in a new generation of politics on the American left, Representative Mayra Flores, the non-college-educated Mexican immigrant who won a special election to Congress in 2021 from the rural Rio Grande Valley, personified the GOP's current lurch toward America First nationalism. Flores would lose in her general election matchup, but her rise heralds the emergence of Latina conservatives also becoming politically active on the right.

While only time will tell which, if either, woman's ideological or partisan preferences are most reflective of the emerging Hispanic American plurality, it's undeniable that each woman can legitimately claim that their distinctive brand of politics is genuinely reflective of the values their respective communities represent. Their Latina identity, or Latinidad, is unquestioned even though they represent the two polar opposites of the congressional political spectrum.

Advocates of greater female representation have argued that women tend to be less combative, more solution-oriented, and better collaborators than male politicians. We can hope. What seems more certain is that regardless of the state of our politics, it will be Hispanic women leading the way. And in Mexico, it will soon be a woman leading the way.

What will happen when, as expected, Mexico elects its first woman president in June 2024? The two leading candidates for president of Mexico are both women—outspoken Xóchitl Gálvez, charismatic and brave but unlikely to win, versus Claudia Sheinbaum of the dominant Morena party, led by current president Andrés Manuel López Obrador, the strong favorite. Mexico has never seen anything like how President Sheinbaum could be expected to lead—she's a scientist with a PhD in energy engineering, a true expert on sustainable energy, and she would be both the first woman and the first Jew elected president of Mexico. This will represent a major step forward.

Until recently women have tended to look to make change in their communities through nonprofits, through volunteer work, and through solving these problems, while men tend to pursue the title and the power and the prestige. My mom really was the main provider for our family, not just financially, but spiritually. I grew up as the middle son with an older and a younger sister. And strong female influences have always been a part of my life. I think I'm able to understand the world through a more feminine lens because I've seen it through my mother's and grandmother's eyes. And there's much more of a matriarchy in our families than there ever is a patriarchy.

Certainly throughout U.S. history, we have referred to America as feminine, and illustrations over the years often have depicted the country as female, but our understandable fascination with the Founding Fathers sets the stage for a perception of our origin as revering a male mindset that borders on turning the Founders into religious deities. Moreover, the ubiquitous image most widely recognized around the world for the United States, arguably more than even Lady Liberty, would have to be Uncle Sam, an older white male often pictured looking aggressive and arrogant—a figure first introduced after the War of 1812, a notable change from the original depiction of America in the eighteenth century as Columbia, a woman, holding out her arms in a welcoming gesture.

Nevada: Labor and Working-Class Latinos

The 2016 Democratic presidential primary election offered a case study in how a growing generational divide in the party is redefining the approach and tactics used to engage Latino voters. The Hillary Clinton campaign entered the Nevada caucuses confident that they would beat back the insurgent Bernie Sanders campaign with a reliably strong performance from Latino voters, whom they had come to expect similar results as those from Black voters. This statewide campaign has largely been forgotten in the history books of presidential elections, but it marked the first true break within the Democratic Party that made clear the generational divide was here to stay. The Clinton campaign relied on calcified tactics and antiquated structures of former presidential campaigns that had always been used by Democratic candidates and Latino political appointees to deliver in a community where the voter base had dramatically changed.

Looking at Nevada in 2024, the state offers a crucial test case of how Democrats can do better with Latinos, especially younger Latinos, the very voters who defected from Hillary to Bernie in large numbers, helped along in some cases by the role of labor unions. Nevada's huge Latino immigrant population comprises the essential service economy in Clark County that makes Las Vegas work. More than anywhere else in the country, it is in Nevada that the organizational power of labor unions among Latino voters has flexed its strength. Over half of the powerful Culinary Union is Latino—54 percent—and is largely credited with turning the state blue.

When Hillary's advisers urged her to present herself to Latino voters in Nevada in 2016 as a relatable grandmother type—the *"abuelas"* for whom our maternal culture holds so much reverence—going into the state's February 20 caucuses, I knew she had a big problem. Hillary, a former secretary of state as well as former First Lady, had positive attributes she could present, but being a relatable or grandmotherly Latina were not among them.

Having announced that Hillary was soon expecting to be a second-time grandmother, some social media staffer thought it would be a great idea to post the list "7 Things Hillary Clinton Has in Common with Your Abuela." The list included things like: she cares for all children, she reads to her grandchild before bedtime, and she doesn't tolerate disrespect. The seemingly innocuous strategy just days before Christmas backfired and lit up the internet like a Christmas tree. It began with small quote tweets on Twitter about how one's immigrant grandmother bore no relatability to the Wellesley-educated former First Lady. The contrast between the grandmother Hillary Clinton and the story of our own grandmothers wasn't just unrelatable, it was downright offensive. I remember scrolling through my Twitter feed as dozens, hundreds, then thousands of Latinos weighed in with the hashtag #NotMyAbuela. Thousands of stories about immigration, struggling with poverty, barely scratching out a living became a breathing story of the young Latino community pushing back on the hierarchical structure of a party that was growing unrelatable itself. It felt like a community was growing in real time that transcended politics by sharing its experiences and telling its stories in contrast to the old stereotype that not only didn't work for them, but never worked for their parents or grandparents, either. This was a profound moment.

As a political professional watching this unfold in real time, I immediately recognized that Latinos significantly over-index in the use of social media (years later they continue to be and are very early adopt-ers of emerging social media channels), meaning this younger demo-graphic was more likely to be found and reached on social media than other groups. This was organic. It wasn't organized. It couldn't be be-cause it was happening spontaneously in response to what the Clinton campaign was putting out.

This was a new generation finding its voice. It wasn't the typical anti-Republican messaging I had grown used to over the years. This had the feel of a movement where the adherents weren't just cranky agitators, they were telling their own distinct stories and saying to the power structure that "you're not one of us."

Two months later, Hillary Clinton would win the Nevada caucuses as predicted, but the race would reveal a larger undertow that the campaign had not seen coming. Entrance polls to the caucus showed that Bernie Sanders secured 54 percent of the Latino vote—a result the Clinton campaign vociferously rejected. To prove that it had won the Latino vote, the Clinton campaign publicly issued precinct results from Hispanic-dense neighborhoods showing Clinton winning—not by very much, but winning. This was the first time I had seen a Demo-cratic campaign panic this way and it told me two things: first, the reli-ance on Hispanic-dense precincts to prove your victory in this close a race was unreliable evidence at best, but more important, even if Clin-ton had barely won—that meant the Democratic establishment can-didate *barely* won the Latino vote. Latino voters had moved into new territory and they couldn't be relied upon by Democrats the way they could with Black voters. Latinos were saying something very different than any minority group in the party had before—they were not going to just fall in line. In essence Latinos were saying: We're not Black vot-ers. We're not model minority voters.

Fortunately, there was a test case of this theory just a week later—South Carolina. On February 27, Clinton smashed Sanders in the South Carolina primary, putting to bed the prior week's media frenzy about which candidate won the Latino vote. Clinton would win the South Carolina primary by a landslide margin of more than 47 percent, receiving a larger percentage of the African American vote than Barack Obama in 2008. She routed Sanders among Black voters by a margin of 86 to 14. The Clinton campaign breathed a sigh of relief, but I knew that the campaign had far bigger troubles ahead in the general election.

Latinos in the Nevada caucuses that year forever changed the narrative of what being a minority voter in the Democratic Party would mean. Black voters again demonstrated their reliability in South Carolina as the backstop of the Democratic establishment, while Latinos were saying the exact opposite. But it wouldn't just be a generational transformation within the Democratic Party that would begin in Nevada. Nevada Latinos would also change the electoral map in presidential races and the balance of power in the United States Senate.

Analyzing the 2016 results now, a fact that jumps out is that Latino voters were much more organized and trained for Bernie's effort than Hillary's. Nine days before the caucuses, the Culinary Union, the state's biggest, announced it would not issue an endorsement, which amounted to a de facto victory for Bernie, since the Hillary people clearly felt they were getting that endorsement.

Nevada, a state increasingly defined by a tendency toward extremely close elections, is one of seven states where Donald Trump improved his performance in 2020 over the 2016 contest—in the Las Vegas metro area, the improvement was 1.4 percent, which ranked eighteenth nationally among metro areas moving more toward Trump. With its mere six electoral votes, Nevada is usually given secondary consideration in the swing-state matrix, but as partisanship continues to solidify, the state will grow in importance in electing both the president and U.S. senators. More than any other state, Nevada's Latino political clout has been made crystal clear by the power of labor unions, specifically the Culinary Union, where thousands of Latinos, largely immigrants, feed and care for the millions of gamblers and tourists looking to vacation in the desert oasis.

Former senate majority leader Harry Reid believed that he could move his home state of Nevada into bluer territory by investing heavily in the growing Latino voters that were filling the service sector roles making up the service economy of Las Vegas. As Reid told journalist Eric Garcia, "People used to make fun of me actually, because I went to all the Cinco de Mayo events. . . . I was criticized for spending so much time with Hispanics, because people said there was a lot of them that aren't even citizens. When they are citizens, they don't register to vote, but when they register to vote, they don't vote anyway. We were able to show that that's not true."

Nationally, Latinos have among the lowest rates of unionization, trailing both Blacks (12.8 percent) and whites (11.2 percent) and, at 10 percent, topping only Asian Americans and Pacific Islanders (9.2 percent). Part of Reid's strategy was to broaden the array of issues that unions would advocate, targeting issues of importance to these largely immigrant Latino voters. Civil rights issues and immigration became a central part of union messaging, similar to what happened in California in the wake of Proposition 187, where Miguel Contreras, the iconic head of the Labor Federation, made the concerted decision to lean into the demographic tidal wave sweeping the state in the mid-nineties. Both Reid and Contreras would have their predictions proven right, as both states have undergone a significant leftward shift due in large part to the growing number of Latino voters and the commensurate organizational strength of unions.

To tell the story of the power of organized labor in engaging working-class Latinos in Nevada and turning them out to vote, I reached out to Francisco Ruffino, who was born in Mexico, but has lived and worked in Nevada for three decades. Along with being a cook at the Paris Las Vegas casino, Ruffino is an organizer and activist for the Culinary Workers Union Local 266 and a believer in the strength of union power as a tool to check runaway corporate greed and to lift the lives of people transitioning from the lower economic rungs of American society to the middle class.

"It's in my blood to help people," he says. "I follow what my union believes in, which are things that I believe in, too. I'm not going to speak wrong about Republicans, but they have not done anything to help working-class people. . . . When I was a kid in Mexico, my dad was very political. We went to marches, so politics is in my blood. I'm a Democrat now, but I support politicians who stand for what I believe in."

Ruffino comes from a long family line of political activism, and as a union member, equates union membership with the fight for working-class issues. Nevada, more than any other state, can use that correlation because the strength of the Culinary Union is the center of the Democratic Party's success or failure with Latinos in the state—not so anywhere else. This, at least in part, may explain why Latino working-class voters in Nevada have remained reliably Democratic voters despite a broader working-class rightward shift in the community.

Ruffino comes from a Mexican family that sold churros to survive. His mom died when he was three and his father looked to the United States for salvation from the economic limitations of their home state of Nayarit, where the family lived in poverty. "My dad had a chance to bring some of us to the United States, but not all of us," Ruffino says. Francisco grew up in the U.S. knowing the price that working immigrants pay for the chance to find opportunity in this country.

"I came to the U.S., back in 1989, when I was fourteen years old," he says. Five years later, he traveled from Southern California, where he had gone to high school, to visit his sister in Las Vegas. It was supposed to be a weeklong visit, but he never left. Ruffino has become a key part of a Latino community that is transforming politics in Nevada.

What Ruffino believes in more than anything are the rights of working people, their right to a living wage. He believes in their power in numbers. Working people, many of them Mexican immigrants, who have teamed up in Nevada with other immigrants, with Black people and poor people, to take on the corporations running the biggest and most lucrative casinos in Las Vegas. It's hard to get elected to anything in Nevada without the support of the powerful Culinary Workers Union.

In the fall of 2023, Ruffino was taking his advocacy to a deeper level of commitment. He participated in acts of civil disobedience that got him arrested on the Las Vegas Strip. As a Mexican-born immigrant now in his late forties, Ruffino well knew the dangers of being arrested and taken into police custody. But he was more afraid not to act. He was more afraid of being docile, of not knowing his worth or his power. He remembered the life he had led in Mexico, hand-to-mouth and dependent on good fortune that was elusive for humble people selling delicacies to survive.

"We're fighting for the workers," Ruffino says. "The bathroom attendants, the cooks, the cleaning people. I'm doing this for them, but I'm also doing it for myself. I want to bring food home to our table. To have good insurance for my family, my kids. I want to be able to take my son to college. All of this makes me think about my life and my future and I'm willing to do what it takes to make a better life for my family. I want to see my own family grow here in the United States."

His union, which represents forty-three thousand workers at casinos owned by MGM, Wynn, and Caesars Palace, has helped over eighteen thousand Nevadans become citizens of the United States—and in 2022 helped elect Senator Catherine Cortez Masto, a key win that helped preserve the Democrats' slim majority in the U.S. Senate. They did it by dispatching 450 canvassers to knock on over 1 million doors. That movement turned out more than half the Black and Latino voters in Nevada.

So when Francisco Ruffino got arrested by Las Vegas police while fighting for his rights, he wasn't alone. He was part of a Latino labor movement in Nevada that is winning elections and looks to win them for generations to come.

Florida: The Cuban Exception

Like me, Giancarlo Sopo grew up admiring Ronald Reagan. Unlike me, Sopo is a Miami native and the descendant of Cuban immigrants. Like me, Sopo's admiration of Reagan led him to identify as a Republican at an early age. Unlike me, Sopo's Republicanism is common among the community in which he grew up, Miami's Cuban American population. Like me, Sopo spent years working in politics. But unlike me, Sopo would actually become a Democrat for a time before not only switching back to the Republican Party, but working for Donald Trump. If that back-and-forth movement almost inspires whiplash, it accurately reflects larger trends involving South Florida Cuban Americans, who began to drift away from the Republican Party in the 1990s during Bill Clinton's presidency, but have since returned in overwhelming numbers.

More than any other group of Latinos, the Cuban American diaspora has defined what Latino voters have meant to the Republican Party. However, Florida is actually an outlier as it relates to the Latino vote. While it has always been one of the big three Latino states in the country, along with California and Texas, it has also had an outsized influence in the country's politics and the Latino political narrative. Where California and Texas have been the two largest Latino population states, they are also the two with the highest Mexican American concentrations and have been decidedly one-party states for twenty-five years or more. The largest Latino vote base, the Mexican American vote, has been siloed in two states—one blue and one red—limiting the reach of its explosive growth politically. Not so Florida, which has all but defined the term "swing state" since at least the 2000 presidential election. This has had the effect of giving the Cuban American narrative, a community that is about 5 percent of the Latino electorate, overwhelming overrepresentation in the country's understanding of Latino political priorities.

The Latino vote in Florida has played a central role in each party's efforts going back decades, despite their relatively small numbers. Cuban Americans are the largest Latino group in Florida, but not as decisively as people assume: Cubans make up about 28 percent of Florida Latinos, followed by 21 percent Puerto Ricans, and—ready for it?—14 percent Mexican Americans. Miami Cubans are a proud people, and understandably so, but they have little in common with the majority of Latinos in the United States—60 percent Mexican American and another 10 percent of Central American origin. While small slices of the overall electorate, Florida Cuban Americans and Puerto Ricans have taken on a dramatically exaggerated role in the narrative of what Latino voters want, how they vote, and what both parties are doing in their outreach to this voter group.

South Florida Cuban Americans stepped onto center stage in American politics and brought conviction and passion—and a powerful backstory. The anti-communist zeal during the Cold War, the failed Bay of Pigs invasion, and the Cuban Missile Crisis were central aspects of the American psyche in the Cold War era and American politicians were more than happy to elevate anti-communist voices as freedom fighters among their ranks. Additionally, the Cuban story of leaving family, homes, and businesses behind, forced to flee Castro's communist dictatorship, matched perfectly with the zeal of anti-communist forces in the country centered primarily in the Republican Party.

Cubans are among the few identifiable groups of immigrants and voters who have come to the United States and immediately voted with the Republican Party upon their arrival. Vietnamese, Hmong, and more recently Venezuelan immigrants also fit that profile. They are unique in that these diasporas largely came to this country for political not economic reasons, fleeing leftist dictatorships at home and finding comfort among a political party that strongly opposes leftist regimes.

From the mid-1960s to the mid-'80s Republicans reflexively won sizable shares of the Cuban American vote, but not unlike what we are seeing with second- and third-generation Mexican American Latinos, the voting habits of those immigrants began to change. Cuban Americans were no different. Bill Clinton and Al Gore began making considerable inroads with the Cuban vote, winning nearly 35 percent in 1996. While this may not sound big, it's essentially the reverse partisan mirror image of what Trump got with the Mexican American vote in 2020—a vote share that sent shock waves through the political establishment.

But in 2000, Republican margins among Cuban American voters snapped back to its historical range of an 80–20 split benefiting the GOP. Why? A major factor was the saga of a young Cuban boy caught up in international politics—Elián González, who was just five years old when he was found floating in an inner tube, three miles off the Florida coast, after his mother drowned trying to flee Cuba for a new life in America. More than any other Latino subset, Cuban Americans are animated by anti-communist messaging, as well as international events on the homeland—which is understandable enough, given Cuba's proximity, only one hundred miles from the Florida shore. The Cuban American vote tends to ebb and flow with events that re-animate family experiences, sometimes creating a multigenerational voting bloc and other times waning, so that younger generations drift overwhelmingly to Democrats as issues on the island fade from the diaspora's memories.

Giancarlo Sopo's story is the perfect personification of this trend.

Sopo is a third-generation Cuban American who evolved from admiring Reagan to holding the political views of a moderate Democrat. He began his political activism working on the Obama campaign in 2008. But ultimately he was turned off by the socialism talk of "The Squad" emanating from the Democrat Party during the Trump years. By 2020 the biggest shift rightward in the country was among Cuban American voters under forty, creating a multigenerational voting bloc driven largely by concerns about what they saw as creeping socialism and communism in the Democratic Party.

Sopo's American journey and his political journey were both informed by the experiences of his ancestors, who came to despise all forms of socialism. Some commentators dismiss Miami Cubans like Sopo for continuing to base their political beliefs on a hatred for socialism. Today, that seems very mid-century American. To me, "red baiting" has always been as contemporary as an eight-track tape console or a rotary phone. But to Sopo, a suspicion of socialism in all its forms led him to move away from the Democrats after he voted for Barack Obama. He also voted for Hillary Clinton in the 2016 presidential election.

Sopo didn't like Trump's rhetoric when he ran against Clinton in 2016. He found him off-putting and unlikable. In fact, he based his vote for Clinton on the fact that he was "more turned off by Trump." But after the 2016 election was settled and Trump won, Sopo was turned off by the reaction of his fellow Democrats.

"I saw a lot of people have, for lack of a better word, meltdowns," he says. "We really entered a period of reactionary politics. If Trump did something, the policy substance of it didn't matter. It was just bad because he did it. I was turned off by groupthink. I was turned off by the backlash to Trump. Seeing all the 'pussy hat marches'—seeing all of that unfold on TV—I was like, 'Look, give the guy a chance.' Maybe because I've studied Cuban history, I've always had a moderating temperament. I'm turned off by groupthink and following crowds. I was getting into arguments with people on Facebook. I found myself in a cycle of constantly arguing with people who were on my side."

Sopo began writing articles that criticized Democrats for focusing on inequality and he encouraged them to focus more on growth. Sopo especially disliked "woke" Democratic socialists he saw as gaining currency in the Democratic Party. He was especially put off by Representative Alexandria Ocasio-Cortez, who became a darling of the left and of social media. Sopo found her politics dangerous—more dangerous than Trump, which made sense, given his family's history under Castro in Cuba.

"My grandfather told a friend he wanted to return to the United States," Sopo wrote in *USA Today* in August 2018. "Someone overheard the conversation and reported him to the authorities. For this, the Castro regime threw him in jail. He was later stripped of his job and salary as an accountant and assigned to feed zoo animals. In addition to the emotional distress it caused, this made my family's financial circumstances even more precarious."

A photo of AOC illustrated Sopo's opinion column, which ran under this headline: "My Family Escaped Socialism, Now My Fellow Democrats Think We Should Move the Party in Its Direction."

"Like those of yesteryear, today's socialists believe the government should nationalize major industries, propose eliminating private ownership of companies, and reject profits," Sopo wrote. "In other words, democratic socialism is a lot like the system my family fled, except proponents promise to be nicer when seizing your business."

At that point, Sopo said, he felt homeless politically. He also felt increasingly warm toward Republicans. He felt Democrats were against small-business owners like his mother. His writings were brought to the attention of the Trump administration and he was hired by the Trump campaign to do rapid response messaging in Spanish. "I was turned off rhetorically by both parties," he says. "But when I looked at the policies, I found myself sympathizing with Republicans. Maybe I overrationalized some of Trump's stuff in hindsight, but at the time I also felt it was being taken out of context."

When asked in October 2023 if he would vote for Trump in 2024 if he was the Republican nominee, Sopo said he didn't know. His plan then was to support Florida governor Ron DeSantis.

~

Florida has offered a case study in the deep limitations of how both parties have perceived Latinos going back decades. Since the 1970s, when the Nixon administration first adopted the term "Hispanic" for the U.S. Census to count people from Spanish-speaking countries, the United States has clumsily tried to wrap its arms around a community it didn't understand. The term "Hispanic" referred to all people whose origins were of Spanish-speaking countries or territories. It is a wildly broad characterization for people who are a hodgepodge of race, nationalities, and cultures. The federal government essentially needed a description of white people that were not ethnically of European descent, but rather represented a blend of new- and old-world peoples.

Too loose are the ties that can coalesce a commonality between Afro-Cubans from Florida, Puerto Ricans on the island territory, and Mexican Americans throughout the southwest of the former Mexican nation. Too tight are the commonalities of not being "white enough" to say no bond exists at all. As such, Latinos struggle among themselves to find a narrative that works for their own individual experience and the nebulous community they are all hoping to find, perhaps creating it where it didn't always exist. Amid that struggle is the loud noise of a media trying to justify and monetize a growing market for advertisers and the shrill sound of politicians looking to solidify a voting bloc. Too often the perceptions about Latinos in all aspects of American life remain rooted in the past or are influenced greatly by American foreign policy biases.

Evelyn Pérez-Verdía, a South Florida–based expert on Latino voting patterns, thinks that trends are coming together to help different Florida Latino communities establish more of their own identity instead of being lumped together as "Hispanics." Pérez-Verdía, a Colombian American married to a Mexican American, has often been surprised at assumptions made. "Usually consultants or advisers always say, 'We have to make sure that when it's in Florida, it doesn't have a Mexican accent,'" she said in an interview for this book. "Wait a second! Why do you say that? When I do ads statewide, depending on the area of Florida, I will put a Mexican voice in there so that people feel represented. I did a statewide ad in 2022 in Orlando and used voices that were Puerto Rican, Cuban, Venezuelan, and Colombian, which are the main demographics in Orlando. But then I did one in Sarasota and Fort Myers that was focused on the Mexican community and that had a Mexican voice—because there are many of them who are U.S. citizens, and they're not given the respect that they deserve when they're one of the largest communities in Florida."

Evelyn and I have appeared together on different interview shows and podcasts, usually making differing arguments. For example, we both were on an NPR podcast on March 1, 2022, looking at the problem of disinformation in the Florida Latino community from starkly different perspectives.

For years I was annoyed with talk of disinformation and Latino voters, seeing it mostly as a distraction, but the problem won't go away—and only seems to be getting worse. The rampant spread of disinformation and weaponized innuendo does have to be faced squarely. Evelyn is smart and visionary and did a nice job on that NPR podcast implicitly connecting the problem of Spanish-language disinformation in South Florida with the worldwide problem of governments using information warfare to push the outcomes of elections in other countries—from Brexit to Trump-over-Hillary to the 2024 U.S. cycle to the 2027 French elections in which rightist Marine Le Pen could well end up the winner.

"What we first have to understand is that disinformation is border-less," Evelyn told NPR. "It can be shared in a WhatsApp group from San Salvador, El Salvador, to someone in El Paso, Texas. It's content that is created which is disinformation. We have seen that it's premed-itated to change a discourse in terms of the elections, and we saw a lot of it."

She cited polls showing that 41 percent of Latinos believed conspir-acy theories sent to them, often from people they know, via platforms like WhatsApp, YouTube, Facebook, and (then) Twitter. Anti-leftist messages were effective for example in support of the Ron DeSantis campaign for Florida governor in 2018 against former Tallahassee mayor Andrew Gillum, calling him a "socialist" and comparing him to Stalin and Castro. "They're using *progresista radicales,* which means 'radical progressive,'" she said. "Why are they using this word? Because that word, for some Latin Americans, first-generation voters who now vote here, it can mean socialist and communist. . . . We're making vot-ers practically run the other way by using them."

When it was my turn on the podcast to speak, I mentioned that outside of California and Arizona, the Latino shift toward the GOP was consistent. "There's a very large and pervasive list of issues that are of concern to the Hispanic and Latino community that simply aren't being addressed," I said. "I'm suggesting this is by both parties, incidentally. We really do ourselves and the community a disservice when we start to find these small, tactical ways of trying to find how this could possibly be happening, because it's not just about Spanish misinformation, or disinformation." I talked about how second- and third-generation Latinos were "beginning to take on the characteris-tics of the overall electorate. That's what's occurring. That's why there is this significant shift."

But as the conversation continued, I sounded a different note, making it clear that while I believe the impact of Spanish-language disinformation campaigns was overstated, we must also be vigilant on every front when protecting democracy from nefarious actors: "The problem of misinformation and disinformation is an extremely toxic, corrosive dynamic that is ruining our democracy," I said. "I think we're struggling as a democracy to try to figure out how to combat this."

I offered a personal take. "As a political consultant who has been doing this for thirty years, when I was younger in this profession, the whole craft of the trade was persuasion," I said. "When I see young political consultants now, that's not what they're doing. There are a lot more political consultants who believe that it's okay to just blatantly lie, and it's *deeply* troubling, it's *very* problematic. And I think if we are going to focus on the monolingual Spanish or Spanish-dominant speaker, they tend to be more recently migrated and they tend to be a little more influenced by the way we practice politics here, because they are trying to do their civic duty and show up and vote, and that does create an increased exposure."

I closed by suggesting both federal and state election laws might need to be updated to give us new tools to fight this scourge. "The old idea that more information or more truth—the sunlight will shake away the disease here—is not proving to be correct," I concluded. "And if we don't get this back on track, I'm deeply concerned about the direction we're heading in."

The problem is only getting worse. As one example, looking at 2024, one thing is certain in the world: Vladimir Putin needs a win. He's been humiliated in Ukraine, and he might not be able to hang on to power too many more years if he continues to be humiliated. What are his options? Russian troll farms and hackers did their best to intervene for Donald Trump in the 2016 election—that is fact—and in 2024, it's fair to wonder what Putin's Russia might come up with in the way of new dirty tricks and techniques to swing the U.S. election. If Trump wins, Putin wins, that much is clear—victory in Ukraine, the dissolution of NATO, a fracturing of the Western alliance, all would be likely in short order in that scenario. So Putin is highly motivated, and also highly unpredictable. Russian disinformation efforts in 2024 can be expected to be widespread and creative and will likely push the envelope of what anyone—even some of the smartest people around on this stuff—can see coming.

It's ironic, to me, thinking about South Florida. Putin jails his own people and stifles freedom, the way that Fidel Castro did in Cuba. South Florida Cuban Americans should be among the most vigilant against authoritarianism. So far, it has not played out that way—but these trends need to be followed, because they can take strange twists and turns.

Evelyn Pérez-Verdía's Florida firm, We Are Más, has some interesting data to consider, gathered by comparing Florida Division of Elections book closing numbers for the 2022 general election with information collected by the Univision network. What her group found was the number of registered Hispanic Democrats statewide went from 947,853 in 2020 down to 901,484 in 2022—but according to the group, by May 2023 the number had increased to 967,840. At the same time, the data revealed, the number of Hispanics registered as Republicans fell—from 901,481 in 2022 to 847,774 in May 2023, a decrease of 53,707.

Most dramatically, the number of independents went from 965,795 to 1,137,180 in May 2023, her group found. "That is a very big message to both the Republican Party and the Democratic Party that they are not giving correct messaging to our community," Pérez-Verdía told me. "So really it's up for grabs for whoever shows that they're sincere. We have a big problem in Florida because both parties are using symbolism and messaging that when we come from Latin America and the Caribbean, it could be seen as individuals who are extremists. And examples of this are the raised fist in the air. I can show you pictures of Maduro and Fidel Castro raising their fists in the air, but we also see Trump raising his fist in the air. We see Republicans registering people with the Cuban flag and the raised fist in the air on their shirt. We see

Bernie Sanders and AOC using the raised fist in the air, which is a connection in the world to socialism and communism."

Evelyn believes Florida is a purple state. I see it as decidedly red. But her analysis squares with the points I've been making in this book. "What we're seeing is it's winnable, but really when you have mixed messages going to our community, and not respecting this pain, this is why we have what we have," she said.

Lionel Sosa and I had similar experiences in our youth of recoiling from the Democratic Party because we believed it was anti-rich. The Biden campaign's attempts to woo Latino voters in fall 2023 were in some ways a throwback to those days. A $25 million ad buy targeted swing-state voters with an economic message. "Every action, every policy for Joe Biden is about 'who,'" a narrator says in the ads, which were geared to a Hispanic audience. "And since he's taken office, unemployment in our community has been cut in half. The 'who' President Joe Biden is fighting for isn't the rich and powerful. It's us."

Evelyn was beside herself and was publicly critical, asking the Biden team: "What are you trying to do? People come here for the American Dream, and now you tell them when they make money, they're going to be forgotten about? You're saying once a Hispanic becomes rich, then you're no longer going to be a priority for them. Is that awesome or what?"

– 15 –

North Carolina:
What Opportunity Looks Like

In politics, it's not just what you know, it's when you know it. Small populations of persuadable swing voters can be decisive, especially if they live in a battleground state. That's what makes North Carolina so interesting in the 2024 presidential election cycle. A state in which only 4 percent of the electorate was Latino, at last count, could well flip red to blue—and do so in large part because of the Latino vote. As of 2023, there were approximately 279,409 registered Latino voters in a state Biden lost to Trump in 2020 by less than 75,000 votes.

North Carolina voted for Barack Obama in 2008, but has stubbornly remained a marginally red state in presidential races ever since. Meanwhile, Democrats running for statewide office have succeeded in winning the governor's mansion nine times since 1976 (seven of the last eight election cycles). To the frustration and dismay of Democrats unable to get a good grasp on the brass ring, this success has not translated into the presidential race, which would dramatically change the road map to 270 electoral college votes. Non-college-educated white voters, especially in rural areas, continue to dominate state politics, but there is a realignment occurring that portends an imminent shift. The question is not *if* North Carolina politics are changing but *when* they will change enough to where Latinos are positioned to push North Carolina into Democratic hands.

Some of that starts with mindset—and decisions about where to spend. As *New York* magazine pointed out in a May 2023 article on ever-shifting perceptions about which states are battlegrounds, "[I]t's also important to recognize that there's a risk of perpetually fighting the last war in focusing on the previous election's battlegrounds. In living memory, such highly noncompetitive states as California, Connecticut, Illinois, New Jersey, New York, and Texas have been presidential battleground states. The map never stops changing. We may be reminded of that again in 2024 when things don't go as expected."

I hope not. I hope that before it comes to that, North Carolina can be moved into the category of "Solidly in Play." For me personally, North Carolina represents some unfinished business. Working with the Lincoln Project in 2020, I thought we could move voters the way we did in the other states we targeted, but we fell short. We spent millions of dollars on ad buys in North Carolina over the final months of the campaign—enough to see our targets in the electorate were not budging enough to justify more spending, so we pulled the plug. Four years later, continuing growth in the Latino community provides an opening to spend wisely, as opposed to throwing away money in a big state that can't be turned—Florida ranks at the top of that list.

As my Lincoln Project colleague and one of the best data guys in the business, Lucas Holtz, elaborated in his memo for the Democratic think tank Third Way, "Looking back to the 2020 presidential election, Florida was a massive expense for Joe Biden and his Democratic allies. Data from AdImpact shows that the Biden campaign and their allies poured the most ad investments into Florida of all the battleground states in 2020—more than Arizona, Georgia, Nevada, and Wisconsin combined. Investing so heavily in Florida spread Democratic resources thin, and it precluded Democrats from spending more robustly in flippable states. Democratic allies spent over $108 million in Florida in 2020 and less than $16 million in North Carolina." As Holtz further notes, Biden lost Florida to Trump by three points and barely lost

North Carolina by 1.5 points. The battleground map going into 2024 has shifted: "If Florida is no longer a viable swing state, then Democrats must adapt their strategy and investments. . . . A Democratic win [in North Carolina] would take the wind out of Republican sails and significantly limit the GOP's path to 270."

The GOP's rightward lurch into white grievance politics and appealing to the economic anxiety of voters in rural communities has seen a transformational realignment in the coalitions of both parties— we correctly anticipated this continued trend in North Carolina in 2020, as it was similarly evident in every major battleground state. Republicans have chosen the predictable path of trying to galvanize rural white voters in North Carolina by pushing for policies designed to suggest voter malfeasance by the emerging electorate, choosing the well-worn path of trying to hold up the bursting dam of demographic change by sticking their proverbial fingers in the dike.

North Carolina is a stubbornly entrenched outlier on the verge of a breaking point. The state has transformed over the past few decades along with many Sunbelt states into an economy of financial powerhouses, high tech, biotech, and a growing array of college-educated workers imported from other states. In that way, on paper at least, it looks a lot like Georgia and Arizona. It was a key state we looked at in the Lincoln Project as part of our New Southern Strategy. In fact, here's the demographic breakdown of North Carolina's registered voters: 71.6 percent white, 21.9 percent Black, 2.0 percent Asian, 4.7 percent Latino, and 1.2 percent Native American or Alaska Native.

North Carolina's Black and Latino populations are creeping up on 27 percent of the electorate, and by the time that number hits 30 percent, the state is likely to flip to blue. There's going to be much greater growth in the Latino side of this ledger than other groups, and the faster these voters are registered and brought onto voter rolls, the faster this state is likely to flip to Democrats. Republicans have employed an overtly partisan gambit to draw eleven of the fifteen seats into safe Republican enclaves, even though the state is among the most competitive between the two parties in the country.

"From 2008 to 2020, the western rural and exurban counties of North Carolina's Appalachia swung 12 points right, and Republicans netted nearly 50,000 more votes than Democrats over this time," Holtz explained. "Democrats' saving grace in North Carolina has been capturing and retaining white college-educated voters in the era of the education realignment."

College-degreed and graduate-degreed voters in North Carolina make up 30 percent of the electorate, combined with Black and Brown voters. Democrats can get to 57 percent of a base demographic that has a strong lean in their direction. While it's true that the growing group of white college-educated voters is helping Democrats maintain their competitiveness, it hasn't been enough to close the deal and put North Carolina in a reliable position for Democrats. There simply aren't enough white college-educated or Black voters to put them over the top. That is where Latinos come in. As a group, they are growing faster than white college-educated or Black voters and will ultimately decide the direction of North Carolina's political future.

The North Carolina Latino electorate is overwhelmingly Mexican American and Central American, two historically Democratic-leaning constituencies. According to Carolina Demography, Mexican Americans made up 54 percent of North Carolina's Latino population in 2020, followed by 11 percent Puerto Rican, 6 percent with family ties to Honduras, 6 percent from El Salvador, and 4 percent from Guatemala. And North Carolina's Latinos had a median age of 25.1, compared to a U.S. national figure of 29.8, adding incentive to reach these voters and develop long-range voting patterns. Latinos present Republicans with an opportunity to connect with a constituency where there is considerable overlap on a variety of issues ranging from culture to the economy, but again they are choosing to limit voting access as a way of standing against inevitable change.

The new North Carolina is being shaped by people like Ramiro Rodriguez, who was born in Celaya, Mexico, in Guanajuato, and came to this country with his parents when he was a child, first relocating to South Florida. He has lived in Raleigh, North Carolina, since 2005, has his own start-up, and also works to train immigrants for high-tech jobs as cofounder and chief technological officer of Code the Dream. As his bio at the group's website puts it, "Ramiro knows about the American Dream and he knows about coding."

"I was brought here when I was eight, undocumented, and so I was a Dreamer," Rodriguez says in an interview. "It was a little tough growing up in Florida, not knowing what was going to happen after I graduated high school. I just tried to do my best and study as much as possible. I enjoyed learning."

When he was a sophomore in high school, his grandmother introduced him to *Star Trek*, and he became a fan. His interest in technology and computing took off from there. He focused on science, especially physics, but always had to worry about his own future: What if he was sent back to Mexico? "I was always afraid, what's going to happen once I graduate?" he says. "I always felt like if something doesn't work out here in the U.S. I can always go back to Mexico."

His strong grades and test scores helped him get into Cornell University, which he was able to afford through private grants the school facilitated. He still loved physics, but double-majored in electrical engineering and computer science to bolster his job prospects—in whatever country he found himself. A Cornell mentor, computer science professor John Hopcroft, helped him find funding to continue his studies and earn a master's in computer science. When Obama's DACA (Deferred Action for Childhood Arrivals) policy was announced in June 2012, he was able to move forward with a career in tech.

Now a citizen, he will be able to cast his first vote for president in 2024. "I feel bad saying this, but it feels more like the Republican Party right now is going through some difficult times," he says. "And so, just because of that reason, I think that I'd rather vote for the Democratic Party at the moment. For me, the biggest thing was the January 6 event. That seemed like a really big deal to me."

Asked what he looks for in political leadership, he says he prefers calm over theatrics. "Trying to be rational, I think that's the biggest thing," he says. "If they're not trying to rile up people just because it's going to get them more votes, but they're trying to be as rational as possible and trying to promote education, if they're trying to improve infrastructure, things like that. Things that are good for businesses, but also that are good for workers. I think a combination of that."

Highly educated Latinos like Rodriguez, working in tech, play a key role in helping build a thriving Latino community in the Triangle area. "There's probably two North Carolinas," he says. "There's the North Carolina that's in the cities, and then there's the rural North Carolina. Right here, I'm in the middle of the blue area of North Carolina. There's a lot of Latinos. There's a lot of Latino businesses and just a lot of racial diversity. But sometimes when I have gone maybe on vacation to more rural areas, you do feel that difference where it's like, 'Okay, here's the white population.' You don't really see a lot of Latinos."

Democrats, for their part, have seemed slow to recognize the opportunities presented to them by the growth of the Latino population in North Carolina, and so far have made only modest investments in voter registration and get-out-the-vote, or GOTV, efforts. These are the highly visible parts of campaigns voters see on Election Days with volunteers canvassing neighborhoods or organizing car rides for senior citizens. Many of these tried-and-true practices have been adopted to the changing Latino community, which is younger and more likely to be a first-time voter, afraid or unaccustomed to the process of voting. GOTV efforts in North Carolina, however, continue to largely focus on targeting and resourcing Black voter-mobilization efforts. While Black voters are more reliably Democratic, it's getting more difficult to find enough who have not been targeted before, so Democrats are hitting a rate of marginal return. Latinos are new voters that can be added to the universe of potential voters, and as we've seen in states like California, Nevada, Arizona, and Georgia, it is the influx of these new voters, in addition to other minority voters, that makes all the difference in electoral outcomes.

The arrival of Latinos in North Carolina is mostly a recent story. "As the region has experienced economic growth and increased global competition, industries have sought out the cheap labor of Latino immigrants," Hannah Gill writes in her 2010 book, *The Latino Migration Experience in North Carolina*. "Conditions of poverty, war, and environmental disaster in Latin American countries have also spurred migration to the region. In three decades, the Latino population in North Carolina grew from less than .5 percent of the total population to 7.4 percent—nearly 650,000 people." By the 2020 census, that number had grown to more than 1.1 million—10.7 percent of the North Carolina population listed as Hispanic—and in Duplin, Sampson, and Lee Counties, more than 20 percent were Hispanic.

In many ways North Carolina defines the convergence of race and partisanship that Latinos present to both parties. White college-educated voters are growing in numbers as high tech, biotech, and financial firms increasingly become part of the new economy and bring in trained workers from Sunbelt states who bring their politics with them, tending to vote Democratic. Blacks make up 19 percent of the electorate in North Carolina and vote nearly 90 percent of the time with the Democratic Party.

To highlight just how problematic low voter turnout has been for Democrats in North Carolina, only 14 percent of Latino voters between ages eighteen and twenty-five voted in 2022, according to the *Charlotte Observer*. There are multiple factors to explain that low level of participation, including intimidation and threats, but I'd be willing to bet a combination of effective messaging and significant investment in outreach and advertising could show palpable results. My advice would be to spend early, and move the numbers—forcing Republicans to update their own assumptions about North Carolina.

Award-winning political columnist Mary C. Curtis, a former *New York Times* and *Charlotte Observer* reporter who has lived in Charlotte, North Carolina, since the 1990s, has watched her adopted state—and city—develop a dramatically more diverse and cosmopolitan appeal over the years. She believes the vibrancy and cultural energy that she sees accelerating can also lead to political change.

"I don't think people think of North Carolina as diverse as it really is," she told me. "We have Spanish language newspapers throughout the state, and we have a very engaged, educated population." Curtis moved to Charlotte from New York and has watched social change unfold over the years. "It's been interesting because the Hispanic population comes from all over," she said. "I've been on panels with people whose family country of origin is the Dominican Republic, Nicaragua, Venezuela, Mexico. As a big-city person who has always lived in diverse big cities, you see it in the cultural offerings that come through Charlotte, the singers, the shows, all of those things. To me, that makes the city. And to see the state reflected in that way, I think it just makes it more interesting. It will definitely affect—as someone who covers politics, we'll see who goes out and energizes the voters. Because in North Carolina, a few thousand here or there can make a difference."

Curtis, a columnist for *Roll Call* whose awards include a Nieman Fellowship at Harvard and three first-place awards from the National Association of Black Journalists, has covered every presidential campaign going back to 2008. "In a sense, Democrats have been looking past North Carolina and saying there are other races—Pennsylvania, Michigan, elsewhere—where the money will be better used because they have a better chance. And I think you will see that changing, particularly since the margins are going to be so tight."

As a sign of a state in flux, Curtis points to the energetic leadership of Anderson Clayton, elected chair of the North Carolina Democratic Party in February 2023 at age twenty-five, replacing a seventy-three-year-old incumbent and becoming the youngest Democratic state chair in the country. She grew up in Roxboro, a small town about an hour outside of Raleigh, and will be targeting rural voters, young voters—and Latinos and African Americans.

Asked on CNN how she'd been elected state chair, despite going up against an opponent with strong support from established North Carolina Democrats, Clayton said, "The folks that are really the grassroots organizers—and the folks that put in the work every single year to help get Democrats elected across the state—really got organized and energized by the message that we need to be organizing everywhere, across all 100 counties in North Carolina and also by the fact that everybody is worth investing in. . . . The number one issue, I think, that I'm really focused on is trying to, honestly, promote economic opportunity for folks across our state."

Clayton thinks Democratic Party leaders in North Carolina have looked to demographic change to "save" them, but her approach is to "organize the state that we're in right now," as opposed to where the state might be in ten years. "We're going heavy on candidate recruitment in communities of color," Clayton told NPR in September 2023. "We're trying to make sure that county parties, especially in majority minority counties, are active and organizing and have the support that they need and the resources that they need."

For me, looking in from out of state, I take those sorts of plans with a grain of salt. Many a state chair has been elected talking up fresh ideas for getting more people involved, only to be slowed down by the obstacles of real-life organizing. But Mary C. Curtis, there on the ground in North Carolina, takes Clayton's pitch seriously. "She has said that she is going to take a whole different approach and be much more proactive about running candidates in races that they had not had Democratic candidates, because they didn't figure they had a chance, and into outreach into every community, because she really feels that there is this sleeping giant, as it were," Curtis said. "There are voters that are not voting, voting-age folks who aren't registered. And if you're going for younger voters, of course that would be Hispanic voters, African American voters, voters of color that are growing the state."

- 16 -

Texas and the Rio Grande Valley

I was a teenager, watching the evening news at home with my parents, when I first heard about a place called Harlingen, Texas, a small city of barely forty thousand north of the Rio Grande river along the U.S.-Mexico border near the Gulf of Mexico. I heard about Harlingen because Ronald Reagan, the president of the United States, was talking about a "sea of red, eventually lapping at our own borders," approaching from Central America, the Red Tide of Communism. Reagan wanted $100 million from Congress to arm rebels fighting the Sandinista government of Nicaragua, which he called "a privileged sanctuary for terrorists and subversives just two days' drive from Harlingen, Texas." For a brief moment, Harlingen was flooded with press inquiries, curious if there were any red-tide sightings, but then quickly returned to obscurity, along with the rest of the Rio Grande Valley, tucked away in the bottom corner of Texas along the lazy winding river. Suddenly, in 2020, we all started talking again about the Rio Grande Valley turning red. A new kind of red tide.

The Rio Grande Valley, a four-county working-class region that is currently more than 90 percent Latino, has long been characterized by independent-minded people, making it a fascinating and critical bellwether. Before Europeans arrived, tribes of hunter-gatherers roamed the area, many speaking distinct languages and unable to communicate with each other. People were always coming and going, including runaway slaves in the nineteenth century on their way farther south. In 1836, the area broke away from Mexico, as part of the short-lived independent Republic of Texas. President James Polk annexed Texas in 1845, including the Rio Grande Valley, triggering the Mexican-American War the following year.

For a century, the area was locked in as strongly in support of Democrats, but registration and voter participation rates were low—and so was public trust in the integrity of the voting process. In fact, the situation was grim enough that counties in the area tried creative approaches. An Associated Press article in November 2000 opened: "Hidalgo County will watch Tuesday's elections with eyes that don't blink. Eager to shake a reputation for dirty voting, the Rio Grande Valley county will videotape next week's ballot count with rented cameras. The surveillance equipment will offer an eagle-eye view of the vote counters. . . . Election fraud has long been a touchy subject in the politically insular border valley."

Keeping Rio Grande Valley voters interested and engaged has always been a particular challenge, which makes the area a fascinating riddle to political pros like me. A 1937 headline in the McAllen, Texas, *Monitor* read: "Quiet Ballot Marks Voting," with an article stating: "Exceptionally quiet voting marked the Rio Grande Valley's balloting Monday in the state-wide election on six proposed constitutional amendments, with reports from Hidalgo, Willacy and Cameron counties showing practically no interest. At noon a total of twenty-five votes had been cast in McAllen, sixteen at the South McAllen box and nine at the North McAllen box. . . . Speedy tabulation of returns was anticipated as a result of the exceptionally light vote."

The 1960 presidential campaign of Massachusetts senator John F. Kennedy, which inspired young people all over the country, also motivated many Mexican Americans to get more involved in politics, including in the Rio Grande Valley, often through "Viva Kennedy" clubs. PASSO, the Political Association of Spanish-Speaking Organizations, emerged from those early organizing efforts, focused on getting more Mexican Americans elected and on issues like discrimination and segregated educational facilities. Founded in a spirit of optimism and hope, the group found the going tough. In June 1964, the *Tyler Morning Telegraph* reported, "The Hidalgo County chairman of the Political Association of Spanish-Speaking Organizations (PASSO) will continue its activity in state politics despite the defeat of all five candidates it backed in Saturday's runoff elections." Leo J. Leo told the paper the disappointing results were "but a minor battle in a long-range war against the political oppression of our people."

As early as 1982, when conservative Republican congressman Jim Collins unsuccessfully challenged Lloyd Bentsen for a seat in the United States Senate, representing Texas, Republican strategists had their eyes on the Rio Grande Valley, often ignored and taken for granted by Democrats, as a possible pickup opportunity. Collins hinged his hopes on the Rio Grande Valley—and was disappointed.

Mayra Flores had better luck. Born in Tamaulipas, Mexico, she was six when she moved with her family to Texas. At one point a Democrat who voted for Barack Obama for president, Flores cited strong anti-abortion views in her decision to join the Republican Party. She rose to a leadership position with the Hidalgo County Republican Party, working on Hispanic outreach, and ended up shunning the George W. Bush school of welcoming conservatism that I myself personally embraced and went all in on conspiracy theories, QAnon-coded outbursts, and extreme right-wing political views. She even organized "Make America Great" pro-Trump caravans through the Rio Grande Valley. An evangelical Christian, Flores told the *New York Times*, "I do believe that pastors should be getting involved in politics and in guiding their congressmen. Our pastors know our people better than we do." Sounds like the mullahs in Iran thinking religious extremists should run everything, if you ask me; the Iranian extremists whose capture of U.S. hostages in the Carter years launched me on a life as a Republican.

Nevertheless, Flores made a splash by winning a special election for Congress in June 2022, and doing it in her own, loud, look-at-me way. "Representative Mayra Flores became only the second Republican to represent the Rio Grande Valley after she won a special election last month and flipped the congressional seat from blue to red," Jennifer Medina wrote in the *New York Times*. "She also became the first Latina Republican ever sent by Texas to Congress. . . . [W]hat is most striking is that Ms. Flores won by shunning moderates, embracing the far right and wearing her support for Donald J. Trump on her sleeve—more Marjorie Taylor Greene than Kay Bailey Hutchison."

It might not have been all that smart for Flores to play the MAGA card quite so belligerently, refusing even to confirm to the *Times* in an interview that Joe Biden had been legitimately elected president—and she would last less than a year in Congress. But her election electrified Republicans with a sense of cementing gains in areas where that had been unthinkable, and this was territory that vividly illustrated my point about economic issues motivating Latino voters but Democrats not speaking to those concerns.

Flores may have been a political comet, briefly having her moment, but if so she made the most of it, appearing in photographs with then Speaker Kevin McCarthy and making provocative statements to circulate widely in the right-wing echo chamber. "The national Democrat Party has abandoned the Hispanic community," she told Fox News in October 2022. "They don't represent who we are. We're pro-God, pro-family, all about hard work. That is just who we are in South Texas. The Democrat Party just doesn't represent those values. They have walked away from the Hispanic community."

She was a bomb thrower and a Trumpist, but she was making many of the same points I had already been making for years. "The fact that a Republican won in one of the most Hispanic districts in America is, you know, it's game-changing, regardless of the circumstances," I told *Time* magazine in October 2022. "No serious observer of the Latino vote is saying the Republicans are going to win over 50 percent of the vote. That's not what's happening. But the margins are closing."

I was even more blunt on my podcast, *The Latino Vote*. I taped it the morning after Flores won and I was pretty fired up. "The Democrats have a really, really big Latino problem," I said. "The incompetence and the disregard, it's infuriating. This district that just flipped has been in Democratic control since 1870." To lose a district with the second-highest percentage of Latinos in the country, I said, amounted to "a five-alarm fire for the Democrats heading into the November elections."

That was very much true, and I'd say it again, but it was also worth remembering that fewer than twenty-nine thousand people voted in the special election—this in a district with a population of more than seven hundred thousand—and Republicans went all out, giving Flores a sixteen-to-one advantage in donations. As I have said and will say until Democrats start listening, low turnout is a problem for them, a sign that you lack connection to the fastest-growing part of the electorate. Still, I was genuinely shocked by the result. It was not a result one wanted to shrug off without looking for deeper answers.

"While national observers fixated on Mayra Flores's extremist statements, voters in South Texas found plenty to connect with in her life story," Kyle Paoletta wrote in an insightful *New York* magazine "Intelligencer" piece in October 2022, accurately enough headlined "How the Border Went MAGA: Control of Congress May Depend on the Democrats' Ability to Adjust to Reality."

"Flores came to the United States as a child and spent her summers as a teenager picking cotton in the Texas panhandle," the article continued. "Her upward mobility spoke to the bootstrapping mentality embraced by so many immigrants, while her marriage to one of the more than 3,000 Border Patrol agents stationed in the Rio Grande Valley signaled her commitment to the agency that is thought of as [the] gateway to the middle class for many poor families. As one advertisement that ran on Flores's behalf a few weeks before the special election put it: 'She's one of us.'"

Working-class Mexican Americans residing close to the border had gone with Trump in much larger numbers in 2020 than they had in 2016. In an inverse of what I was focusing on with my Lincoln Project work targeting college-educated women, the reason was often economics. "Aside from Hispanic heritage, most of the Rio Grande Valley and South Texas have similar demographics to Trump's strongholds in rural communities across the country," Representative Henry Cuellar (D-Laredo) had explained to the *Texas Tribune* in November of 2020. "It's homogenous, deeply religious, pensively patriotic, socially conservative, and it's hurting economically."

The 2022 midterm election was not as bad for Democrats in Texas as many had expected—but the extraordinary changes were still undeniable. The Republicans picked up one House seat from Texas, with Monica De La Cruz becoming the first Republican ever to win the state's Fifteenth Congressional District, but Flores lost to Vicente Gonzalez.

Flores's outrage afterward may have had something to do with her sudden realization that she was no longer the flavor of the month in Texas politics, or maybe she had a point in suggesting there were limits to the momentum her win earlier in the year had seemed to set in motion.

"The RED WAVE did not happen," Flores put out on Twitter on Election Night. "Republicans and Independents stayed home. DO NOT COMPLAIN ABOUT THE RESULTS IF YOU DID NOT DO YOUR PART!"

The same could be said of Democrats. As I told *Roll Call* in August 2023, "White college-educated people are pulling the Democratic Party to the left and white non-college-educated people are pulling the Republican Party to the right, and Latinos are coming up in the middle saying, 'I'm not really comfortable with either of you guys.' Latinos are to the right of most Democrats, and they're to the left of most Republicans. And they're the fastest-growing segment of the electorate, so the potential for Latinos to moderate both parties is very high."

Democrats have to realize the importance of Latino voters. They have to drop the denial and frame an economic message to appeal to a Latino voting base that isn't wedded to the Democrats the way many Black voters are—although there has been some erosion, for example, among African American men. Flores's victory in the Rio Grande Valley showed the costs to Democrats of failing to rise to that challenge.

Arizona's Valley of the Sun

In March 2023, Phoenix, Arizona, was one of the host cities for the World Baseball Classic, a rare opportunity for baseball fans around the world to cheer for their favorite players and teams representing their country of origin. Nowhere in the world did fans match the raucous, celebratory mood of Latino fans attending games in Arizona, offering a vivid reminder of what Latino enthusiasm and participation can mean for democracy itself, if only given a chance. The problem with Latino voters has nothing to do with apathy. We Latinos don't really do apathy. It's not our thing. Given a choice between caring too much and caring too little, we throw our hearts at caring too much. But talk past us, take us for granted or ignore us, and yes, we might feel alienated.

Just think how it could look if Latinos in the United States were activated in large numbers to breathe new life into U.S. democracy, the way Latinos are breathing new life into Major League Baseball. Here was the scene in Phoenix in March 2023, as captured by José M. Romero of the *Arizona Republic*:

It took only a split second to see that Sunday was no ordinary night of baseball in downtown Phoenix. Lines to get into Chase Field for the highly anticipated, officially sold out USA vs. Mexico World Baseball Classic Group C game stretched all the way to Footprint Center at one entry. Fans of all ages arrived, decked out in sombreros and lucha libre masks, powdered wigs and glowing cowboy hats. There was a little more red, white and green of Mexico than red, white and blue of the U.S. in the stands, but with an announced crowd of 47,534 packed into the home of the Diamondbacks, there was a lot of both flag colors. Sprinkle in some orange and black of the Hermosillo Naranjeros of Mexican pro ball, a little Dodger blue and D-Backs Sedona red and a lot of split outfits in support of both nations, and the stadium was awash in baseball colors. . . . There was certainly an international soccer type of atmosphere, with noisemakers, alternating chants of "Mexico! Mexico!" and "USA! USA!" and people waving the flags they draped themselves in like capes.

Many fans were cheering for both teams, as I would have been if I was there. Romero talked to one fan at the game, Charles Nield, wearing a baseball cap on which he'd embroidered the name of his great uncle, from Sonora, Mexico, a huge baseball fan. "What's in my heart is the fact that, especially in the northern states of Mexico, baseball is something really special," Nield told Romero. "The fact that we're able to escape and either play or watch this great game is something that I don't think we should ever take for granted. . . . And whether we support the U.S. or Mexico, we're just here to see a great game at the end of the day."

Imagine if Latinos running for office in the United States could tap into that kind of emotional power, that kind of optimism. For two decades from the mid-nineties until recently, the primary campaign message for Democrats has too often been a negative message to Latinos about Republicans on immigrant issues. The same period has coincided with extraordinarily low levels of voter turnout and civic engagement despite exploding population numbers. While negativity can be accurately described as an early useful tool for galvanizing Latino voters in the mid-nineties, there have been far more elections since with extremely low turnout numbers, suggesting the overuse of negativity in campaigns has further alienated Latinos from both parties and helped drive down civic participation.

Arizona jumps out as an example of a state where Democrats have shown some ability in recent years to learn their lessons and push forward in a more constructive direction. Through 2024, one of Arizona's two United States senators has been Kyrsten Sinema, a one-time progressive activist who, as she once told the *Arizona Republic* in her role as spokesperson for the Green Party, was focused on "disaffected young people." In a letter to the editor, she sounded like your typical self-absorbed campus progressive: "Until the average American realizes that capitalism damages her livelihood while augmenting the livelihoods of the wealthy, the Almighty Dollar will continue to rule." Then she was elected to the Senate as a Democrat, and was soon making headlines for all the money she'd taken from, apparently, any group who would pay her—even as she gave Latinos in Arizona little sense of caring about their concerns and priorities.

Sinema's successor could end up being Democrat Ruben Gallego, a former member of Congress who served in Iraq with the U.S. Marines and saw his unit take heavy losses. At times, watching his race unfold, I had the feeling Gallego's team was reading drafts of this book. Gallego does not want to flog grievance politics. Having grown up poor, to an immigrant family—mother from Colombia, father from Mexico—he talks about cleaning toilets to earn money, but moves on quickly to emphasize the need for a broader optimistic vision that can bring people together. He doesn't want to dwell on recent Arizona political history, like the virulent and visible racism of Maricopa County sheriff Joe Arpaio, a national lightning rod, but to move forward.

"Arizona is now a very welcoming state," Gallego told the *Washington Monthly* in July 2023. "Some of the worst divisive politics was really happening in Arizona. Now, Maricopa County is the fastest-growing county in the country. We have first-generation, second-generation, and third-generation Latinos, but we also have people coming in from all over the world that are really trying to make their American dream in Arizona. I think that's the one thing that is a very big unifier: Everyone in Arizona is just trying to live their best lives. And that's something that is very much unifying—versus before, there wasn't a unified Arizona idea. [Now] everyone wants to buy a house in Arizona. Everybody wants to be successful. They want to have a stable life."

As of January 2024, Kari Lake had announced her candidacy—and Sinema was still weighing her options.

I haven't seen enough of Gallego to evaluate whether he's the kind of breakthrough political talent who can set an example for others to follow, but I know Arizona, as it continues to develop in the 2020s, is the right place to try. You have to love the state's history of launching political mavericks, from Barry Goldwater—Reagan before there was Reagan, in some ways, in other ways not—to John McCain, who I both liked and admired. Gallego would like to fit into that tradition, as a Latino Democrat. As the *Washington Monthly* article put it, Arizona could be "a crucible for a next-generation style of American politics. . . . [W]hat Gallego and other Democrats are building could help the national party rally fresh support among Latinos while also charting a confident, center-left path that drains support from at least small numbers of Republicans fed up with the MAGA bandwagon while navigating political landmines like race and immigration."

According to data from Pew Research, 41 percent of Latinos in Arizona are Democrats or lean Democratic, and 31 percent are Republican or lean Republican. Among whites, those numbers were 34 percent and 49 percent. Overall, Pew found, Republicans had a narrow edge over Democrats among all voters, 40 percent to 39 percent—but with each cycle, more Latinos register and more Latinos overall vote.

In large numbers, Arizona voters—and Latinos in particular—are put off by the kind of extremism represented by Kari Lake and Donald Trump. That was why, in my Lincoln Project work in 2020 trying to defeat Trump, I saw Arizona as my backstop. Other states we were focused on might not go our way, but in the end, I was sure Arizona voters would vote Trump out of the White House.

No Democrat had carried Arizona since Bill Clinton in 1996, and before that none since Harry Truman in 1948, but I knew if we invested in Arizona, we would be rewarded. If it was late on Election Night, I told people, and things were breaking toward Trump, which they tend to with an incumbent, and we ended up with Arizona as the decider, then we were going to win the race. We focused on Maricopa County, the largest in the state—and fourth largest in the country—more than 30 percent Latino, mostly Mexican American. We did a little buy in Yuma-Pima to close the margins of the Republican victory there, but we knew Maricopa County was the key.

We were targeting the same demographic everywhere: college-educated Republican women, focusing on variations on the shame argument. For thirty years, country-club Republicans were motivated by economics. They tolerated the socially cultural stuff believing these conservative positions, especially overturning abortion rights, would never come to pass. Basically: *We'll go along with the churchgoing crowd, just give me my capital-gains tax cut. In fact, we don't even go to church on Sundays—we're at the country club, having brunch. But we'll vote with you because we've got industries we need to protect that make us money.* In 2020, for the first time, the analytics showed it was cultural issues that were moving these voters.

Sure enough, on Election Night, Maricopa County went for Joe Biden, the first Democrat to carry the county in a presidential election since Truman, and he won by more than 2 percent—45,109 votes, according to the final tally. That's close, but not as close as many expected.

We'd done our jobs and exceeded my Bannon Line predictions: Biden peeled off 9 percent of Republicans and 10 percent of conservatives, according to exit polls, and won 58 percent of independents. Among Arizona Latinos of Mexican family background, Biden carried

65 percent, compared to 59 percent overall support by Latinos nationally. In 2020 the Latino vote stood at 18 percent of the Arizona electorate, up from 15 percent in 2016. In 2024, don't be surprised to see
that figure climb north of 20 percent—and keep going from there in
future election cycles.

Arizona is the perfect petri dish for exactly what I'm pushing for in
this book, a better message for Latinos that can be part of a better overall message for America. When Ruben Gallego kicked off his Senate
campaign with an optimistic, morning-in-America kind of spot, I had
to think back on my friend Lionel Sosa and the themes he emphasized
in his work.

"Growing up poor, the only thing I really *had* was the American
Dream," Gallego says on the voiceover in the three-minute spot, which
opens with him driving through a stunningly beautiful morning landscape in Arizona. "Opportunity, it's the one thing that we give every
American, no matter where they're born, in life," he continues. "It was
actually something to believe in and to fight for."

That to me is pure Lionel, in a good way—and the spot moves on to
powerful biographical material. It's smart. Gallego was already known
in the state as a congressman, but why not introduce yourself all over
again? There's a still shot of Gallego's hardworking immigrant mother,
and he explains: "I slept on a floor, on a couch, on a roll-out mat, hearing her cry every night, being stressed out about how she was going to
raise four kids on a secretary's salary, you know, with an absent father."
The spot circles back to the theme of hope, as its foundation, touching
on Gallego's experience as a marine in Iraq, losing so many friends in
combat, suffering PTSD afterward, then it takes a twist different than
what Lionel or I might have advised. "The rich and the powerful, they
don't need more advocates," Gallego says. "It's the people that are trying to decide between groceries and utilities that need a fighter for
them. There is no lobbyist for working families."

Interestingly, the consultant working with Gallego as senior adviser was Chuck Rocha, a Texan best known for his Latino outreach work with the 2020 Bernie Sanders campaign, which might help explain the flourish at the end. Chuck and I have our differences on policy, and politics, but we share a similar sense of mission to help activate Latino voters, and I know Chuck is very good at what he does. That strong video helped the Gallego campaign come out of the gate with energy, posting strong early fundraising numbers, and putting in the miles around the state for Gallego to meet voters one-on-one, which he enjoys.

"He's raising a lot of money, he's connected to the community, so I think he's in the catbird seat," Rocha told me in September 2023. "I look at optimism the same way I look at aspiration, and I think what people, especially folks in Arizona, look for are true believers in the American Dream. I think that's what you saw in Ruben's launch. Anything is possible if you work hard, play by the rules, and show up every day. This poor kid who grew up in Chicago, who finds himself at Harvard by happenstance, who then is overseas in one of the most battle-ridden units of the Marine Corps, and then would go on to work in local politics and be elected to office. That doesn't happen that much anymore. Then to be Latino and bilingual on top of that, I think pulls at a lot of the strings of what makes him so powerful in a place like Arizona, because he has so many commonalities of people."

Chuck, a Latino himself, has a story that inspires. "I've never been to college, I was a teenage father, I've got a criminal record," he says. "Ruben and I are both examples of what's possible in American politics, and I think that's what draws us together. That's why you constantly hear me talking about success for Democrats will only happen when we return back to the messaging that got us to where we are—what I would call blue-collar messaging, which is a place where Ruben's very comfortable, because that's where he's from."

Gallego may or may not be able to hit on an approach that others can emulate. Scarred by war, a Harvard grad after growing up sleeping on floors—he somehow wears it all lightly. "Certain things he's had to overcome help him have a lot of commonality with the regular person, because he wasn't given anything. He didn't have a safety net. There was nothing he was going to fall back on. When he came back from war, he was homeless. His mama really didn't have room for him in Chicago. He was dating a woman who would end up being Kate Gallego. He moved back to live with her in Arizona, and that's how he got there, because he didn't have a place really to go. These are real-life experiences that really ground him in experiences that lots of us have had. Politicians today talk about experiences their mothers and fathers lived through, and sometimes their grandparents. The difference with Ruben is he's been very close to that pain and suffering, and so he understands that. He has a real sense of understanding of what average working Americans are going through."

Where does Chuck see Latino politics going in the future?

"This wake-up call of 2020 really made people realize that something needed to be done differently, and a lot of these white consultants at the Democratic Party are trying to feel their way through that process. You have somebody like Ruben pop up who's giving them the template, much like I did with Bernie.... At his core, he's a union, populist, progressive, commonsense Democrat who can be with the unions, be with the Chamber of Commerce, be with the Indian tribes, because all of that's rooted in what's best for people. He'll always pivot back to that point, while a lot of these campaigns who have well-intentioned white consulting firms who've been around for a long time are still trying to feel their way through this."

The Challenge for Republicans

Not so long ago, Republicans were on track to earn record numbers of Latino voters. They had a likable candidate who genuinely sought the support of Latinos and put them at the center of his two successful presidential campaigns. They were leading on policy solutions prioritized by the community and they struck the perfect tone of aspiration and optimism in their national narrative. This happened only twenty years ago with George W. Bush scoring over 40 percent of the Latino vote in 2004. According to Pew, that's a higher percentage of the Latino vote than any Republican presidential candidate has earned before or since.

What the Bush campaign achieved could be a model for Republicans to emulate as the pool of Latino voters grows substantially over the next twenty years. Though they haven't done much in the past decade to earn it, Republicans have momentum with Latino voters going into the 2024 election cycle for the first time since Bush. That momentum speaks to how strong the potential growth could be for Republicans. In recent elections, Latinos in key states have shown a willingness to vote GOP, in part because of both strategic and tactical mistakes made by Democrats, but also because Democrats are drifting away from their traditional working-class roots and the cultural and economic issues that define the American working class. But even these GOP successes with Latinos have produced only mixed results.

The rightward shift and low Democratic turnout among Latino voters in U.S. politics that occurred in three of the last four national elections is real, but is happening despite Republicans' best efforts, not because of them. Republican support levels are growing as Latinos are increasingly U.S.-born and make up more and more of the blue-collar workforce. The rightward shift is a function of economic populism, Democratic cultural drift, and Latinos assimilating into the blue-collar culture of America. Whether this shift continues in the direction of a realignment or swings back to the Democrats is completely up to the Republicans.

The GOP could do much better by targeting Latino voters aspirationally, as Bush and Reagan once did, but Republicans have been stuck in a trap of their own making: their North Star has been non-college-educated white voters as their path to victory. It's a game plan that comes naturally to them, since the GOP is an overwhelmingly majority-white party. In California the Republican Party is nearly 80 percent white by registration in a state that is only 34 percent white by population. Nationally the number is reportedly even higher, though that's difficult to quantify because all states record registration differently, if at all. Republicans maintain a rabid focus on stopping immigration, building walls, banning Muslims, preserving "Judeo-Christian values," opposing the manufactured specter called "critical race theory," and vilifying any group that criticizes or questions the dominance of white Christians within the American story. This reflects the GOP's shift toward isolationism, protectionism, and nativism in the wake of 9/11.

Republicans just keep using racial wedge issues, including demonizing Latin American immigrants, to get their voters to the polls. They have been content to stay with this strategy, despite clear evidence that it is costing them dearly over the long run. Unrelentingly negative, scorched-earth tactics caused college-educated white Republicans, particularly women, to defect from the Republican ranks in the 2018 midterm elections. This phenomenon cost Republicans the White

House in 2020, despite their success with Latino voters. It failed to work as a primary message for Republicans in the 2022 midterms as they fell far short of historical trends and expectations in the minimal number of House seats they picked up in what should have been an extraordinarily strong year for their party.

It's clear to me that Republicans just can't help themselves; this is who they are. If Republicans could ever develop comprehensive strategies to attract working-class and middle-class Latinos, along with working-class whites, they would be in a much stronger position to regain the White House and establish majorities in Congress. Why don't they? It starts with Republican racial and ethnic biases that I used to fight against until I didn't want to fight anymore. Whenever I proposed recruiting more Latinos to the GOP, I would get one of three responses: I would get asked, "Why can't we all just be Americans?" Or I would get accused of "playing the race card." Or I would get ignored.

These GOP biases go all the way to the top of the party structure. They speak to an insular, sometimes bigoted GOP core that fears non-white voters precisely because they are different. At the core of the present-day Republican voter is a base fear: a fear of a changing America, a fear of loss of status, of income, of history. Make no mistake, the biggest purveyor of identity politics in America today is the Republican Party. It's just that when it's white-identity politics they don't consider it identity politics at all. When I was younger I didn't understand why it was so difficult to get Republicans focused on courting Latino voters with a message of economic mobility for themselves and their families. Economics was a central part of the Republican message before the Trump era, and polling showed it was a top priority for Latino voters.

As I got older, I understood that nativist beliefs and the politics of white identity were much more dominant drivers among the Republican base than economic issues. The economic issues I found so compelling for helping lift people up were just not important to most Republican politicians and voters. Donald Trump removed any doubt about that. Republicans are addicted to white identity and race denialism.

Ronald Reagan was wrong to assume that Latinos were predisposed to be Republicans any more than Democrats today believe they are predisposed to be Democrats. They weren't then and they aren't now. But they can be won over—if the GOP does not want to squander that opportunity.

In the wake of the infamous "GOP autopsy" commissioned by the Republican National Committee after Mitt Romney's loss to Barack Obama in the 2012 presidential election, professional GOP consultants saw the demographic writing on the wall. The controversial report warned that without expanding its vote base to non-white and nontraditional constituencies, the GOP was destined to lose the popular votes by greater and greater numbers. While the backlash would come at the grassroots level and respond to Trump's overt and vulgar appeals to white racial identity, the essence of the dismissed report is now quietly being reconsidered. Even Trump—who famously kicked out iconic Univision reporter Jorge Ramos from a 2016 press conference—began the 2024 primary season with a friendly, if controversial, sit-down interview with the media giant.

I would argue, as the 2012 autopsy report did, that Republicans will keep losing the popular vote in presidential elections by growing margins and be forced to settle for congressional wins, so long as they stick with appealing to white identity as a strategy. It's not as if Republicans are asking themselves what kind of policies they can refine to attract Latino voters. It's that Latinos in blue-collar industries are naturally gravitating toward the GOP's protectionist and anti-regulatory message. If you work in the energy patch of the Rio Grande Valley of Texas, the Central Valley in California, or southern New Mexico; or if you work in the housing construction industry in Las Vegas or Phoenix, or in the agricultural industry in Iowa or Wisconsin, or manufacturing in Virginia or North Carolina—then Democrats are often viewed as one of the greatest threats to your income. It's not that there's an anti-regulatory ideology in Latino culture, it's that there is an existential threat to your income.

My advice to Republicans? Don't be racist. This is a low bar, obviously, but until Republicans banish Trumpism, they will remain a party preaching to a white, shrinking minority. The data clearly shows that if the Republicans moved beyond white grievance, they would do better in national elections. To be sure, Trump is winning a greater share of nearly all working-class non-white voters, but let me ask you to consider why from the perspective of someone who has run campaigns. Are these voters moving to Trump or away from the Democratic Party? The answer to this isn't merely semantic, it's definitive in how the parties should approach Latino voters.

Ron DeSantis winning 57 percent of Latinos in Florida in 2022 would suggest there's far more upside for Republican candidates beyond Trump himself. And it's not just a Florida phenomenon. Texas governor Greg Abbott got 40 percent in 2022 and 42 percent in 2018, beating Trump's Texas performance of 34 percent in 2016 and essentially matching him with 41 percent in 2020. In other words, Republican candidates are getting at least Trump numbers and, in some cases, far better.

It's not that Trump is doing so well with Latino voters, it's that Republicans would be doing far better without him. If the GOP were more pro-immigrant, if they moved away from nativist positions and relied largely on traditional economic messaging of cutting taxes, easing regulatory burdens, and a free market economy, Republicans could return to support levels of Ronald Reagan, who was nearing 40 percent, and George W. Bush, who got upward of 44 percent in the 2004 election. Not surprisingly, it was Ronald Reagan and George W. Bush who got the highest level of Latino support, and they also happen to be the most pro-immigrant Republican presidents since the end of the Second World War. Republicans need to build a strategy around the economy, jobs, and upward mobility. The next step for Republicans is to target second- and third-generation Latinos, the sons and daughters and grandchildren of migrants. Republicans need to speak directly to them.

Assimilation and the culture war can cut both ways. Second- and third-generation Latinos (in particular Latinas) are voting their generation and gender more than their ethnicity and religion. And they are going to continue to do so. There is a huge yield of votes in this group. The Latino who is turning eighteen, who is going to be the dominant demographic of the voting bloc in the future, is not migrating here and naturalizing as a citizen. Republicans are scaring these voters on the cultural issues and angering them on the racial issues.

The strategy Republicans are relying on is predicated on the belief that if they double down on messaging to their aging white male Christian base they will ultimately be the beneficiaries of a U.S.-born, assimilating Latino male that is rapidly replacing them in the population. There is some rationale for this, and the rightward shift does provide some evidence that this could work in the long run. However, for the next decade, simple math doesn't justify this approach. It's apparent that Republicans are alienating college-educated whites and U.S.-born Latinas with this strategy at a rate faster than they are picking up Hispanic men.

Republicans are making all these unforced errors because they are still controlled by Trump. They can't quit him (even though they ultimately lose with him more often than they win). Yes, Trump attracted a percentage of Latinos that surprised some, but it shouldn't have. Latino voters are like other voters. They can be swayed. But ultimately, Trump's message is limiting, and it repels more voters than it attracts.

- 19 -

The Challenge for Democrats

President Barack Obama commanded 71 percent of the Latino vote nationally in 2012, and in 2016 Hillary Clinton held on to two-thirds (66 percent), but by 2020 Latino support had slid to 59 percent for Joe Biden at the head of the Democratic ticket. Going into the 2024 election, Latino support for Biden is weaker for a Democrat than at any point in recent memory. In three of the last four election cycles, Democrats have lost their share of the Latino vote or failed to bring voters who swung to Republicans back into their fold. Once can be an anomaly, twice can be a coincidence, but three is a trend. In the most recent election, the 2022 midterms for Congress, Latino support for Republicans rose 10 percent over where it had been four years earlier. When one looks deeper at the data in the last decade of election cycles, there is a message screaming out at Democrats: you are losing your once indisputable share of Latino voters and that trend looks to continue as the American-born Latino population grows.

Democrats have been losing Latino vote share as they have become a party of white, progressive, college-educated voters who prioritize cultural issues over blue-collar economic concerns. Recent years have seen way too much denial in the Democratic Party. Many on the left wrote off the Latino rightward shift as assimilating Latino whiteness or self-loathing. Too much was made of the impact of disinformation efforts in Spanish-language social media platforms. Still others claimed that the shrinking margins were nothing to worry about, so long as the growing numbers of Latino voters continued to favor Democrats. Perhaps most pernicious is that many of the Latino professionals in the Democratic Party that were hired for these efforts have consciously chosen to drive the narrative that this isn't happening. I've watched it for thirty years; every time Republicans have made serious inroads into the Latino vote, there's an attack on the media, attacks on polling methodologies, and attacks on math and science. I saw it with George W. Bush and I watched it happen with Donald J. Trump. Denial is a helluva drug.

Democrats haven't felt enough urgency to come up with a fresh playbook to account for the complexity of the Latino identity, relying instead on old clichés and tired tactics. Locked into a pattern of seeing everything in terms of "minority" politics, Democrats have too often conflated a politics of victimization onto all non-whites—a strategy whose shelf life looks finally to be expiring as the number of American-born Latinos continues to grow faster than any other segment of our community. The 12.4 million Latinos who turned eighteen between 2000 and 2018 accounted for 80 percent of the growth among the population's eligible voters during those years. Democrats are seemingly stuck in addressing Latino issues as those of the immigrant (particularly the undocumented), while the vast majority of Latino voters are not immigrants, nor prioritize that experience as a primary concern when voting.

Democrats and the media have often portrayed U.S. Latinos as strangers in a strange land, when the opposite is true. We are not all lying awake at night worrying about deportation. We are not all working in harvest fields for shit wages. We are not all motivated by culture wars or political labels. Despite the clear indications of Latino upward mobility, Democrats have been stuck reinforcing stereotypes that are not characteristic of the Latino electorate as it is emerging. Every year in which Democrats focus on policy priorities exclusively for the poor and the recently migrated is another year the Democrats lose out on attracting the assimilating and upwardly mobile Latino voters whose numbers are growing—and whose support is vital to the party's (and country's) future.

Latinos are aspirational voters, largely working poor, working-class, and middle-class, and for the last decade Democrats have become more the party of economic extremes. For the last three presidential elections since 2012, the wealthy have voted in majorities for Democrats and not Republicans, reversing a long-standing trend. At the same time, Democrats are the party of the very poor. Meanwhile, Republicans are increasingly becoming the party of the working class and middle class. According to the U.S. Department of Labor, Hispanics are projected to account for 78 percent of net new workers between 2020 and 2030. The U.S. labor force growth rate has slowed over the past couple of decades—and what growth has occurred is largely due to the increasing number of Hispanic workers. (Non-Hispanic growth was negligible over the past ten years, at just 0.5 percent. With Hispanic workers' growth factored in, the nation's overall labor force growth rate clocked in at 4.5 percent.)

It's in blue-collar sectors that Latinos are having the most impact. The sector with the highest concentration of Hispanic workers is farming, fishing, and forestry at 43 percent. In second place is building and grounds cleaning and maintenance, at 37.9 percent; followed by construction and extraction at 35.7 percent; food preparation and serving at 27.3 percent; and transportation and material moving at 23.9 percent. Hispanics remain overrepresented in service occupations, where they now make up 10.7 percent of workers in management jobs, up from 5.2 percent in 2000.

One of the most jaw-dropping statistics to me is from the National Association of Home Builders, which reports that one in three workers in the U.S. construction industry is Hispanic. And it's not just that the home-building industry is reliant on Latino labor, it's that Latino households are also reliant on construction jobs. According to the National Community Reinvestment Coalition in September 2023, one in five Hispanic men were employed in construction or related industries. This is a staggering figure and alone explains a significant amount of the economic anxiety felt by Latinos in a time of slow building and higher interest rates. Neither party can have a Latino economic policy without home building and construction as a centerpiece for both income-producing jobs and to bring down the price of homeownership.

While Democrats still garner a majority of working- and middle-class voters, the numbers are slipping away from them as the "diploma divide" reshapes the country. More than income, it is having or not having a college degree that is reshaping America's political allegiances. Among adults ages twenty-five and older, 61 percent of Asian Americans have a bachelor's degree or higher education, along with 42 percent of white adults, 28 percent of Black adults, and 21 percent of Hispanic adults, according to 2021 data. This divide is showing the rapid consolidation of voters with a college degree under the banner of the Democratic Party—those without are moving toward Republicans. Because Latinos comprise one of the fastest-growing segments of the non-college-educated workforce, we should not be surprised that they are mirroring the attributes of their non-Hispanic white colleagues. This is especially true, as U.S.-born Hispanics don't view themselves all that differently from a racial and ethnic perspective. Democratic messaging to Latinos is overwhelmingly racially and ethnically focused and it's landing flat with these voters. To quote an old Bill Clinton line: It's the economy, stupid.

Latino voters are the Democrats' to lose, but if the Democrats do lose them, they will pay a steep political price for their denial. Have the Democrats caught up with the fact that six of ten Latinos in America are of Mexican descent? They have not. Democrats are simply not persuading Latinos to go with them. This should be an issue of house-on-fire urgency, but Democrats in the main don't seem moved to respond to the defection of Latino voters. The trend was apparent well before the 2022 midterm elections, but according to the Third Way, a Democratic research group in Washington, D.C., 10.8 percent more Latinos voted Republican than Democratic in California's fourteen Latino-majority congressional districts, compared to the 2020 presidential election. These margins were critical in the victories of two Republican congressional candidates in rural California districts—David Valadao of Hanford and John Duarte of Turlock—and one suburban district with Mike Garcia of Santa Clarita—which were key in giving the GOP its narrow edge in the 118th Congress of only nine seats. The rightward shift also occurred in Hispanic border communities like New Mexico's Second Congressional District and the Rio Grande Valley of Texas.

"Those losses helped give Republicans majority control of the U.S. House of Representatives," Democrat Anna M. Caballero, a California state senator, wrote in the *Sacramento Bee* in March 2023. "These outcomes, plus razor-thin victories by other Democrats in the Central Valley congressional races, should signal to the national Democratic Party that serious adjustments need to be made to compete for votes. The Central Valley electorate is becoming younger and increasingly Latino. As a result, the traditional Democratic playbook can no longer be counted on to win elections or to build broad-based political strength in California's key emerging power center."

Caballero was advised in 2010 to focus on "Valleycrats," or "Blue dog" moderate swing voters, and did—and lost. In 2018, she ignored the advice and focused instead on Latino voters—and won. "Does the California Democratic Party really believe in and understand Central Valley voters?" she asked in that *Bee* article. "[I]t would be a mistake to depend on efforts funded by urban-based philanthropic foundations that parachute their agendas and resources into rural, farmworker communities, with no comprehension of the social, economic and political challenges faced by Central Valley residents or the solutions they want."

Latinos regularly have the lowest turnout rates of any of the four major racial/ethnic groups in the country over the past few decades, clear proof that these voters are not being cultivated with a compelling message. Low voter turnout is not a sign of loyalty to a party. It's the exact opposite. It is a sign that your message does not resonate with a community. The poor don't always have the luxury of civic engagement and often don't feel a stake in society. That's a threat to democracy. It doesn't matter whether you're poor and Black in Mississippi or poor white in Appalachia or poor and Brown in East Los Angeles. If you're poor, the likelihood that you don't vote grows exponentially. Combine poverty with noncompetitive elections, and it's a perfect recipe for low voter turnout.

While Democrats consistently point to the trope of voter suppression as a reason for low minority turnout, this excuse falls short of explaining the bulk of the problem. There is perhaps no state in the union with more varied ways of voting than California. You can vote weeks before an election or even register and vote the same day. You can vote from the convenience of your living room, a standard polling place, or in a vote center. California has adopted nearly every imaginable method and process for voting, and for Latinos, voter turnout remains abysmally low. That's an obvious sign that we do not have a voting process problem, at least not in the largest Latino state in the country.

Democrats are uncomfortable talking about poverty as the primary driver of low civic engagement. This phenomenon is nonpartisan; we are creating underclasses of Latinos in red states and blue states. The growing Latino population and voter base has never shown a proclivity to turn out in large numbers, not just because party leaders are ignoring their clamor for an economic agenda—but because the limited upward mobility of Latinos has stifled the political class representation in both parties that we would expect to see in a healthier, more balanced democracy.

Latinos outside California are shifting right faster than they are in the state because they have greater upward mobility outside of the state rather than in it. When adjusted for housing costs (as they should be), national poverty statistics clearly show Latinos in California are dramatically overrepresented among the state's poor and among the groups least likely to be able to afford housing—a critical component of achieving middle-class status. California Latinos are relatively poorer and more likely to be renters than Latinos in other states. Poverty is a key indicator of low civic engagement.

Democrats still lean on the same crutch they have for years: they seek turnout based on opposition to Republicans rather than support for what they are selling. It's easier to "go negative" than to do the hard work of fixing problems, but at least for the time being, Latino voters aren't adopting the voting behaviors of rage that have consumed older white voters. Negative ads don't have the staying power for them that they do for whites. This is likely due to remarkably higher optimism and confidence in institutions than older white voters. While Latino voters have responded to attacks on the community, they don't seem to last beyond one or two election cycles. Latino voters will clearly reject a party when it advances racially charged policies attacking it, but that doesn't mean they give their loyalties to the other party. Not voting is a much more conscious action than the Democratic Party would like to admit. It's the most tangible rejection of both parties that neither is paying attention to.

Articulating what and who you are against and not what you are for creates an unhealthy society—and electorate. It makes for a tepid relationship between Latinos and the Democratic Party. Latinos are not voting *for* the Democratic Party so much as *against* the Republican Party. That may work in the short term, but Democrats could bury Republicans, particularly in congressional elections, if they could energize a larger share of the Latino voting base. If Democrats had taken the Latino vote seriously over the past decade and built an aspirational multiethnic working-class agenda focused more on economics and pocketbook issues than the current emphasis on race and ethnicity, it is entirely conceivable that they could still be winning 70 percent of the Latino vote. Had they heeded the warning signs made clear in three of the last four elections, both houses of Congress would comfortably be resting in their hands and Donald Trump would be a distant terrible memory.

EPILOGUE

A Case for Optimism:
Pluralism over Tribalism

A spectacularly ostentatious resort rose up in the distance, thirty miles south of Lviv in the fertile farmlands of western Ukraine. The resort resembled an Italian emperor's villa complete with man-made lake, hunting grounds, eighteen-hole golf course, and an ornate gold foyer that would make Donald Trump blush. The artwork and antiques were original throughout, making it clear this preposterous exercise in excess had been the dacha of some Russian oligarch, its garishness serving as an indictment of the corrupt system that produced it. We were told to wait, and so we waited and waited.

Sometime after dark a convoy of black Suburban SUVs pulled up into the rounded driveway. After the expected contingent of battle-tested body guards spilled out of the vehicles and fanned out, a balding, bearded man of medium build stepped out. His warm smile, humble manner yet dominant presence made it instantly clear he was a man of consequence. This was Rustem Umerov, the second most important man in Ukraine after Volodymyr Zelensky—then chief negotiator with Russia, since elevated to defense minister. He had a calm, methodical demeanor and confident gaze that immediately left me wondering if I could handle myself so well if my country was under siege, facing annihilation by the Russian war machine.

Rustem was remarkably gracious and crisp in his thinking. He insisted everyone eat before he did, and easily adjusted to focus on the questions we asked, despite being repeatedly interrupted to take urgent calls dealing with momentous issues related to life, death, and war. His English was flawless—"boarding school in Pennsylvania," he explained with a smile—and there was an uncanny certitude in his voice for a man whose role as chief negotiator for Ukraine with Russia and, as a Crimean Tatar and Muslim, a family history of ethnic strife were a brutal reminder of Russian aggression.

"The war began in Crimea and it will end in Crimea," Rustem explained to us, ignoring the assortment of food around him.

"Not because this is a fight over territory—although it certainly is that," he continued. "This is a different war than the last European war. It's not as simple as a struggle between authoritarianism and democracy, although it is that, too."

I was riveted. Astonished at the easy gravitas this man summoned. And I was gobsmacked when he told my Lincoln Project colleague Ron Steslow and me: "This is about seeing if a pluralistic democracy can work."

That was when it dawned on me: the Ukrainians are fighting *for* something, not *against* something. In backing them, in tandem with our European allies and despite the opposition of Russia-funded fifth columnists in the Republican Party, we are fighting *for* something, not *against* something. And in writing this book, and hitting the road to talk to people in this pivotal national election year, I am, above all, fighting *for* something, not *against* something, and this is a positive, optimistic vision of a truly pluralistic American political culture that pulls us into the future and takes us back from a dark and dangerous period of angry tribalism run amok.

~

In many ways, the cultural superpower Latinos bring to U.S. politics is the characteristic that defines them as a mixed heritage people— neither fully Indigenous nor fully white, representing every race. Here is what neither political party understands: Latinos are redefining the mythology of the American melting pot. They are not and don't want to be treated as victims, or even as minorities. The sheer size of the transformation occurring is going to require American society to melt into a Latino pot as much as the other way around. Latino voters do not fit the ideological boxes both parties create for them, and American institutions are struggling with how to deal with that.

Winning future elections will be a test of which party can be more introspective and more capable of setting aside ethnic and racial biases while embracing the opportunity of attracting Latino voters. Right now, the average Latino voter is under the age of thirty. This is a young electorate. In many respects, they are just reaching the stage when people become higher-propensity voters. They are voters who are just coming into their own as workers, homeowners, parents, and all the other characteristics that define high-propensity voters.

America's youngest voters, Gen Z voters, are best understood by recognizing that a huge swath of Gen Z voters are Latino. According to Pew Research, 38 percent of Gen Z voters aged eighteen to twenty-five identified as people of color. Fully 25 percent of Gen Z is Latino compared to 52 percent white. Compare this to baby boomers—the largest voting-age cohort, who voted for Donald Trump by over 50 percent and identify as 79 percent white.

If the 1960s catalyzed our modern culture wars, the demographic changes sparked in the Southwest during the 1990s left no doubt we were also in the early throes of a battle for our racial and ethnic identity. There's a fine line between culture wars and race wars in the country today. The 2016 presidential campaign began what will likely be a two-decade struggle through a painful national demographic transformation.

Make no mistake, the decline of civic virtue and engagement, distrust in social institutions, loss of empathy for each other, loss of compromise for the common good as a virtue, among other pernicious characteristics during this new age, signal a dangerous climate for the continuation of this American experiment in self-governance. If just enough people lose confidence in it, there is no Constitution that can be written to safeguard us from the slide into authoritarianism that we all feel around us.

Only a changed culture can save us, one where we are more committed to a sense of community and to each other's well-being as much as the individual. A culture that is aspirational, optimistic, and confident about the promise of America and her future. A culture with a heightened sense of trust in social and democratic institutions like government, the media, the academy, our educational system, the Church, law enforcement, and the military. America is at a point where those who hold power and wealth have lost their capacity to keep the flame of what generations before us have handed down for two and a half centuries. Americans over fifty have been endowed with the most prosperous, privileged, and peaceful era in U.S. history and yet have the most negative view of this country and its future of any generation in the history of modern polling.

The strain, pressure, and distress we feel comes from the realization that an old America is indeed dying, but we are simultaneously giving birth to something new. This new chapter promises to continue our arc of justice toward a more perfect union, another struggle to remind ourselves that the limits of our Constitution are met when we expand our conception of who is American, a reminder of the true American political tradition brought to the forefront by Jefferson in the Declaration of Independence and again by Lincoln's speech among the dead in a field outside of Gettysburg that "[a]ll men are endowed by their Creator with certain unalienable rights. . . ." That is our charge. That is the test of younger Americans from the millennial and Gen Z generations. If we are successful, it will be because we were saved from within.

Latinos, perhaps as a function of youth and the relatively recent arrival of so many who have placed us on a pedestal, are as a group much more oriented toward an optimistic, positive vision. That is a generalization, but it is one based on deep knowledge, decades of polling data—and deep truth. Latino immigrants specifically poll as much more optimistic than other Americans.

The U.S. experiment depends on new waves of immigrants to breathe energy and life into our belief in our country, and our conviction to try to live up to our better selves. Latinos embody that powerfully, which is one reason why—I can tell you this as a political pro—negative advertising doesn't seem to work as well in mobilizing these voters to go to the polls. There are exceptions. For some Latino populations, smearing Democrats as *"comunistas"* or *"progresista radicales!"* has provided some traction for Republicans, and I've witnessed a generation of Democrats running on nothing but anti-Republicanism in California, but in general, Latinos—especially Mexican Americans—find negative spots confusing, off-putting, unrelatable, and even annoying.

The question in their minds is: *What does any of this have to do with my family and me and making a better life?* Given our cultural traditions, we do not hold up ideals of humanity as perfect or perfectible. Instead, we're deeply instilled with a sense of the duality of human nature. You don't need to knock would-be heroes off their horses for us. For those that have lived in Latin American countries and immigrated here, it's common sense to recognize that as difficult and challenging as life is here, it is decidedly better than life in the countries from which they came. Republican attacks on school performance or teachers unions often backfire when the schools your children attend are often better than schools in the old country. Democrats' attacks on the wealthy fall flat when this country, unlike those back home, actually allows lower classes to rise.

Latinos are the perfect audience to help Democratic and Republican leaders get their groove back. We've been taken for granted for decades now on the assumption that our support is easy to line up.

It's not. It takes honest and persistent outreach, but at the same time, we're open and ready to be persuaded. And it's time: this book has been nothing if not clear on the Category 5 catastrophic event brewing for our democracy if Latinos continue to be ignored and taken for granted. Our democracy might not survive that. How do we rebuild trust in our democratic institutions? Latinos already have that. How do we moderate the political parties overrun by hyper-partisanship and extremism? Latinos already do that. How do we find a new way to discuss race that emphasizes our blended reality and not the dysfunctional bipolarity of the past? Latinos do that, too.

Can we, at long last, move in the direction of freedom? Freedom for all? A place for all? To do that, pluralism must win out over tribalism. The two are in some ways similar, and yet utterly different. Tribalism is a very negative, close-minded, isolationist, threatened, cowardly way of viewing the world. It lacks confidence at its core because it's fear-based and fear leads to anger and anger leads to conflict. Pluralism is an idea that we can transcend these base instincts that can be activated by any sense of threat, whether because someone else looks different or speaks a different language or worships in a different church. Differences don't have to inspire fear. I don't need to kill you. You're not a threat. You're not here to take my stuff. In fact, we could both have more if we worked together.

"Pluralism and tribalism both stress that people have different interests and identities arising from their particular group involvements and that such differences result in political conflict, but these perspectives are very different," writes former University of Kansas political science professor Paul Schumaker, an academic expert on pluralism.

> Pluralist societies have many cross-cutting group involvements such that no particular interest or identity predominates; indeed, in pluralist societies, groups realize that their limited size and power precludes domination and thus they seek cooperation, accommodation,

and compromise with other groups. Tribal societies have cumulative group interests and identities, such that one set of interlocking groups is strongly loyal to one tribe (or party or ideology) while another set of interlocking groups is strongly committed to an opposite tribe. Tribes seek domination over their tribal opponent; in pursuit of domination, they stereotype, marginalize, and oppress those groups that are part of the opposite tribe.

Tribalism is like a failed version of pluralism. Or better yet: the undead form of pluralism. It's like a zombie. It looks the same and it can walk around the same, but it's empty, it's hollow, it's soulless, and it's dangerous. Tribalism is a degenerate form of pluralism. What's different is the way you perceive society. If you're fearful, if you're afraid of change, if you lack confidence in who you are, then you are easily pulled toward tribalism as well as nativism, jingoism, isolationism, protectionism—all those dangerous isms. If you have a more expansive, confident, optimistic view of humanity in your country, and your ideals and your beliefs and your values, they're no threat at all.

Tribalism seeks first to defend its members and leaders regardless of the cost to the broader society. Both of our political parties have devolved into tribes, viewing themselves as the saviors of their respective views of democracy and members of the other tribe as an existential threat to the country. It's human nature. It's what the Founders knew when they crafted this elegant solution to a timeless problem—how do we protect ourselves from ourselves?

If you're focused through a lens of individualism and nativism, then you end up with tribalism, which is the first step toward war and conflict. You slide downward into me-ism. It's not even decadence. Rome collapsed because of decadence and bacchanalia. We don't even have that. It's a regression into a preadolescence where entitlement is everything, a feeling that if you just kick and scream long enough, you'll get what you want.

If you have a limited sense of the world and fear everything, then tribalism is likely the belief system that you're going to find. If you have a respect for the universality of the American idea, then you not only believe in pluralism, you *require* pluralism. When you lose that as an anchor, it devolves into tribalism.

Pluralism is opportunity. That comes across to people of widely divergent views the more they understand how pluralism works. As I mentioned in the prologue, new research shows that, despite so much fearmongering, the prospect of an increasingly Latino United States, when accurately explained, had positive associations even among conservatives. "Notably, the narrative of racial blending was especially reassuring to white Republicans, who felt most threatened by the conventional majority-minority account," the *Atlantic* article reported.

It really depends on how you view the world. Recent years have shown that America's insecurity about itself runs deeper even than we thought. Our lack of confidence in whether we can measure up to who we have always said we are is now oozing out of our pores—and, unfortunately, materializing in tribalism. The U.S. experiment in democracy really represented the apex of the individualist thinking of the European Enlightenment. It could only have been European Protestants who brought forth a government where people could govern themselves. That is a great gift to humankind, the elegance of what they created—life, liberty, and the pursuit of happiness—and that vision begins with the individual.

Latin American culture does not begin with the individual. Going back to its roots in Indigenous culture, it begins at the other end of the spectrum, which is with the bedrock conviction that the success of the individual can only be meaningfully viewed within the construct of the success of the family and of the community. The larger whole matters, not so much the component parts.

I've spent most of my life trying to reconcile those two as I've been assimilating as a third-generation Mexican American in California, understanding the history of my grandparents as immigrants, my parents' struggles to move up the economic ladder and find economic mobility, losing my language, keeping my religion, understanding that my perspective at home was different than the perspectives of my friends at school, and trying to thread this needle in a very American way. That story, that struggle, multiplied by millions, is what's happening in America. The story isn't new, but the size and scope of it is and that's why this century will be a different American century.

In a changing country, it will increasingly become a question of whether you view the world first and foremost through the eyes of individualism or do so through a broader familial and community lens. That is the fault line between tribalism and pluralism. To move from old myths of individualism to a more twenty-first-century awareness of global interconnectivity with a more contemporary sense of pluralism being the driver of renewal and rebirth, that can be a painful process.

To make that leap of faith requires a sturdy sense of self-confidence—a quality represented by both John Kennedy and Ronald Reagan—that our country currently lacks. We're an American experiment, but are we truly a nation, anchored together by a common set of beliefs? I don't know. The evidence isn't looking very strong. We fought the Civil War over slavery, the North won, and 150 years later, we're still dealing with systemic racism and the inability to overcome these foundational wounds. We've come a long way, but still have a long, long way to go.

The largest Protestant sect in the United States, the Southern Baptist Conference, was created to give religious legitimacy to slavery. Just think about the ramifications of that. If you can use the message of Christ to justify slavery, there's a long runway of shit you can justify once you start to rationalize along those lines. It's about protecting power, protecting the gains of earlier generations, and keeping others out.

Here is where Latinos come in: we can no longer be ignored, and the message we're delivering to the political parties and anyone else who would claim to be a cultural leader of this country is not complicated. When I first began this journey, and throughout my career and lifetime, the question I was pressed to ask myself was found in an authoritative book by the scholar Peter Skerry titled *Mexican Americans: The Ambivalent Minority*. The question he posed was not will Mexican Americans join the American mainstream, but how—as a traditional immigrant ethnic group or as an aggrieved racial minority? This was the fundamental question of both my personal search for understanding and my professional attempts to help guide the direction of my community and country. I have spent the past thirty years watching Democrats unsuccessfully argue that it is the latter, while I have watched Republicans unsuccessfully argue it is the former.

From my unique perch in American political history I can now say that the answer has never been clear because the question was wrong. The question that needs to be asked is, if Latinos are to help guide this American experiment into a new century, how will they take their experience as both an aggrieved racial minority and a traditional ethnic immigrant group and transform that perspective into the American mainstream? The question I initially sought to answer was posed in the last American century and that is where it belongs.

Like Latinos themselves, we are not facing the either/or proposition I felt required to make as a Republican or as a Democrat. Or the choices my mother made as choosing to emphasize her Hispanic identity or her white one. Both can be wholly true at the same time. Latinos are not a Rubik's Cube. We are not a puzzle. And we are not a riddle. We are a population of Americans who want to see this country thrive and grow, and want to be accepted and embraced and allowed to be ourselves equally as individuals and as members of a distinct, yet nebulous community as we make vital contributions and begin to take the reins of power to design the country's future.

Talk to us about solid middle-class values, and hopes and aspirations. Talk to us about jobs and the economy. Talk to us about education. Respect the struggle of the immigrant and the least among us. For 2020s fundraising, both Democrats and Republicans fill inboxes with sky-is-falling alarm every day, negative, negative, negative, all about pushing down the other guy, the other party. It's like watching a bad rerun of a tired old prime-time drama that no one liked the first time. It's boring and it's insulting, and no wonder Latinos—like a lot of other people—are fed up and increasingly alienated.

My parents preached personal accountability to my sisters and me. My parents refused to see themselves as victims and they refused to let their children become victims. We did not dwell on issues such as ethnic or racial discrimination. Culturally, we could walk and chew gum at the same time. What I mean by that is this: We were proud of our Mexican roots, but we were Americans first. We pledged allegiance to the Stars and Stripes. The fierce eagle on the tricolored flag of Mexico is a wonderful symbol that we appreciated, but the red, white, and green was not our flag and my parents were never confused by that.

I am optimistic because I believe the struggle to connect with Latinos will force one or both national parties to reinvent themselves. As a political operative, I tend to focus on mistakes made on individual political campaigns and, in particular, how both Republicans and Democrats have missed out time and time again on the chance to make fresh inroads with Latinos. As an author, I need to take a larger perspective. I need to acknowledge that the Leninist project on which Steve Bannon launched Donald Trump, the tearing down of institutions, the continuing degradation of Washington politics, has by design turned people off from anything to do with politics, especially Latinos. The work of getting government itself going again will not be easy. And it will not be quick. It will require a slow rebuilding of trust.

At least I can now be sure that leaders see the Latino challenge with the same urgency with which I've approached these issues my whole life. A drumbeat of media accounts has started to catch up with the warnings I've made for years—step up and talk to Latinos like real people, not props in an old movie, or pay the consequences.

America, as she has many times before, stands on the cusp of profound change. This newest challenge comes from within, and those are often the most difficult to face. If we can get beyond our old conceptions of our American identity and embrace something new but truer to our founding principles, this can be yet another American century—a Latino century.

Acknowledgments

This book began thirty years ago in a dorm room at Georgetown University, where a young Mexican American kid from Southern California struggled and questioned his own past, place, and destiny in the years that would unfold over his lifetime. It has been a great gift to imagine what my country would look like as I pondered the future demographic numbers over the coming decades and considered what our great experiment might look like. To have been able to make my own projections, be directly involved in democracy as a practitioner guiding Republicans and Democrats, and now, take what I have learned to explain and guess again at what America will be as a non-white European country going forward. I was so blessed to have been born to loving parents Louis and Rosalina who, through extraordinary sacrifice and support, made that imagining possible. For their faith, optimism, and hope in life and their children, especially when there was little reason for it, I am so grateful. To my sisters, Juliet and Gina, who showed me the strength and power of Latinas and taught me, the only boy, to see the world through their eyes. My children, Andrew (the logical data scientist), Madeline (the passionate artist), and Grace (the gifted people person), who bless me every day with what they share with our world.

Because this work has encompassed so much of my life, I will invariably forget too many impactful people that brought me to this point. I regret that I will not be able to mention all of you here.

I want to thank the remarkable professionals who made this all possible, beginning with my agent, Johanna Castillo, at Writers House. I couldn't ask for a better advocate, support system, and guide through an extraordinary chapter in my life. After thirty years of guiding candidates on the scariest adventure of their lives, I found myself in the same spot, deciding to write a book. Johanna was the first person I had to turn over control of everything to professionally, and the trust and confidence I have placed in her were among the best decisions I've made on this journey. A very special debt of gratitude to Mindy Marquez, who believed in this book, believed there was a place for it, trusted me to author it, and built the team to make it all come together. Such an exceptional partner! This book and its story are the result of her commitment to it, and I am so appreciative of her and the entire Simon & Schuster team.

To my dear friend Marcos Bretón, who agreed to go on this journey with me and provided not only the historical perspective that was required but whose own life experiences made the tough discussions and long, hard, honest examinations of my past more approachable. It's rare that two people can go through this process and not only remain friends but be better for it (*muchisimas gracias hermano*). To my new friend and consigliere Steve Kettmann, whose love of baseball, politics, and all things Latino made him a natural for the project and whose tireless work made this possible: I'm not sure I can offer up how much you meant to this project other than to say I know this was a labor of love in part inspired by a deep friendship with the late Pedro Gomez. I hope you find him present throughout these pages.

More than any other person who has helped me understand the complexity, beauty, and struggle of ethnicity, culture, and race in America today is the brilliant essayist Gregory Rodriguez. One of the many lessons I've learned from him is to never waver when you are presenting ideas that are ahead of their time and to not be afraid to move on when the world finally catches up. To my good friend whose career origins as a Sacramento journalist dovetailed with mine years ago, Anthony York, who not only endured three decades of discussions on this subject but provided clarity, inspiration, and grounding through all of it. To Mary Anna Mancuso, who refused to allow doubt into the room and who believed in this book, especially when I didn't.

To my business partner Robb Korinke, who remains the best personal and professional decision I've made and whose trust in me has always inspired greater confidence. You remind me every day that shared values overcome political differences every time. Thank you to Glen and Sally Becerra who were there from day one. To Paul Mitchell, Dustin Corcoran, and Scott Lay (who left us too early), our friendship, support, and loyal opposition helped us define a generation in Sacramento and brought us right where we were destined to be: We did good for a bunch of community college kids. I'd like to thank three giants in the political consulting profession who operated with not only great talent but great integrity and served as excellent role models and mentors as professionals and as men—Stu Spencer, Lionel Sosa, and Dan Schnur. It would be impossible not to recognize the integrity and resolve in the face of enormous pressure among three individuals who shared a foxhole with me during the most consequential presidential race in the last century, my fellow Lincoln Project cofounders George Conway, Ron Steslow, and Jennifer Horn.

I want to thank the special group of young professionals who comprised the best political and data team of my career on that race—Zack Czajkowski, Conor Rogers, Lucas Holtz, and Spencer Harrison. You guys made history and I'm proud to have been alongside you.

To the many elected officials who inspired and encouraged me, especially those that became friends: U.S. Senator Alex Padilla, Mayor Antonio Villaraigosa, Senator Jim Brulte, Assemblyman Rod Pacheco, Assemblyman Nao Takasugi, Assemblyman Chad Mayes, and Speaker John Pérez. A special thanks to all of the journalists with whom I've spent hundreds of hours over the years doing my best to explain this unfolding story.

And finally, to the millions of Latino voters whom I have polled, focus grouped, analyzed, examined, counted, organized, persuaded, researched, and written about for three decades: This grand experiment is counting on you to revitalize and re-instill the values and confidence that have made this country work (if imperfectly) for 250 years; we are counting on you to make America great again.

Notes

Prologue: It's Not All Black and White

1 *As essayist Richard Rodriguez once put it:* Richard Rodriguez, *Brown: The Last Discovery of America* (New York: Viking, 2002).

8 *As Richard Alba, Morris Levy, and Dowell Myers reported:* Richard Alba, Morris Levy, and Dowell Myers, "The Myth of a Majority-Minority America," *Atlantic*, June 13, 2021, https://www.theatlantic.com/ideas/archive/2021/06/myth-majority-minority-america/619190/.

11 *When the country was founded:* The first United States census, in 1790, recorded more than 700,000 enslaved people, about 18 percent of the U.S. population at the time.

12 *In 1908, a stage play premiered:* *The Melting Pot*, a play by Israel Zangwill, depicts the life of a family of immigrant Russian Jews.

Chapter 1: The Latinization of America

18 *By 2040, 70 percent of new homeowners will be Latino:* Laurie Goodman and Jun Zhu, *The Future of Headship and Home Ownership* (Washington, D.C.: Urban Institute, 2021), https://www.urban.org/research/publication/future-headship-and-homeownership.

23 *Only 26 percent of Hispanic men:* "Analysis: Degree Completion Gaps for Hispanic Students Are Widening," Excelencia in Education!, July 19, 2023, https://www.edexcelencia.org/excitings/analysis-degree-completion-gaps-hispanic-students-are-widening.

Chapter 2: Lessons from My Nana

29 *Future presidential candidate John Kerry:* "By 1967, Kerry received his commission and his first assignment: cleaning the USS Gridley, a missile frigate . . . off the Vietnamese coast. . . . The USS Gridley and Kerry arrived back in California on June 5, 1968, the day that one of his heroes, Sen. Robert F. Kennedy (D-N.Y.), was

shot." Lois Romano, "Keen Focus on Lt. Kerry's Four Months Under Fire," *Washington Post*, April 23, 2004, https://www.washingtonpost.com/archive/politics/2004/04/23/keen-focus-on-lt-kerrys-four-months-under-fire/ae47dafb-0255-4e7b-8647-32f623f6681a/.

34 *When we first got to Moorpark:* Moorpark population in 1970 was 3,380. U.S. Bureau of the Census, *Census of Population: 1970*, vol. 1 *Characteristics of the Population*, part 6, California—Section 1 (Washington, D.C.: U.S. Government Printing Office, 1973), https://www2.census.gov/prod2/decennial/documents/1970a_ca1-01.pdf.

Chapter 3: Becoming a Republican

41 *When Reagan traveled to Berlin:* "June 12, 1987: President Reagan Says, 'Tear Down This Wall,'" ABC World News Tonight, June 6, 2017, https://abcnews.go.com/Politics/video/june-12-1987-president-reagan-tear-wall-47874686.

Chapter 4: Political Director of the California Republican Party

48 *a former Ziegfeld Follies showgirl:* "Born in New York, [Robert] Dornan moved west with his family as a child. His mother was a Ziegfeld showgirl. . . . An unbridled showman, Dornan was trained in the theater arts when he was growing up in Beverly Hills." Eric Bailey and Peter M. Warren, "Dornan Loses Officially, but Is Not Giving Up Fight," *Los Angeles Times*, November 23, 1996, https://www.latimes.com/archives/la-xpm-1996-11-23-mn-2095-story.html.

59 *we lost by only 192 votes:* "In the last county race to be decided, Wildman's margin over GOP businessman John Geranios in the Nov. 5 balloting was a slim 192 votes." Nancy Hill-Holtzman, "Wildman Declared Winner in Close Assembly Contest," *Los Angeles Times*, November 23, 1996, https://www.latimes.com/archives/la-xpm-1996-11-23-mn-2086-story.html.

Chapter 5: *Un Nuevo Día*

73 *in 1981, he started his own agency, Sosa & Associates:* "Sosa & Associates began in 1981 with a single account—Westinghouse—and $50,000 a year in billings. Eight years later, billings are about $55 million a year." "Ad Agency Successful in Hispanic Promotions," *Odessa American*, August 13, 1989, https://www.newspapers.com/image/300632723/?terms=%22lionel%20sosa%22%20largest%20hispanic%20advertising%20agency%20the%20country&match=1.

77 *Meanwhile, the tradition:* "Mexican governors attended the gubernatorial inaugurations of Ann Richards, George W. Bush and Rick Perry. But in a break with tradition, they won't be in Austin when Gov.-elect Abbott takes his oath of office." Julián Aguilar, "Mexican Governors Won't Be at Abbott Inaugural," *Texas Tribune*, January 19, 2015, https://www.texastribune.org/2015/01/19/mexican-governors-wont-be-abbotts-inauguration/.

Chapter 6: First He Came for the Mexicans

81 *Except for Arnold Schwarzenegger:* Steve Poizner was elected insurance commissioner of California, running as a Republican, in 2006, the same year Schwarzenegger was reelected as governor. Poizner subsequently left the Republican Party to run as an independent. "Steve Poizner, the wealthy Silicon Valley tech entrepreneur and 2010 Republican gubernatorial candidate, has announced he'll seek statewide office as an independent in 2018—marking a high-profile defection from the state Republican Party as President Donald Trump's approval ratings sink in California." "Top California Republican to Run Statewide as an Independent," Politico, February 12, 2018, https://www.politico.com/story/2018/02/12/top-california-republican-to-run-statewide-as-an-independent-406171.

81 *Even George P. Bush came out for Trump:* "George P. Bush, the Texas land commissioner, is breaking with his father, a former Donald Trump Republican primary rival, to back the GOP nominee." David Mark, "George P. Bush Urges Republicans to Back Trump," CNN, August 8, 2016, https://www.cnn.com/2016/08/07/politics/george-p-bush-donald-trump-jeb-bush/index.html.

Chapter 7: Political Odd Couple

101 *vying with Republican John Cox:* "[B]ackers of Villaraigosa—who is scrapping with Cox for the second spot in the primary—are airing an ad on Fox News and other stations that paints Cox as a Chicago carpetbagger and onetime Democrat who can't win elections. While living in Illinois, Cox unsuccessfully ran for office multiple times. During a testy televised debate earlier this month in San Jose, Newsom was asked whom he would prefer to face in the general election. The lieutenant governor quickly said he hoped to battle a Republican. 'A Republican would be ideal in the general election,' Newsom said with a grin, then glanced over at Cox and [Travis] Allen. 'Either one of these would do.'" "Trump Endorses Republican John Cox for California Governor," *Los Angeles Times*, May 18, 2018, https://www.latimes.com/politics/la-pol-ca-john-cox-trump-endorsement-20180518-story.html.

Chapter 8: The Lincoln Project

103 *what I called "fumigating the Republican Party rather than reforming it":* Madrid: "I do believe that there are conservative ideas that need to be fought for that California and this country desperately need right now. I'm not trying to save the Republican Party. I'm trying to fumigate the party, and there is a wing that needs to be pushed out and denounced. I do believe that the Republican Party's brand has become so toxic that there are a lot of millennials—a lot of Latinos, African Americans, Asian Pacific Islanders and white progressives that will never vote Republican, at least not for a generation. And in California that's 80 percent of the state!" Patt Morrison, "The New Year's Resolution That Can Save California's

Shriveling GOP: Don't Be Evil," *Los Angeles Times*, December 26, 2018, https://www.latimes.com/opinion/op-ed/la-ol-patt-morrison-madrid-gop-20181226-htmlstory.html.

106 *"The American presidency transcends the individuals who occupy the Oval Office"*: "The president and his enablers have replaced conservatism with an empty faith led by a bogus prophet." George T. Conway III, Steve Schmidt, John Weaver, and Rick Wilson, "We Are Republicans, and We Want Trump Defeated," *New York Times*, December 17, 2019, https://www.nytimes.com/2019/12/17/opinion/lincoln-project.html.

111 *the far-right disinformation website Breitbart, which even Bannon himself called "alt-right"*: "In July, Steve Bannon, who was the executive chairman of Breitbart at the time, told a *Mother Jones* reporter, 'We're the platform of the alt-right.' Earlier this month, Bannon became the 'CEO' of the Trump campaign. Dexter Thomas, a former reporter at the *Los Angeles Times* who covered online communities, describes the alt-right as 'racists with a marketing strategy.' He adds, 'They're making being racist cool again for a certain class of people.'" Chava Gourarie, "How the 'Alt-Right' Checkmated the Media," *Columbia Journalism Review*, August 30, 2016, https://www.cjr.org/analysis/alt_right_media_clinton_trump.php.

Chapter 9: The Bannon Line and the New Southern Strategy

121 *"Mendoza Line"*: In baseball, a player who has a batting average of .200 or more has cleared the Mendoza Line, named for Mexican shortstop Mario Mendoza, who failed to clear the Mendoza Line in five of his nine seasons in the major leagues, playing for Pittsburgh, Seattle, and Texas from 1974 to 1982. The term was used in a Peter Gammons *Boston Globe* column on May 17, 1982, quoting George Brett: "We read the names of the guys below the Mendoza Line: all the guys hitting below .200." https://www.newspapers.com/image/437074691/?terms=%22We%20read%20the%20names%20of%20the%20guys%20below%20the%20Mendoza%20Line%3A%20all%20the%20guys%20hitting%20below%20.200.%22&match=1.

Chapter 10: The Latino Voter

144 *The Hispanic Consumer Sentiment Index:* Florida Atlantic University's Hispanic Consumer Sentiment Index, down to 74.3 percent in the third quarter of 2022, rebounded to 85.3 percent in the fourth quarter of 2022. For the first quarter of 2023, the index fell back to 80.2 percent, then inched up to 83.4 percent in the second quarter and slid back to 74.7 in the third quarter. https://business.fau.edu/departments/economics/business-economics-polling/bepi-hics/.

Chapter 11: Beyond the Politics of Immigration

149 *a cultural drift probably best summed up with one word: "Latinx":* First found in published references in the 2010s, the term generated controversy from the

beginning. The first appearance of "Latinx" in the *New York Times* was not until 2016, and its second usage in the *Times* came in an April 2, 2017, article, "Readers Respond: Which Racial Terms Make You Cringe?" Carmen Erasmus wrote: "The new term 'Latinx.' I don't think the term Latino or Latina needs to be revised. I also cringe when 'Latino' is labeled as a race. There are many races within the Latin ethnic designation." https://www.nytimes.com/2017/04/02/us/racial-terms -that-make-you-cringe.html?searchResultPosition=2.

150 *an August 2020 Pew Research Survey*: Luis Noe-Bustamente, Lauren Mora, and Mark Hugo Lopez, "About One-in-Four U.S. Hispanics Have Heard of Latinx, but Just 3% Use It," Pew Research Center, August 11, 2020, https://www.pewresearch .org/hispanic/2020/08/11/about-one-in-four-u-s-hispanics-have-heard-of -latinx-but-just-3-use-it/.

152 *Pew Research Center data published in September 2022*: Jens Manuel Krogstad, Khadijah Edwards, and Mark Hugo Lopez, "Most Latinos Say Democrats Care About Them and Work Hard for Their Vote, Far Fewer Say So of GOP," Pew Research Center, September 29, 2022, https://www.pewresearch.org/race-ethn icity/2022/09/29/most-latinos-say-democrats-care-about-them-and-work-hard -for-their-vote-far-fewer-say-so-of-gop/.

155 *In an April 2022 poll*: Vianney Gómez, "As Courts Weigh Affirmative Action, Grades and Test Scores Seen as Top Factors in College Admissions," Pew Research Center, April 26, 2022, https://www.pewresearch.org/short-reads/2022/04/26 /u-s-public-continues-to-view-grades-test-scores-as-top-factors-in-college-admis sions/.

Chapter 12: The Flip Side of Machismo

160 *a translator to Hernán Cortés*: Malinche—also given the name Marina—translated for Cortés during his famous November 1519 first meeting with Moctezuma, emperor of the Aztec Empire.

Chapter 13: Nevada: Labor and Working-Class Latinos

169 *As Reid told journalist Eric Garcia, "People used to make fun of me actually, because I went to all the Cinco de Mayo events"*: Eric Garcia, "What Harry Reid Told Me About Reaching Latino Voters—and What He Can Teach Democrats," *Independent*, December 30, 2021, https://www.independent.co.uk/voices/harry-reid -democrats-latino-voters-b1984664.html.

Chapter 14: Florida: The Cuban Exception

175 *winning nearly 35 percent in 1996*: In the 1996 presidential election, Bill Clinton and his running mate Al Gore won Florida by more than 5 percent over Bob Dole and Jack Kemp, an outcome made possible in part by support among Cuban Americans. As Miami Cuban leader Jorge Mas Canosa told Robert Novak for a September 30, 1996, column in the *Washington Post*: "Clinton has been better

than we expected.... To be honest, he's been better than Bush." https://www.washingtonpost.com/archive/opinions/1996/09/30/courting-the-cuban-vote/076ffbe8-78d4-419e-b96a-4d91de05f15b/. Overall, Clinton earned 72 percent of the Hispanic vote in 1996, compared to 62 percent in 1992, according to Voter News Service. In Florida, again based on Voter News Service exit poll data, Clinton in 1992 "appeared to win about 20 percent of the Cuban-American vote; this time, about 35 percent," according to Robert Joffee of the Mason-Dixon Florida Poll. "Clinton Won Florida Because He Gained in Key Voter Groups," *Stuart News*, November 10, 1996, https://www.newspapers.com/image/801333236/?terms=clinton%20cuban-american%20vote&match=1.

175 *A major factor was the saga of a young Cuban boy caught up in international politics— Elián González:* David Adams, "Elian Swings Cuban Voters Back to GOP," *Tampa Bay Times*, November 5, 2000, https://www.tampabay.com/archive/2000/11/05/elian-swings-cuban-voters-back-to-gop/.

Chapter 15: North Carolina: What Opportunity Looks Like

187 *demographic breakdown of North Carolina's registered voters:* Figures based on data gathered by the U.S. Census Bureau, reported in November 2021 by WNCT Channel 9 in Greenville, South Carolina. https://www.wnct.com/news/politics/7-7-million-votes-see-the-demographics-of-north-carolinas-voting-population/.

Chapter 16: Texas and the Rio Grande Valley

195 *"sea of red, eventually lapping at our own borders":* Bernard Weinraub, "Reagan Steps Up His Drive to Give $100 Million to Nicaragua Rebels," *New York Times*, March 6, 1986, https://www.nytimes.com/1986/03/06/us/reagan-steps-up-his-drive-to-give-100-million-to-nicaragua-rebels.html.

Chapter 17: Arizona's Valley of the Sun

205 *Gallego told the* Washington Monthly: Steve Kettmann, "Ruben Gallego and His Intriguing Bid for the U.S. Senate," *Washington Monthly*, July 19, 2023, https://washingtonmonthly.com/2023/07/19/ruben-gallego-and-his-intriguing-bid-for-the-u-s-senate/.

Chapter 18: The Challenge for Republicans

214 *"GOP autopsy":* The so-called GOP autopsy, officially known as the *Growth & Opportunity Project*, which based its findings on thousands of online surveys and group listening sessions, as well as hundreds of conference calls and a reported fifty focus groups, was a Republican National Committee–commissioned report issued in 2013, the year after Obama defeated Romney. https://www.wsj.com/public/resources/documents/RNCreport03182013.pdf.

Chapter 19: The Challenge for Democrats

219 *According to the U.S. Department of Labor:* Kevin Dubina, "Hispanics in the Labor Force: 5 Facts," U.S. Department of Labor Blog, September 15, 2021, https://blog .dol.gov/2021/09/15/hispanics-in-the-labor-force-5-facts.

219 *from the National Association of Home Builders:* Na Zhao, "One in Three Workers in Construction Is Hispanic," Eye on Housing National Association of Home Builders Discusses Economics and Housing Policy, June 23, 2022, https://eyeonhousing.org/2022/06/one-in-three-workers-in-construction-is -hispanic/.

Epilogue: A Case for Optimism: Pluralism over Tribalism

225 *since elevated to defense minister:* Andrew E. Kramer and Anushka Patil, "Who Is Rustem Umerov, Zelensky's Nominee for Defense Minister of Ukraine?," *New York Times,* September 4, 2023, https://www.nytimes.com/2023/09/04/world/europe /defense-umerov-zelensky-ukraine.html.

230 *University of Kansas political science professor Paul Schumaker:* "Pluralism and Tribalism," Paul Schumaker: Advancing Pluralism, October 28, 2018, https:// paulschumaker.com/2018/10/28/pluralism-and-tribalism/.

Index

Abbott, Greg, 78, 84, 155, 215
ABC, 39, 41, 54
abortion, 151–54
Access Hollywood tapes, 84
AdImpact, 186
advertising campaigns
 Latino voters as audience of, 71, 73,
  104, 108, 115–22, 179
 negative advertising by Democratic
  Party, 223–24
affirmative action, 155–56
AFL-CIO, 138
Alba, Richard, 8
Alejo, Luis, 100
"alt-right," 111
Amandi, Fernand, 140
"The American Dream" (*El Sueño
 Americano,* Republican Convention
 slogan), 69
America's Voice, 137
Arguelles, Jesus, 31–32
Arizona
 Gallego's U.S. Senate campaign, 205–6,
  208–10
 Lincoln Project's 2020 strategy and,
  116, 118, 126–27, 130, 206–7
 Maricopa County and Arpaio, 21, 205
 voter turnout need for, 203–5

Arizona Republic, 203, 205
Arpaio, Joe, 21, 205
Asian Americans
 on affirmative action, 155–56
 intermarriage of, 8–9
 unionization and, 169
 working- and middle-class statistics,
  220 (*see also* economic issues)
assimilation. *See* generational differences
 among Latino voters
Associated Press, 101, 104, 114, 134, 196
Atlantic magazine, 8–9, 108, 232

Ballesteros, Leonides, 31–34, 36–37,
 57–58
Bannon, Steve, 3, 111–12, 113–15,
 120–22, 235
Barabak, Mark, 63
Bayh, Birch, 52
Becerra, Glen, 55–56
Bendixen, Sergio, 135
Bendixen & Amandi International, 140
Bentsen, Lloyd, 197
Biden, Joe
 Arizona vote and, 207–8
 on immigration, 54, 149
 Lincoln Project on Biden campaign,
  117, 119, 127–31

Biden, Joe (*cont.*)
North Carolina vote and, 185, 186
presidential campaign (2024) of, 2,
83, 217
presidential election (2020) of, 109,
143
Texas vote and, 198
Black voters
on affirmative action, 155–56
COVID and Black "essential workers,"
145
Latino voter block size and, 135
in North Carolina, 187, 188, 190–94
in South Carolina, 168
unionization and, 169
working- and middle-class statistics,
220 (*see also* economic issues)
Bonilla, Henry, 72
border security, 147–49, 199. *See also*
immigration
Breitbart, 111
Brulte, Jim, 102
Bush, Columba, 68
Bush, George H. W., 44, 82
Bush, George P., 68, 81
Bush, George W., 67–78
Latino support for, 2, 211, 212, 215
9/11 terror attack and, 45
Un Nuevo Día advertising campaign of,
73–78
pro-Latino stance of, 67–71, 79, 82
Republican National Convention
(2000) and, 67–71, 73
Sosa and, 67, 68, 71–74
Bush, Jeb, 81
Bush, Laura, 68

Caballero, Anna M., 221
California
blanket primary of, 64
Community Colleges Board of
Governors, 56
Democratic Party challenge for future,
221, 222
Democratic Party victories, election
(1998), 64–65
gubernatorial elections of, 96–102, 136
Latino population increase, 2, 57, 173
Latino voter registration in, 144
polling data (1990s), 134
Proposition 187, 21, 47–48, 62, 80, 90,
144, 148, 169
Republican Party voter profile, 212
State Assembly of, 59, 64, 89, 90
State Lands Commission, 36
undocumented immigrants of (1990s),
13
Ventura County, Mexican American
population of, 31–38, 40
women legislators of, 162
See also California Republican Party;
*individual names of California
politicians*
California Republican Party, 47–65
GOP Hispanic Summit (1997), 61
immigration and public opinion, 53–57
Madrid's consultant role in, 102
Madrid's director roles in, 47–48,
60–65, 71, 89, 102, 110
Madrid's early political career and, 2,
48–52, 56–60, 133
Proposition 187 and, 47–48, 62
Cantinflas (comedian), 28
Cardona, Maria, 130
Carolina Demography, 188
Carter, Jimmy, 39–40, 41, 135, 197
Catholics, 10, 26, 151–54, 160. *See also*
religion
Census Bureau, U.S., 17–18, 178, 191
Center for American Progress, 145
Centers for Disease Control and
Prevention (CDC), 125
Central American voters, of North
Carolina, 188

Charlotte Observer, 191

Chavez, Cesar, 35, 68

"Chicano" terminology/identity, 26–27, 150

Church, Frank, 52

"City on a Hill" (speech, Reagan), 42–43

class issues of voting. *See* economic issues

Clayton, Anderson, 193

climate change and environmental issues, 138, 156–57

Clinton, Bill
  Arizona voters and, 207
  domestic vs. foreign policy of, 45
  "It's the economy, stupid" slogan of, 220
  scandal publicity about, 64

Clinton, Hillary
  Latino support for, 217
  presidential campaign (2016), 128, 139, 140, 165–68
  Villaraigosa and campaigns of, 94

CNN, 63, 68, 141

Code the Dream, 189

Cold War, end of, 39–46

Collins, Jim, 197

Columbia (patriotic figure), 164

communism, Cuban American voters on, 174–76, 180, 183

community vs. individualism, 231–33

Confederate flag, symbolism of, 108

Congress, U.S.
  Democratic Party challenge for future of, 221–24
  Flores and Rio Grande Valley voting, 197–201
  Gallego's U.S. Senate campaign, 205–6, 208–10
  Republican voters reflected by, 120
  Trump's first impeachment hearings, 104–6
  women legislators of, 162
  Zelensky's address to, 5

Conservative Political Action Conference (CPAC), 85, 86–87

Contreras, Miguel, 169

Conway, George, 104

Conway, Kellyanne, 104, 110

Cortés, Hernán, 160–61

Cortez Masto, Catherine, 171

"country-club Republicans," 109, 117, 207

COVID pandemic, 125–26, 145

Cox, John, 101

Cruz, Celia, 69

Cruz, Ted, 110

Cuban American voters
  identity of Latino groups and, 178–83
  Lincoln Project's 2020 strategy and, 113, 129
  profile and Republican Party loyalty of, 17, 19, 20, 173–78
  Trump votes by, 140
  See also Florida

Cuellar, Henry, 200

Culinary Union, 166, 168–71

culture war. *See* generational differences among Latino voters

Curiel, Gonzalo, 82

Curtis, Mary C., 192–94

Czajkowski, Zack, 120–21, 124

data and research, 133–45
  exit polling data, 134
  generational differences and polling importance, 141–42
  language and polling importance, 136–41
  Latino voter registration rates, 143–44, 182, 188, 190–94
  Latino voters on economic issues, 144–45 (*see also* economic issues)
  microtargeting (polling marketing strategy), 52
  polling methodology, overview, 133–36

data and research (*cont.*)
    population density and polling
      importance, 139–40, 142–43, 167
    See also Latino voters
Davis, Gray, 64
Decker, Cathleen, 63
Declaration of Independence, 228
Deferred Action for Childhood Arrivals
    (DACA), 189
De La Cruz, Monica, 200
De León, Kevin, 90
democracy, worldwide threat to, 7
Democratic Party
    border security and, 147, 148
    California white Democrats on
      immigration (1990s), 53
    challenge for future of, 217–24
    Democratic National Convention
      (2012), 94
    education of voters in, 149–51 (*see also*
      education level of voters)
    Latinos and diverse voter
      characteristics, 4, 15–22 (*see also*
      Latino voters)
    North Carolina chairperson, 193
    research by (*see* data and research)
    socioeconomic reputation of members,
      72, 183
    *See also individual names of Democratic
      politicians*
demographic change and trends. *See*
    Democratic Party; Latino voters;
    Republican Party; *individual names
    of states*
DeSantis, Ron
    Latino vote for, 84, 140–41, 215
    Lincoln Project 2020 strategy and, 126
disinformation campaigns
    Breitbart and, 111
    by Russia, 181–82
    Spanish-language, 83, 179–80
"Dixiecrats," 75

Dobbs v. Jackson (2022), 151–54
Dominican Americans, voting by, 19, 192
Dornan, Robert "B-1 Bob," 48, 60
Duarte, John, 221
Ducey, Doug, 126
Duffy, Kay, 49–51

economic issues
    Democratic Party and challenge for
      future, 217–24
    Democratic Party and its
      socioeconomic reputation, 72, 183
    labor unions, 35, 165–71
    Latino diversity and, 4, 15–22
    Latino working-class perspective as
      unifier, 22, 144–45, 214–15
    Los Angeles drugs and gangs of late
      twentieth century, 30
    Nevada's Latino voters and, 65–71
    racial/ethnic divide and class issues, 19
    Republican Party and challenge for
      future, 213
    Republican Party and "country-club
      Republicans," 109, 117, 207
    Villaraigosa's gubernatorial campaign
      on, 100
    See also education level of voters
Economist magazine, 63
Edel, Anastasia, 112
Edison (exit polling data), 140
Edmund A. Walsh School of Foreign
    Service (Georgetown University), 2,
    58–59, 133
education level of voters
    border security issue and, 149
    Democratic Party voter profile, 149–51
    "diploma divide," 23, 100, 118, 128–29,
      149–51, 220 (*see also* economic
      issues)
    Latino college enrollment, 18, 23
    Lincoln Project on voter demography
      change and, 118, 123, 128–29

Republican Party "country-club"
profile, 109, 117, 207
Republican Party voter profile, 123,
128, 185, 200, 212–16, 220
Villaraigosa's gubernatorial campaign
on, 100
Eisenhower, Dwight D., 72
environmental issues, 138, 156–57
Estefan, Emilio, 69
Estefan, Gloria, 69
exit polling data, 134

Facebook, 114
fear
politics motivated by, 96
of Republican Party on changing
demographics, 11, 80, 213–16
Feinstein, Dianne, 100
Ferguson, Anita Perez, 48
Fiedler, Bobbi, 48
Finkelstein, Arthur, 51–52
"Flag of Treason" (advertisement), 108, 118
Flores, Mayra, 163, 197–201
Florida
Cuban American voters of, 17, 19, 20,
113, 129, 140, 173–83
DeSantis and Latino voters, 140–41
as Latino population "big three" state,
173
Latino vote and polling
miscalculations, 140
Lincoln Project's 2020 strategy and,
113–14, 123, 126–27, 129, 130
Republican Party challenge for future
in, 215
Florida Atlantic University, 144
Floyd, George, 118
Fox News, 125, 126, 198
Fukuyama, Francis, 44

Galen, Reed, 103
Galen, Rich, 103

Gallegly, Elton, 48–51, 53–55, 81, 135
Gallego, Kate, 210
Gallego, Ruben, 205–6, 208–10
Gálvez, Xóchitl, 164
Garcia, Domingo, 130
Garcia, Eric, 169
Garcia, Mike, 221
generational differences among Latino
voters
Democratic Party challenge for future
and, 217–19
Gen Z Latino voters, 227
"melting pot" and assimilation, 11–12
polling importance and, 141–42
Republican Party challenge for future
and, 216
social media and, 166–67
Georgetown University, 2, 58–59, 133
Georgia, Lincoln Project's strategy in,
113, 116, 118, 126–27, 130
Geranios, John, 59
Gill, Hannah, 191
Gingrich, Newt, 64
"Girl in the Mirror" (advertisement),
118–19
Goldwater, Barry, 206
Gonzalez, Vicente, 200
"GOP autopsy" (Republican National
Committee, 2012), 214
GOP Hispanic Summit (Los Angeles,
1997), 61
Gorbachev, Mikhail, 41
Gore, Al, 70
"great replacement" as perceived threat,
11. See also fear
Guatemalan Americans, voting by, 19, 188
Guerra, Frank, 72, 74
gun rights/gun control, 154–55

Hahn, Jim, 92–93
Hahn, Kenneth, 92
Haley, Nikki, 60

Harrison, Spencer, 124–25
Havice, Sally, 59
Hemmer, Bill, 68
Hidalgo County (Texas) Republican
    Party, 197
Hispanic Business magazine, 48
Hispanic Chamber of Commerce, 77
Hispanic Consumer Sentiment Index,
    144–45
Hispanic Summit (Los Angeles, 1997),
    61, 129
"Hispanic" terminology, identity of
    Latino groups and, 178–83
Hitler, Adolf, 112
Holtz, Lucas, 186–88
Honduran Americans, voting by, 188
Hopcroft, John, 189
House of Representatives, U.S. *See*
    Congress, U.S.
housing and homeownership
    affordability, 92, 95–96, 100, 223
    construction industry, 214
    Latino voting rates and
        homeownership, 18, 33

identity. *See* Democratic Party; Latino
    voters; pluralism; Republican Party
immigration
    border security, 147–49, 199
    California, undocumented immigrants
        of (1990s), 13
    California public opinion (1990s) on,
        53–57
    "City on a Hill" (speech, Reagan) and,
        42–43
    COVID and immigrant "essential
        workers," 145
    DACA, 189
    George W. Bush vs. Trump on, 77–78
    Latino immigrants vs. U.S.-born
        Latinos, statistics, 17, 20
    Latino voters on, 137–39, 143, 147

independent voters (Florida), 182
individualism vs. community,
    231–33
intermarriage of Latinos, 8–10, 17–18
Iran hostage crisis, 39–40, 197

Jefferson, Thomas, 13, 228
Jennings, Peter, 41
Johnson, Ron, 126

Kansas City Star, 64
Kemp, Jack, 81, 101
Kennedy, John F., 196, 233
Kerry, John, 29
Koppel, Ted, 39
Kushner, Jared, 114

Labor Department, U.S., 219
Labor Federation, 169
labor unions, 35, 165–71
Lake, Kari, 206
Lambros, Rich, 47, 62
Lambros, Richard, 59–60
language
    Mexican American identity and, 28
    polling importance and, 136–41
    Spanish-language disinformation
        problem, 83, 179–80
    Spanish political advertising, 71
Latinization of America, 15–23
    defined, 13
    Latinas' role as future of, 23, 159–64
        (*see also* women voters)
    Latino, defined, 15
    Latinos and diverse voter
        characteristics, 4, 15–22
Latino Century, 1–14
    defined, 4
    democracy challenges and, 7
    demographic transition in United
        States, 1–4, 235–36 (*see also* Latino
        voters)

identity and future of United States,
10–14
liberty and symbolism for, 4–7
racial discourse importance, 7–10
See also pluralism
Latino Decisions, 137–39
The Latino Migration Experience in North Carolina (Gill), 191
The Latino Vote (podcast, Madrid), 199
Latino voters, 133–45
advertising targeted to, 71, 73, 104, 108, 115–22, 179, 223–24
COVID and Latino "essential workers," 145
demographics (2000 and 2004), 76–77
generational differences and polling importance, 141–42 (*see also* generational differences among Latino voters)
George W. Bush and, 67–78 (*see also* Bush, George W.)
identity and diversity among, 10–14, 26–28, 37–38, 63–64, 142, 150, 178–83, 226–27
intermarriage of Latinos and, 8–10, 17–18
"Latino Mirage," 136
Lincoln Project on Biden campaign and Latino vote, 127–31 (*see also* Lincoln Project)
patriotism of, 28–29, 235
polling methodology, overview, 133–36 (*see also* data and research)
population density and polling importance, 139–40, 142–43, 167
rightward shift of, 139
Trump's appeal to, 83–89
turnout rates, 21, 98, 137–39, 199, 203–5, 208, 222–24
voter registration rates, 143–44, 182, 188, 190–94

working- and middle-class statistics, 220 (*see also* economic issues)
See also economic issues; education level of voters; immigration; language; Latinization of America; Latino Century; political issues for Latino voters; *individual ethnic group names*
"Latinx" terminology, 149–51
League of United Latin American Citizens (LULAC), 130
Leguizamo, John, 130
Lenin, Vladimir, 111–12, 235
Leo, Leo J., 197
Levy, Morris, 8
Lincoln, Abraham, 228
Lincoln Project, 103–12, 113–31
advertising campaign (2020) by, 115–22, 186
Arizona and 2020 strategy, 116, 118, 126–27, 130, 206–7
"Bannon Line" strategy of, 113–15, 120–22
on Biden campaign and Latino vote, 127–31
cofounders of, 2, 5
COVID strategy of, 125–26
criticism of, 116
on cultural vs. economic issues, 117–19
data used by, 123–25
goal and founding of, 103–12
Hispanic Summit, 129
New Southern Strategy of, 126–27, 187
podcast of, 121
threats to founders of, 107–8
López Obrador, Andrés Manuel, 164
Los Angeles Times, 42, 55, 62, 63, 93, 100

Madrid, Gina, 34
Madrid, Juliet, 29, 32
Madrid, Louis, 26–27, 29–34

Madrid, Michael
California Republican Party work of,
47–48, 56–65, 71, 89, 102, 110 (see
also California Republican Party)
early life and family background of,
25–38, 48, 49, 55, 57, 235
George W. Bush campaign work of,
67–78 (see also Bush, George W.)
The Latino Vote (podcast), 199
Republican Party affiliation of, 39–46
Trump criticism by, 86–87
Villaraigosa working relationship with,
89–90, 96–102 (see also Villaraigosa,
Antonio)
See also Lincoln Project
La Malinche, 160–61
Marin, Rosario, 130
Marine Corps, U.S., 205, 208, 209
McCain, John, 82, 84, 142, 206
McCarthy, Kevin, 198
McClatchy (news service), 85
McGovern, George S., 52
Medina, Jennifer, 198
The Melting Pot (play), 12
"melting pot" and assimilation, 11–12
Mendoza, Mario, 121–22
Mexican Americans
Democratic-Republican voting
statistics, 17, 129
identity of, 26–28, 37–38, 150, 178–79
as Latino majority in United States, 19,
220–21
matriarchal figures in Mexican culture,
160–62, 164
move to suburbs by, 25–38, 40
of North Carolina, 188–90
Trump's rhetoric against, 79–87
Mexican Americans: The Ambivalent
Minority (Skerry), 234
Mexico
border security and, 147–49, 199
Sheinbaum's presidential candidacy, 164

Michigan
Lincoln Project's 2020 strategy and,
130
presidential election (2016) and, 80
microtargeting (polling marketing
strategy), 52
Mi Familia Vota, 138
Miller, Jason, 127
Moctezuma, 160
Monitor (McAllen, Texas), 196
Moorpark Community College, 48, 55
Mulholland, Bob, 61
Myers, Dowell, 8

National Association of Home Builders,
219
National Association of Latino Elected
and Appointed Officials (NALEO),
138, 163
National Community Reinvestment
Coalition, 220
National Conference of State Legislatures,
162
National Council of La Raza (UnidosUS),
138
National Hispanic Caucus of State
Legislators, 162
National Public Radio (NPR), 193
National Review magazine, 63
National Shooting Sports Foundation,
154
Nevada, Latino voters of, 165–71
New Mexico, Second Congressional
District of, 221
New Republic magazine, 63
Newsmax, 122
Newsom, Gavin, 97, 100–101, 136
New Southern Strategy, 126–27
Newsweek magazine, 129–30
New York, polling data (1990s), 134
New York magazine, 186, 199
New York Times, 52, 63, 106–7, 197, 198

New York Times/Siena poll, 141
Nicaragua, Sandinista government of, 195
Nield, Charles, 204
Nightline (ABC), 39
9/11 terror attack, 45
North Carolina
    Democratic shift of, 185–94
    Lincoln Project's 2020 strategy and, 130
Un Nuevo Día advertising campaign, 73–78. *See also* Bush, George W.
Núñez, Fabian, 90

Obama, Barack
    on DACA, 189
    on immigration, 53–54, 137
    Latino vote and, 143, 217
    North Carolina vote and, 180, 185
    presidential election (2008), 168
    presidential election (2012), 81, 83, 214
Ocasio-Cortez, Alexandria, 163
Ohio, Lincoln Project's 2020 strategy and, 123
Orange County Register, 98–99
O'Rourke, Beto, 155

Pacheco, Rod, 98, 131
Pacific Islander Americans, unionization and, 169
Padilla, Alex, 90
Paoletta, Kyle, 199
Parscale, Brad, 108, 110–11, 123
patriotism
    Cold War end and, 44
    misconstrued loyalties of Latinos, 28–29, 235
    Statue of Liberty symbolism, 4–5, 73, 161
    Uncle Sam and Columbia symbolism of, 164
Pennsylvania, presidential election (2016) and, 80

Perez, Cris, 36
Pérez, John, 90
Perez, Miguel, 70–71
Pew Research Center
    on Arizona voters, 206
    on COVID and "essential workers," 145
    on Cuban vote (2016), 140
    election (2020) ballot statistics, 117
    on Gen Z Latino voters, 227
    on George W. Bush and Latino vote, 211
    on individual issues of voter concern, 147–50, 152–55
    on Latino evangelicals, 76–77
    on Latinos and American identity, 17
    polling research standards of, 134
    on U.S.-born Latino population growth, 143
pluralism, 225–36
    democracy and worldwide threat, 7
    diversity and identity within Latino communities, 27, 63–64
    Gen Z Latino voters and, 227
    importance of, 227–30, 232–36
    Latino Century, defined, 4
    Latinos as mixed-heritage people, 226–27
    tribalism vs., 228–33
    as Ukraine's goal, 225–26
Political Association of Spanish-Speaking Organizations (PASSO), 196–97
political issues for Latino voters, 147–57
    affirmative action, 155–56
    border security, 147–49, 199
    Catholicism and abortion, 151–54
    climate change and environmental issues, 138, 156–57
    gun rights/gun control, 154–55
    "Latinx" terminology and, 149–51
    See also immigration
Politico, 87, 140
Polk, James, 196

polling. *See* data and research
population density and polling
importance, 139–40, 142–43, 167
poverty. *See* economic issues
"P.O.W." (advertisement), 108
Proposition 187 (California), 21, 47–48,
62, 80, 90, 144, 148, 169
Protestants, 21, 22, 76, 232, 233. *See also*
religion
"Protestant work ethic" and
individualism, 21
Puerto Rican voters
on abortion, 152
identity of Latino groups and,
178–79
Latino population of United States, 19
Lincoln Project's 2020 strategy and,
113–14, 129
North Carolina voting by, 188
Republican shift of, 141
Putin, Vladimir, 5, 82

racism
immigration and public opinion, 54
racial discourse importance and, 7–10,
22
Republican Party accused of racism by
Latinos, 91–92
Republican Party challenge for future
and, 211–16
Radosh, Ronald, 112
Ramaswamy, Vivek, 60
Ramos, Jorge, 214
Reagan, Ronald
"City on a Hill" speech, 42–43
"Eleventh Commandment" of, 103–4
Goldwater and, 206
Latino vote and, 74, 75, 142, 212, 214,
215
legacy of, 40–41, 44–46
on Nicaragua, 195
pro-Latino stance of, 79, 81, 82

Ronald Reagan Presidential Library
and Museum, 58
Record (Bergen, New Jersey), 70
Reid, Harry, 169
religion
Catholicism and abortion, 151–54
Catholic vote, 10, 26, 151–54, 160
Flores on Republican Party influence
by, 197
George W. Bush's voters and, 76–77
Latino evangelicals, 76–77
Lincoln Project on cultural vs.
economic issues, 117–19
Protestant vote and, 21, 22, 76, 232,
233
"Protestant work ethic" and
individualism, 21
Republican Party voter profile, 212
slavery and, 233
Virgin of Guadalupe (La Virgen de
Guadalupe), 5, 20, 160, 161
Republican Party
author's affiliation with, 39–46
challenge for future of, 211–16
Cold War end and, 39–46
"country-club Republicans," 109, 117,
207
education of voters in, 123, 128, 185,
200, 212–16, 220
fear of changing demographics by, 80,
213–16
"GOP autopsy" by Republican
National Committee (2012), 214
Latinos and diverse voter
characteristics, 4, 15–22
Latino voters' rightward shift, 139 (*see
also* Latino voters)
Lincoln Project on cultural vs.
economic issues, 117–19
Republican National Convention
(2000), 67–71, 73
research by (*see* data and research)

Rio Grande Valley (Texas) and
   Republican shift, 195–201
socioeconomic status of members, 72
Trump's decision to run as Republican,
   45–46
Trump's support by, 79–87, 101
See also California Republican Party;
   *individual names of Republican
   politicians*
Republican Women's Federated, 49–50
Richards, Ann, 77
Ridge, Tom, 64
Rocha, Chuck, 21, 130, 209, 210
Rodriguez, Ramiro, 189–90
Rodriguez, Richard, 1
Roe v. Wade (1973), 151–54
Roll Call, 192, 200–201
Romero, José M., 203–4
Romney, Mitt, 81, 140, 214
Ronald Reagan Presidential Library and
   Museum, 58
Roosevelt, Theodore, 12
Ruffino, Francisco, 169–71
Russia
   Bannon as Leninist, 112, 235
   Russia-Ukraine War, 5–6, 181–82,
      225–26
Ryan, Paul, 81, 82

Sacramento Bee, 221
Salvador Americans, voting by, 19
Sanchez, Gabriel, 139
Sanchez, Leslie, 74
Sanchez, Loretta, 48, 60
Sanders, Bernie, 165, 167–68, 209, 210
Sandinista government (Nicaragua), 195
San Francisco Examiner, 62, 63, 64
Schneider, Bill, 63
Schroeder, Michael, 60
Schumaker, Paul, 230–31
Schwarzenegger, Arnold, 81
Scott, Tim, 60

Senate, U.S. *See* Congress, U.S.
Sheinbaum, Claudia, 164
"Shrinking" (advertisement), 108
Sinema, Kyrsten, 205, 206
Skelton, George, 63, 100
Skerry, Peter, 234
Smith, Betty, 25
socialism, Cuban American voters on,
   176–77, 180, 183
social media, Latinos' use of, 166–67
"sombrero politics," 20–21
Sosa, Lionel
   George W. Bush's 2000 campaign and,
      67, 68, 71–74
   Reagan and, 42
   voter turnout and work of, 208
Sosa & Associates, 73
South Carolina, Latino voters of, 167–68
Southern Baptist Conference, 233
Spanish-language disinformation
   problem, 83, 179–80
Statue of Liberty, 4–5, 73, 161
Steslow, Ron, 226
Stevens, Stuart, 117
Stewart, Potter, 20
St. Louis Post-Dispatch, 63
"El Sueño Americano" ("The American
   Dream" Republican Convention
   slogan), 69

Tarrance, Lance, 74, 75
Tarrance Group, 140
Texas
   border security and, 147–49
   Department of Public Safety (DPS),
      148
   George P. Bush's defeat in, 81
   George W. Bush as governor of, 72
   as Latino population "big three" state,
      173
   Lincoln Project's 2020 strategy and,
      126–27

Texas (*cont.*)
National Guard, 148
polling data (1990s), 134
Republican Party challenge for future in, 215
Rio Grande Valley's Republican shift, 195–201
Texas Hispanic Policy Foundation, 141, 148
Texas Monthly, 72
Texas Tribune, 200
Third Way, 186, 221
Time magazine, 93–94, 198
Torres, Art, 13
Tower, John, 73
A Tree Grows in Brooklyn (Smith), 25
tribalism vs. pluralism, 228–33. *See also* pluralism
Truman, Harry, 207
Trump, Donald
Arizona vote and, 206–7
Bannon and, 3, 111–12, 113–15, 120–22, 235
Cuban American voters on, 140
election of (2016), 99, 101, 109–12
first impeachment hearings, 104–6
Flores's support for, 197–98
on immigration, 54, 77–78
Latino voter turnout and, 21
Lincoln Project's goals and, 103–12 (*see also* Lincoln Project)
North Carolina voters and, 185, 186
presidential campaign (2020) and, 168
profile of supporters of, 227
racist rhetoric of, 79–87, 214–16
Republican Party and motivation of, 45–46
Trump University, 82
2020 election and, 29
turnout of Latino voters, 21, 98, 137–39, 199, 203–5, 208, 222–24. *See also* Latino voters

Twitter, 166
Tyler Morning Telegraph (Texas), 197

UCLA Latino Policy & Politics Institute, 162
Ukraine
Russia-Ukraine War, 5–6, 181–82, 225–26
Trump's first impeachment and phone call to, 104–6
Umerov, Rustem, 5–6, 225–26
Uncle Sam figure, 164
United Farm Workers (UFW), 35
Univision, 91, 139, 140, 182, 214
USS *Gridley,* 29

Valadao, David, 221
Venezuelan Americans, Republican Party and, 17
Ventura County Star, 61
Vietnam War, 26–27, 30
Villaraigosa, Antonio, 89–102
California gubernatorial run by, 96–102
early life and career of, 90–92
as L.A. mayor, 92–95
Madrid's working relationship with, 89–90, 96–102, 131
Vindman, Alexander, 104–5
Virgin of Guadalupe (La Virgen de Guadalupe), 5, 20, 160, 161
voter registration rates, Latino, 143–44, 182, 188, 190–94. *See also* Latino voters
voting trends. *See* Latino voters; women voters

Wall Street Journal, 73
War Room (podcast, Bannon), 122

Washington Monthly, 205, 206

Washington Post, 63

Weber, Max, 21

We Build the Wall, 122

What Is to Be Done? (pamphlet, Lenin), 112

WhatsApp, 83

White House Initiative on Educational Excellence for Hispanics, 74–75

white voters
on affirmative action, 155–56
Republican Party voter profile, 212–16
working- and middle-class statistics, 220 (*see also* economic issues)
See also economic issues; education level of voters

Wildman, Scott, 59

Wilson, Pete, 48, 55–56, 58, 62, 81

Wilson, Rick, 104, 108

Winthrop, John, 42–43

Wisconsin
Lincoln Project's 2020 strategy and, 116, 118, 126, 130
presidential election (2016) and, 80

women voters, 159–64
Access Hollywood tapes, 84
Latinas' role as future of America, 23
Lincoln Project data and strategy for, 117–19, 129
matriarchal figures in Latino culture, 160–62, 164
Republican Party challenge for future of, 212–13
women's leadership and Latino culture, 159, 162–64

Wooldridge, Adrian, 63

Yaqui people, 31

Zelensky, Volodymyr, 5, 105, 225